Garden *and* Climate

Garden *and* Climate

Chip Sullivan

Foreword by Marc Treib

McGraw-Hill
New York
Chicago
San Francisco
Lisbon
London
Madrid
Mexico City
Milan
New Delhi
San Juan
Seoul
Singapore
Sydney
Toronto

McGraw-Hill

A Division of The McGraw·Hill Companies

Cataloging-in-Publication Data is on file
with the Library of Congress

ISBN 0-07-027103-8

Designed by Marc Treib

The sponsoring editors for this book were
Scott Grillo and Wendy Lochner, the editing
supervisor was Steven Melvin, and the production
supervisor was Pamela Pelton.
R.R. Donnelley & Sons Company was printer
and binder.

For

Frank James
who drew me to the Academy in Rome

Marc Treib
who has guided me through academia

Elizabeth Boults
who is my beacon of light

Book III: **Air** *133*

Book IV: **Water** *191*

Foreword

The ubiquity of effective climate control has made us forget, to a large degree, what living was like before technology granted us such independence. Now we close the windows and doors, flip a switch, and our heating and air-conditioning systems take over. The latitude, the season, the temperature, and the humidity have little relevance to our thermal sensations and daily patterns. A simple setting of the thermostat maintains a certain temperature and a certain humidity; comfort is assured. Or so it at first seems; but we do pay a price for such climatic independence.

We pay the price financially: with high heating and cooling bills, an enormous expenditure of energy per capita, the depletion of fossil-fuel reserves, and the complex infrastructure required to maintain it all. We also pay the price psychologically (some might say spiritually, as well), loosening if not losing the bonds with our locality. These two types of loss, and how we might avoid them, are what Chip Sullivan explores in this book *Garden and Climate*.

In the past, when shelter and garden were essentially climatic mitigation, we were more rooted to our landscape. In hot, wet climates, we built minimally to provide shade from the sun and to facilitate the flow of air. The garden contributed to comfort as well, addressing many of the same issues as building, while adding the kinetic pleasure of moving leaves, bursts of floral color, the heady fragrance of tropical blooms, and seasonal change. In cooler climates, garden and building reverse these purposes and means, attracting and trapping the sun and its accompanying heat and light, extending those times of the year when the outdoors could be enjoyed as pleasant or at least benign. And in the temperate zones, landscape and architecture straddled both tasks bringing warmth during the cool months and freshness when the temperatures were sultry. A device as simple as a deciduous tree or vine could thwart the entry of solar rays in summer but admit them abundantly in the cold of winter. Intelligent environmental design was a necessity, with the perception and judgment of its effects immediately apparent.

Many gardeners, landscape architects, and architects know the benefits of such thinking. Students of folk architecture learn from the lessons of vernacular buildings, knowledge acquired over the course of centuries through trial and error and social acceptance or rejection. The built landscape is rarely in complete accord with its environment, however. Seldom does climate determine house and garden form completely. At some point, social aspects come into play, and aesthetic issues as well.

Japan offers a poignant example of imperfect environmental modulation and the social acceptance of discomfort. In Japan, the traditional house was essentially a steeply pitched thatch roof with a raised platform for living. In the summer months, when the air is set at high temperature and laden with humidity, the house form is almost ideal. Its veranda serves as an active setting for living, sheltered from the sun by the eaves yet open to the flow of air even in the midst of torrential rainstorms. Southeastern orientation best addresses solar exposure and maximizes the breeze; trees planted to the south further shade the house and veranda. Gardens near the house rarely feature extensive paved areas, because these hard surfaces would serve as thermal mass holding the sun's heat long after it had set. Instead, a field of raked gravel or sand might fracture the sunlight and reflect it deeper into the house—light rather than heat. Or, in the smaller gardens of the domestic sphere, shrubs and ground covers absorbed the warmth, offering instead a pleasantly textured field upon which to gaze.

But the very features that make the house more comfortable in summer make it almost unbearably cold in winter. The deep thatch roof retards the passage of warmth to the interior, which remains cold and dark. The veranda in such instances is often no colder than the spaces within the house; in fact, given the radiant heat of the solar rays, the open veranda may actually provide greater comfort than those zones well within the building's interior. The garden here is of little thermal benefit, except as a subject for contemplation and beauty that transcends feelings of discomfort.

Lessons such as these seem so obvious that it is difficult to understand why so much of this knowledge has been disregarded or lost during the last century. Technology, as noted above, is partially to blame, but it is not the sole reason. Also at fault is the schism between the garden makers who view landscape more as a work of art and those of a more technical bent. There have been numerous books on passive solar design (that is, the use of landscape and architecture to modulate climate with active technology) taken from a technical standpoint. These are often difficult for the layperson to comprehend and even more difficult to apply to a garden design task at hand, especially a small one. On the other hand, there have been relatively few books on architecture and climate—and even fewer on landscape and climate—that approach the subject with an admission, if not an overt desire, that beauty can serve as the principal goal in creating a landscape. Olgivay's *Design with Climate* remains the classic in the field, balancing technical information with solid common sense. Lisa Herschong's *Thermal Delight in Architecture* opened eyes for all those interested in the impact of climate (and its regulation) on living in the house—more particularly how we use architecture in terms of climate. Nothing similar to it addresses landscape design, however. More social than technical, more anecdotal than coherently doctrinaire, the book is a quiet plea for considering climate as a social consideration when designing environments for human use.

In the field of landscape architecture, there is precious little that weds a consideration of climate with those of living, formal, and spatial issues. And it is at just this intersection that Chip Sullivan makes his most significant contribution to designing landscapes. Climate is not the by-product of an a priori aesthetic decision—it is the root of that design. Mr. Sullivan shows us how historical landscapes, many of them the great gardens we know from books and travel, have addressed these very issues of climatic comfort, making them more thermally palatable—and beautiful. He pairs

technical information garnered from his years of observation with a projected reading of the designer's intentions. His question remains constant: Just how does a consideration of climate inform the making of landscapes?

His corpus spans the Mediterranean with some excursions as far east as Persia. For the most part, however, we are looking at the gardens of southern Spain and those of Renaissance and Baroque Italy. These are not the vernacular gardens of the people, but those with patronage from kings, emperors, popes, and nobility. Presumably, however, the lessons drawn from these gardens applied equally to smaller domestic gardens as well, as part of a continuum of landscape intelligence, and would apply to our own gardens today. Rarely, in this book, do we read of any garden as a whole, although several of the great works will appear in the book more than once. Instead, with Mr. Sullivan's guidance, we examine discreet areas or features of the historical garden. We learn of the cool cryptoporticus, hot seats and cool walks, pools and ponds, and astute plantings. His sketches and commentary are analytical x-rays that see beyond the surfaces of places we may already know, and which look instead at the ideas behind the forms and spaces.

This is not to say, however, that *Garden and Climate* is a historical study alone, although it would certainly engage those more interested in landscape history than contemporary applications. But the author's intention is quite the contrary. Chip Sullivan here proposes that the historical practices of Mediterranean garden making remain valid—indeed, necessary—in our field. While many of us will not possess the land or the means to replicate many of the features he cites, we can abstract these ideas and utilize them in smaller contemporary applications. A summary follows each of the postulates, extracting from historical observations more general ideas valid still for contemporary application. In some places we may laugh at the author's personal idiosyncrasy; but even these are sound in terms of intention if not in their particular form. Try to find the lesson at the core of each example.

The book is ordered classically, structured in separate books around the four elements: earth, fire, air, and water. We can accept the author's conceit with little difficulty because one structure is probably as acceptable as the next: Consider the book more of a lexicon of passive environmental devices than a didactic treatise. Through a series of marvelous analytical sketches, Mr. Sullivan examines these thermal mitigations most often in section (key to understanding solar rays and air flow), but also in plan — and almost always accompanied by a perspective sketch or photograph. He wants us to consider not only how the feature functions environmentally but what it looks like and how it fits within the design of the garden and the life of its occupants. These concerns constitute the book's most important contribution.

One can only hope that the lessons in *Garden and Climate* will be taken seriously and applied broadly. In the past two decades, a number of influential publications on xeriscape and drought-tolerant gardens have helped to develop landscapes better adjusted to their climatic and topographic situations. But these books have rarely addressed the use of the garden: What if we consider landscape design from the aspect of human occupancy, as well as that of water consumption? In that very way this book is different and significant. While almost all of the conditions drawn and described here do address horticultural and topographic issues, the author's final goal is landscapes that are environmentally sound and yet successful in their provision of comfort without elaborate technology and depletion of resources.

A most worthy goal. An important book.

Marc Treib
University of California, Berkeley

Introduction

The spark for *Garden and Climate* ignited in the early 1970s, when a multitude of events forced me to reflect on the connection between landscape design and energy conservation. The first oil crisis in 1973 became a major issue for me, just as the first oil embargo of 1973–74 alerted the world to its overdependence on diminished fossil-fuel reserves. At that time, building and growth patterns had become extremely wasteful due to the prevailing attitude that our energy supplies were inexhaustible. Many architects and landscape architects began to investigate how we could use passive design methods as a means of transforming the built environment from its energy-intensive state. (Today, the United States devotes roughly 30 percent of its energy budget to the heating and cooling of buildings.)

As a landscape architect, I embarked on a journey to create a new energy-efficient landscape design philosophy. However, I found a number of obstacles blocking this path. The typical architectural and engineering solutions to the "energy crisis" concentrated on the old active models of making buildings more efficient for mechanized heating and cooling. With increasing frequency, buildings became hermetically sealed to protect the artificial interior climate (Figure 0-1). Building codes were revised to require fewer windows in order to keep "conditioned" air from leaking out. Not only were there fewer windows, but also fewer and fewer windows that actually opened to the outside world. Insulation standards increased in pursuit of the ideal of sealing out the natural world. Moreover, no landscape specifications were developed to encourage more energy-efficient design.

In rethinking my design philosophy, I researched historical precedents on my journey toward a new garden form (Figure 0-2). I found that many past cultures had integrated metaphysics into their gardens as an adjunct to microclimatic and habitat design. For example, the Persian garden was

Figure 0-1
Hermetically sealed glass building, Miami, Florida.
(Photo: Author)

considered a sacred place; not just beautiful, but also instilled with a deeper sense of meaning. It symbolized a journey that was intended to impart knowledge to all those on the path of wisdom. My studies of these garden mystics led me to an awareness of their passive design qualities and the commitment of these designers to maintain and enhance the vital connection with nature by learning directly from it.

Through this exploration of historic models of garden metaphysics, I came to realize that the metaphysics of the contemporary garden should be a balanced interweaving of proportion, function, and comfort, and energy conservation and passive design. When these ideals merge together, the contemporary garden has the potential to become not only a place of functional utility, but also of spiritual enlightenment.

Since, until that time, I had lived primarily in the Sun Belt of the United States, I decided to focus my research on historic gardens in similar climates—namely Roman, Islamic, Italian Renaissance, and Hispano-Moorish gardens. I saw the garden's role in history essentially as one of ornament, notwithstanding its metaphysical qualities. I believed, with the late Ian McHarg, that all formal gardens were created merely as separate aesthetic adjuncts to the dwelling—simple, artfully created exercises in geometry and order "imposed on an unknowing and uncaring nature."[1] It soon became apparent that I had grossly underestimated the full breadth and nuance of these gardens. Starting with Georgina Masson's classic book, *Italian Gardens*, I began to understand how these historic gardens expressed not only great beauty and order, but also possessed ingenious passive methods to control climates and microclimates. As my research continued, I found hundreds of examples of such passive design features. A most intriguing paradigm emerged, that the harsher the climate, the more ingenious the devices and methods became for creating physically comfortable spaces.

Figure 0-2
The garden as an extension of the building.
(Photo: Author)

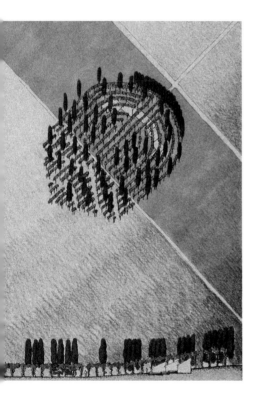

To learn more about these climatic inventions in historic
gardens, I embarked on a rigorous schedule of drawing as
direct experience. By conscientiously drawing in the field,
diagramming historical documents, and using travel sketches,
I developed an immediate visual contact with the subject.
The process of redrawing extant plans of Italian, Roman,
and Hispano-Moorish gardens proved not only an important
learning tool, but also allowed me to develop constantly
new ideas.

After I had collected sufficient data from the many inspiring
examples of historic gardens, I began designing passive garden
prototypes (Figure 0-3). These experimental gardens were
contemporary applications of the historical lessons I was
learning in how to reduce energy consumption. I spent several
years creating over 90 passive garden prototypes. These
prototypes became the bases for built gardens which clients
began employing me to design to help them reduce their
energy costs. Plant and garden structures were manipulated
into new systems where energy conservation was merged
with aesthetics.

In 1984–85, I was a Fellow at the American Academy in
Rome, developing my ideas for this book. My experiences
there allowed me to bridge my earlier research on historic
gardens with my practical experience on energetic land-use
analysis. The location proved more than inspiring: The
Academy sits on the Janiculum Hill overlooking the Tiber
River and Rome; the McKim, Mead and White building,
completed in 1914, is a neoclassical structure that I came
to understand as an interpretation of a historical precedent
itself. The rich vocabulary of architecture and garden design,
combined with the serene atmosphere of contemplation,
taught me that the environmental devices of the past were
not dead, but very much alive.

The daily climatic nuances of the built environment became evident throughout my tenure at the Academy. I realized that understanding the exact location and movement of the sun, during the day and throughout the year, stands as one of the most important factors in climatic design. Architects and designers in the past had an intimate and keen understanding of this movement, and I knew I had to develop the same sensitivity to solar orientation.

My daily routine of study and observation quickly became dictated by the changing patterns of sunlight and weather. I spent the daylight hours either in my studio, or on day excursions, making detailed studies of the sun's effect on microclimates in the built environment. After dinner, I would make my way to the Academy library, passing through the *cortile*, or courtyard. The courtyard, enclosed on four sides by a loggia, was always a comfortable place to sit and think; one could find a shady seat in the summer or a protected corner in the winter. A four-square garden, edged with boxwood hedges, filled the courtyard and enclosed a central fountain, surrounded by four stately cypress trees. The high walls of the loggia framed the sky (Figure 0-4). The gentle splashing of the fountain, the scent of the elegant cypress trees, and the patina of the ochre walls created an enthralling and inspiring daily experience. Passing through this space during the year, I was both an observer and a participant in the changing seasons. For me, the courtyard represented a frame of reference for the dynamics of the garden and the passage of the sun; a living map of the year's journey through time, an alchemical transmutation of climate and architecture into an allegory of nature and design.

From my experience and research at the Academy, I came to realize that my original thesis was fundamentally flawed. Reflecting on my time at the Academy and the current state

Figure 0-4

The cortile at the American Academy in Rome.

(Photo: Marc Treib)

of architecture in the United States, I reached an entirely different point of view that broke from McHarg's impression of the uselessness of classical formal gardens. My findings indicated that passive garden design could be both functional and beautiful. The conclusion of my journey pointed to the many new and exciting possibilities that lay ahead for the creation of gardens designed for energy conservation.

The great environments of the past were a subtle, but thorough blend of metaphysics, passive design, and art. The great microclimates of the past were created through intuition, common sense, and an intimate connection to the seasons. We don't need complex computer models or data graphs, but rather a sympathetic understanding and appreciation of how the sun moves through the heavens. Sometimes, all that is required is time and patience. Just walk outside and observe the position of the sun.

Current events only serve to reinforce the necessity for more energy-conscious landscape design applications. Scientists have succeeded in documenting that human behavior is changing regional weather patterns. The burning of fossil fuels is warming the atmosphere through the greenhouse effect, producing "urban heat islands" and raising the temperature of the earth.[2] At the close of the twentieth century there were power shortages throughout the country as the demand for heating and cooling increases. California is currently experiencing rolling blackouts and power outages in an effort to conserve what limited energy is available. The Silicon Valley technology lobby is particularly concerned with rising fuel costs, as the computer industry burns 16 million kilowatt-hours worth of electricity annually; in contrast, the Detroit auto manufacturers use 9.2 million kilowatt-hours each year.[3]

As we march into the new millennium gasoline prices continue to climb across the United States, reaching over $2 per gallon in northern California. America, with 5 percent of the world's population, consumed 25 percent of the world's oil. Our Congress has yet to significantly raise fuel efficiency standards (which have actually declined since the 1970s); instead it is considering opening the Arctic National Wildlife refuge to drilling. To date, there is little mention from our political leaders about conservation or a national public-transit plan.

While the environmental future may look grim, these extreme conditions do provide opportunities for innovative planning and design. Many new and exciting opportunities lie ahead for the creation of garden forms that not only conserve energy, but are also works of art and places of spiritual renewal. By describing and detailing little-known inventions of our ancestral garden designers, I hope to generate both new ideas and modern adaptations of old ones — tools with which to build modern gardens that help save and preserve our natural environment while enhancing the spaces in which we live and work. My vision of the future foresees the flowering of new passive garden communities and the retrofitting of existing communities for the reduction of energy consumption. This vision could be a first small step in a strategy for moving our culture toward the creation of a more sustainable environment by incorporating the principles in this book into the planning and design of new communities.

Garden and Climate has been divided into four books. The four elements — earth, fire, air, and water — are the organizing divisions that categorize each book's garden inventions. The Greek philosopher Empedocles was the first to devise a system of four elemental bodies to explain the nature of reality. These eventually became known as the four Platonic solids. Plato assigned each element a geometric form: Earth

was represented by a cube; Fire, a tetrahedron; Air, an octahedron; and Water, a dodecahedron (or icosahedron). Plato
believed these basic units to be the building blocks of the
universe. In addition, these same four elements have long
been considered sacred by many cultures and formed the
symbolic typology of the traditional Islamic garden. Earth is
the surface on which we live; Fire is the sun that warms us;
Air is the cool breath of life; and Water quenches thirst and
sustains the living.

Each of the four books unfolds with its corresponding
Platonic solid, along with a discussion of its relationship
to the introductory thesis. A specific postulate opens each
chapter. The postulate defines the passive garden device that
will be examined in the body of the chapter. Each chapter
establishes a vocabulary by defining a historical context for
each passive device, and provides a thorough analysis of
prime examples, explaining how the garden device moder-
ates a microclimate.

Each book summarizes its design vocabulary in a contemporary garden prototype. The prototype synthesizes the
metaphysical journey, the benefits of passive design, and the
idea of the garden as art. The garden's context, location,
and environment are detailed, and each passive device and
function is described. The design summarizes how knowledge of the past can be refined and adapted to the present.
The conclusions bring the journey to an end with a brief
discussion of the wonders and marvels that follow in the
next book.

> If the world is to make great gardens again, we must both discov-
> er and apply in the changed circumstances of modern life, the
> principles which guided the garden-makers of the Renaissance,
> and must be ready to learn all that science can teach us concerning
> the laws of artistic presentment.[4]
>
> Sir Osbert Sitwell, *On the Making of Gardens*, 1909

Notes

1. Ian L. McHarg, [1969] 1971. *Design with Nature*. Garden City, NY: The American Museum of Natural History; Doubleday/Natural History Press, p. 71.

2. Jim Doyle, "Hot: Heat Rising from Cities Appears to be Changing Regional Weather Patterns," *San Francisco Chronicle*. March 6, 2000, Science, Health and Environment, p. 1.

3. A. Clay Thompson, "Power Hungry in Silicon Valley," *San Francisco Bay Guardian*, June 21, 2000, p. 16.

4. Sir Osbert Sitwell, *On the Making of Gardens*, New York: Charles Scribner's Sons, 1909, p. xix.

Acknowledgments

I am eternally grateful to the American Academy for awarding me the Rome Prize to embark on this voyage of *Garden and Climate*. The Department of Landscape Architecture, College of Environmental Design at the University of California, Berkeley established a positive climate for my explorations that has proven extremely productive. The Beatrix Farrand Research Fund has been a tremendous resource over many years; without this source of funding this book would have been nearly impossible. The Committee on Research, University of California, Berkeley, helped facilitate much of the production work for *Garden and Climate*.

Randy Hester's early support and continued commitment to the ideals of this book have always kept me focused. I would also like to sincerely thank all of my research assistants over the years: Paul Smith, Jennifer Madden, Catherine Harris, Annie Admunson, and Patrick McGannon for their long and arduous hours of reviewing, editing, and preparing the many drafts of this manuscript for publication. I must also thank Sheila Madden for her constructive editing of the first draft. I am indebted to Kathryn Drinkhouse for the very difficult task of formatting, organizing, and word-processing the original draft of the manuscript. Her perseverance and dedication are to be admired. Lisa Micheli contributed an ecological overview, and her insight emphasized the manuscript's environmental design potential. It was a pleasure to work with Elizabeth Byrne, Head Librarian, College of Environmental Design, University of California Berkeley, who magically could find the most obscure references when I was at my most helpless. Waverly Lowell, head of the Environmental Design Documents Collection, graciously supplied many photographic references. Wendy Lochner, the original editor of this book, was instrumental in bringing *Garden and Climate* into print. I thank her for her foresight. And, for her methodical scrutiny of the final text, I am especially grateful to my mother.

A Bogliasco Fellowship at the Ligurian Center for the Arts and Humanities in Genoa, Italy, provided an outstanding climate and atmosphere for me to complete the final draft. I was fortunate to receive a Rockefeller Foundation Fellowship at the Bellagio Study Center in Lake Como, Italy, where I had the most magnificent studio in the world to finish these illustrations.

Marc Treib has been an influential force throughout the history of the manuscript. We first met at the American Academy in Rome when we toured many of these gardens together. Since then he has become not only a great friend, but a mentor as well. His faith and guidance since the inception of this book have been invaluable. Marc not only reviewed, critiqued, and edited the manuscripts, but also designed a magnificent book. I wish to express my sincere gratitude to him.

Most important, Elizabeth Boults's assistance with editing and rewriting the final draft was critical to the successful completion of this book. Her positive energy, enthusiasm, and creative inspiration have been paramount in keeping me afloat through the endless obstacles that attempted to keep this project from fruition. I cannot thank her enough, for without her optimism and encouragement I could not have made it.

Garden *and* Climate

Book I: **Earth**

Yesterday I came to the villa at Careggi, not to cultivate my fields but my Soul.[1]
Cosimo de Medici

Earth is the most fundamental of the four elements that constitute the physical world. Plato represented earth as a stable cube, the primary geometrical solid from which were generated the other more ephemeral elements of Fire, Air, and Water. Earth may be understood both as a structural foundation and as a source of sustenance, not only for physical life, but also for the spirit. It can be cultivated to provide nourishment, and, as Cosimo de Medici stated, to comfort the soul.

The physical and chemical properties of earth make it an effective starting point for the design of passive microclimates. Due to its capacity for insulation, earth is an ideal building material. This humble substance also supplies the nutrients necessary for the growth and development of plants, which in turn produce cool, shady environments that generate oxygen and purify the air.

In addition to the earth's potential to support life and mitigate extremes of climate, there are aesthetic and psychological aspects resulting from its role in the landscape. It can be molded into forms that both shelter and inspire us. It is traditionally associated with images of fertility and fecundity, and, too, with ideas of the underworld. In Greek and Roman mythology many natural forces were personified by deities connected with the earth. Earth was an integral part of the Roman belief system as demonstrated in the design of their built environments.

A reconsideration of historical precedents, such as those created by the Romans in the design of passive microclimates, has become imperative given the harmful and dangerous building practices and attitudes of contemporary culture. Asphalt and concrete change the permeability of the earth's surface and disrupt the natural traffic patterns of water and heat in the environment. In contrast, Roman and Italian

Renaissance designers understood earth's role in modifying microclimates and developed methods and practices that took advantage of earth as an important design element. Thick walls of earth or stone address hot and dry climates by delaying the transmission of heat (a property known as thermal mass). Heat transfer works as follows. The earth or stone cools during the night. Throughout the day these surfaces, particularly those facing south and west, receive considerable radiant heat from the sun, which is absorbed by the earth or stone. But it takes a long time for this heat to penetrate through these materials, so that by morning the heat has dissipated and the cycle begins anew, with the space remaining cool throughout the day.

In Book I, we examine architectural and landscape elements that successfully combine the scientific and ecological aspects of earth with its potential as a powerful design medium. At the close of the historical discussion, guidelines postulated at the beginning of each chapter will be applied to the design of a contemporary garden prototype. The goal is to create beautiful and functional passive microclimates that address the needs of both body and soul.

Postulate I: **Earth Seats**

● The earth seat is a simple block of compacted soil, usually planted with aromatic ground cover or turf, which uses the earth's cooling properties to provide comfort and repose on hot summer days. Ideally, earth seats occupy shady zones beneath trees or along a garden's edge and are planted with wildflowers. Whether constructed of soil, brick, wood or stone, an earth seat may take the form of an architectural element to soften the transition from building to landscape. It can nest in small intimate locations or extend along the entire edge of large outdoor spaces (Figure I-1).

In all your Gardens and Orchards, bankes and seats of Camomile, Peny-royall, Dasies and Violets, are seemly and comfortable. [2]
W. Lawson, The Country Housewife's Garden

The simple idea of a bank of grass-covered earth, high enough to sit upon and perhaps blanketed with flowers, remains enchanting to this day. As moisture transpires between grass, flowers, and soil, the earth remains cool and comfortable. It is not through the sense of touch alone that the earth seat comforts its users; when crushed, the flowers planted upon the seat release a pleasing fragrance. Visually, too, one finds ease in the earth seat, as green, the color of grass, is known to be soothing to the eye.

First recorded in medieval paintings and through the ballads and poems of troubadours, earth seats have been integral to the creation of passive microclimates, and have remained popular for centuries. From the early botanically correct illustrations of maidens sitting on earthen seats in lush walled gardens, to the 1478 agricultural treatise *Ruralium Commodorum* by Pietro de Crescenzi, the garden context of the earth seat has been described as "shaded by a vine pergola and sweet scented and blossoming trees like cypress, bay, apples, pears and pomegranates planted round the walls."[3] In these settings, earth seats often occupied a portion of the perimeter wall of enclosed gardens and were built from the same material (Figure I-2).

While earth seats may properly be called "turf seats" when they are composed entirely of grass, the term is used here to include any cool and peaceful garden seat that utilizes the earth's natural cooling properties. Because of the short life-span of its living material, few historical examples of true earth seats survive. The medieval turf seat can perhaps be understood as evolving into the carved stone bench of Renaissance gardens (Figure I-3), wherein the grass and flowers have been replaced with the natural coolness of stone shaded from sunlight.

Freestanding stone benches, or seating niches carved from natural stone outcroppings, were a more permanent device in creating comfortable microclimates. One of the most imaginative of this style can be found at the Villa Rupert on the island of Majorca in Spain. On a cliff overlooking the Mediterranean Sea, this ingenious seating pocket sinks deep into the earth (Figure I-4). The surrounding walls reach well above the eye level of the average person; a continuous stone bench runs along its base. The thick stone walls sunken into the ground retain the coolness of earth and keep the temperature quite pleasant even during the hot summer months (Figure I-5). A table carved from the same stone occupies the center of the shaded seating area.

Many of us have fond memories of lying in the cool grass in summer and watching bees buzz over a carpet of flowers. Perhaps one of the earth seat's charms is the opportunity it gives adults to enjoy this wonderful childhood activity. As garden forms evolved through history, and garden elements acquired increasingly sophisticated functions, the earth seat too became more complex. While the earth seat relies on the earth for insulation and on the circulation of cool air, seating areas carved more deeply into the damp recesses of the earth are known as grottoes. They are described in the next chapter.

● Figure I-I *(opposite)*
The earth seat as passive microclimatic design element.

Figure I-2
Typical earth seat built against a garden wall of brick.

Figure I-3 *(below)*
Villa Orsini, Sacra Bosco, Bomarzo, Italy

A sensuous stone bench carved from the tufa rock at
the garden of Bomarzo, Italy.
(Photo: Marc Treib)

Figure I-4 *(opposite top)*
Villa Rupert, Palma, Majorca, Spain.

Earth seat cut deep into a cliff next to the sea.

Figure I-5 *(opposite below)*
Villa Rupert, Palma, Majorca, Spain.

Gnarled trees shade the sunken seating pocket.

Earth Seats
Contemporary Applications

1. Construct earth seats to the same height as typical park benches, about 18 inches high. The structure can be formed of any building material such as brick, stone, or concrete. Build a planting cavity a minimum of 1 foot deep and approximately 2 feet wide to retain soil on four sides.

2. Seed the potting soil of the turf seat with grass and flowers. Use flowers or herbs like thyme that when crushed will add a pleasant fragrance to the air.

3. Planted with grass, the cool green of the turf seat will soothe the eyes.

4. Turf seats can be built into the base of exterior building walls, fences, or courtyards to make green backdrops and garden borders.

5. When excavated from soil or stone, the top of the earth seat must be above the average person's head to take advantage of the natural cooling properties of the earth. Plant trees along the edges of the excavated seating area to provide for shade by which to keep the seat cool.

Figure I-6   *(opposite)*

April, Hall of the Months,
Il Palazzo di Schifanoia, Ferrara, Italy.
Fifteenth century. Francesco del Cossa.

In this allegorical painting representing the month of April and the triumph of Venus, the Goddess of Love, an amorous young couple sits on an earth seat constructed of stone and planted with grass. Other couples make music in a lush garden. The rabbit beneath the seat symbolizes fertility.

(Courtesy Musei Civici Arte Antica, Ferrara)

Figure I-7

The tree seat, reminiscent of a medieval style.

A composite of numerous sources yielded a common variation on the earth seat: the "tree seat." Circling each trunk of selected trees, the earth was confined by wattle-woven fencing and covered with a cushion of grass. Not only do the earth and grass provide a cool seat, but the tree's canopy offers a shady retreat.

Figure I-8

Orsini Park, Pitigliano, Italy.
1560. Niccolo IV.

A stone variation of the earth seat can be found inside Orsini Park, near the lake of Bolsena. Built along a promontory on a tufa-rock plateau, a large, arched niche was carved to create a shallow cavern. A seat, also of tufa, fills the back of the cavern. This seating nook affords a view of the landscape from inside the shadows of the cool earth and provides a comfortable summer microclimate.

Postulate II: **Grottoes**

● The grotto is an earth-sheltered construction that has many applications in the design of passive microclimates. Imitating a natural cave or cavern, the grotto is a dark, mysterious hollow that may be decorated with natural materials such as shells, river stones, petrified rocks, and volcanic glass. These rustic follies were dug into the earth or built into hillsides, open to the prevailing winds for maximum cooling (Figure I-9). The cavelike atmosphere also lent an air of mystery and drama to a garden.

Grottos were above all sacred places: where homage was given to the divinities of sources and water. [4]
Naomi Miller

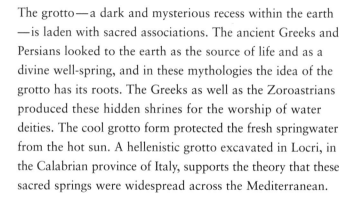

The grotto—a dark and mysterious recess within the earth—is laden with sacred associations. The ancient Greeks and Persians looked to the earth as the source of life and as a divine well-spring, and in these mythologies the idea of the grotto has its roots. The Greeks as well as the Zoroastrians produced these hidden shrines for the worship of water deities. The cool grotto form protected the fresh springwater from the hot sun. A hellenistic grotto excavated in Locri, in the Calabrian province of Italy, supports the theory that these sacred springs were widespread across the Mediterranean.

The grotto as natural shrine slowly evolved into a more artificially constructed form with increasingly secular functions. Domestic grottoes proliferated in the homes and gardens of the patrician class during the Roman republic. As classical themes were revived during the Renaissance, elaborately decorated grottoes were popular additions to Italian villa gardens of the fifteenth and sixteenth centuries. The grotto remained a sanctuary in the sense that it was a haven safe from the harsh rays of the summer sun; it took on an expanded role as a place of refuge from everyday realities. The cool shady retreats were used for "delight, meditation, rest, relaxation. For feasting and fooleries."[5] As a place

● Figure I-9 *(opposite)*
The grotto as a passive microclimatic device.

Figure I-10a
Villa Orsini, Sacro Bosco, Bomarzo, Italy.
Entrance to the grotto.

Figure I-10b
Villa Orsini, Sacro Bosco, Bomarzo, Italy.
Interior of the grotto with seating and table.

where wild nature ran free, the walls of a grotto were often adorned with satyrs.

The grotto symbolized the power of the earth to cool the body and refresh the spirit. It is both a delightful retreat and a functional device that uses the density and mass of soil to retain coolness. Designed with natural elements such as moss and stalactites, and kept cool by the naturally insulating ability of the earth, the grotto recreated the mystery and drama of being inside a cave. To heighten the subterranean experience, water was often introduced either through naturally occurring or engineered springs. These theatrical effects were important considerations in the design of Italian renaissance and baroque gardens.

A most bizarre example of an Italian Renaissance grotto lurks on a hillside in the park of Bomarzo in Lazio. Piero Francesco "Vicino" Orsini, the Duke of Bomarzo, built the garden between 1553 and 1560 in a woodland at the foot of the hilltown. In its original layout, the visitor passed through formal gardens before entering the "sacred wood," as the Duke had named it. Climbing to a second garden terrace, one is still greeted today by a horrific giant monster face on the grotto (Figure I-10a). The facade, carved from a low hillside, faces slightly east. The visual impression of the exterior is so overwhelming that people often overlook the grotto's interior space.

The mouth of the dreaded monster opens into a cave, and its eyes act as an *oculus*, which is a term for a round opening usually in a ceiling (Figure I-10b). Over the huge mouth reads the inscription "Leave every care, you who enter here." On the other side of this grotesque facade is a dark and pleasantly cool grotto. Looking out into the woodland from a carved stone bench along the rear wall inside (Figure I-11), the monster's "tongue" is read as a table, and the

Figure I-11
Villa Orsini, Sacro Bosco, Bomarzo, Italy.

The monster's face as a window.
(Photo: Catherine Harris)

Figure I-12a *(opposite above)*
Villa Garzoni, Collodi, Italy.

Rusticated entrance to the grotto.

Figure I-12b *(opposite below)*
Villa Garzoni, Collodi, Italy.

Section through the grotto located at the midpoint of
the garden.

courageous visitor is rewarded with a remarkable view. Bright light streaming through the eerie eyes and mouth contrasts with the dark stillness of the deep interior. The monstrous head is transformed into an agreeable, if unusual, place to spend a hot summer day.

A very different style grotto can be seen in the small town of Collodi, near Lucca, in the ornate baroque gardens of the Villa Garzoni. Completed in 1652, the hillside terrace grotto is found on the second terrace of the garden's central axis, facing south. The grotto, deep and spacious, is entered through a large rusticated portal (Figure I-12a). The inner walls support fountains and built-in seats, and are decorated with pebbles, stones, and other earthen treasures (Figure I-12b). From the perspective of a person seated on the stone seats, the grotto's portal frames a vista of the valley below and the region's hillside agricultural terraces, while the lower gardens seemingly disappear. The cool cavernous grotto is a refuge from the blistering Italian sun. As the central feature in the garden in both plan and elevation, the grotto offers an ideal place to rest, as one begins the climb up the steep slope to the upper garden levels (Figure I-13).

The grotto has evolved from the form of a natural sacred cave to a highly ornamental and pleasurable retreat, all the while using the earth as insulation to maintain lower temperatures. The next chapter, Subterranean Rooms, also examines cool spaces carved from the earth, but these passive microclimates are of a much different scale and have more diverse uses in the landscape.

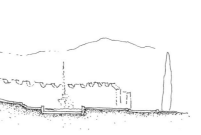

Figure I-13 *(opposite)*
Villa Garzoni, Collodi, Italy.

View from the lower garden to the grotto entrance.
(Photo: Marc Treib)

Figure I-14a
Villa Cicogna, Bisuschio, Italy.
Redesigned in the sixteenth century;
gardens by Gianpietro Cicogna. Section.

The Villa Cicogna has a functional and spacious grotto located in a sunken courtyard on the southern side of the villa. The grotto's entrance faces north leaving it in shade year-round. From the inside, the grotto walls frame two small pools, each with elevated basins with single jets of water. The splashing from these fountains reverberates within the cavern while reflections from the pool dance on the walls.

Figure I-14b
Villa Cicogna, Bisuschio, Italy. Plan.

Encircling the central grotto is a narrow corridor obscured in shadows. One enters through one of three small, rock archways, which produce the illusion of being surrounded by an intricate system of tunnels. The mysterious passageways contribute psychologically cooling effects by creating a feeling of being deep within the earth's recesses.

Figure I-15 *(opposite left)*
Giardino dei Giusti, Verona, Italy.
Mid-sixteenth century, designer unknown.

The Giardino dei Giusti, built against the steep hillside of San Pietro, combined trompe l'oeil effects within the grotto form. These elaborate illusions once made the garden one of the most famous gardens in Italy. An allée of cypress trees forms the garden's main axis, leading to a series of stairs, and terminating in the large grotto carved from rock. A mirror, once located in the rear of the grotto, reflected the sky and, when viewed from the allée, a tunnel seemed to penetrate the hill.

Figure I-16 *(opposite right)*
Giardino dei Giusti, Verona, Italy.
(Photo: Marc Treib)

Like the grotto at Bomarzo, a monster face looks out from the apex of the cliff to the central allée below, and dominates the features of this garden. From this cool grotto perspective, the views of the city of Verona are particularly grand.

The grotto demonstrates how both aesthetics and technics combine to form effective landscape spaces.

Figure I-17
Giardino dei Giusti, Verona, Italy.
[Painted by Kitty Sullivan, the author's mother]

According to historical accounts, a most unusual use of the grotto created a gripping spectacle: The smoke from a fire built inside the mouth of the monster would exit the eye sockets, creating a fearful apparition. As a grand finale, the coals would be tossed from the mouth, producing the effect of a fire-spitting monster.

Grottoes
Contemporary Applications

1. Constructed to resemble a cave, the true grotto will provide a cool interior offering protection from the hot sun.

2. Exploit the natural insulating properties of the earth by burrowing the grotto directly into a hillside, or by covering the structure with an earthen layer that is a minimum of 8 feet deep.

3. Locate the grotto as a central focal point in the garden where it will become a destination and hidden retreat, or place the grotto within the main architectural structure.

4. The threshold of the grotto is an ideal space for imaginative designs. Draw people inside by transporting them through fantastic portals.

5. The interior of a grotto should be large enough to constitute a small room. Place comfortable seating along its interior walls.

Figure 1-18
Isola Bella, Lago Maggiore, Italy.

Isola Bella's highly ornate grottos are not excavated from the earth, but built into the south basement of the huge villa; their windows open to the lake, encouraging the flow of cool air directly into the rooms. In the Isola Bella gardens, the grotto form becomes thoroughly integrated with the structure; it is a perfect example of how traditional passive devices can be artfully merged with contemporary building patterns.

● Figure 1-19 *(opposite)*
Nature recreated in a subterranean room.

Postulate III: **Subterranean Rooms**

● Subterranean rooms combine the climatic benefits of earthen insulation with the aesthetics of a contained interior garden space. They are built into the earth, usually under architectural structures, and are intended as living spaces (Figure I-19). The smooth, thick walls of subterranean rooms are often decorated in trompe l'oeil garden scenes or paintings of nature, and their ceilings may create the illusion of sky, complete with clouds and birds.

These underground corridors and chambers provided with fountains were meant especially for hot regions; they provided cool and shaded spaces in which to walk or repose, in the manner of ancient Romans, while protected from the heat of the sun.[6]
Giovanni d'Vincenzo Scamozzi

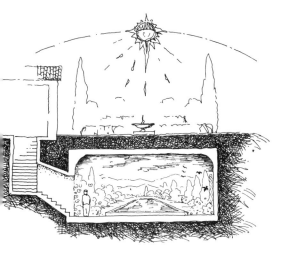

The very origins of human dwelling may indeed be traced to the cave. As discussed in the section on grottoes, the ancient Romans incorporated cavelike forms into their architecture to encourage passive cooling. These forms evolved into more architectural spaces that I term "subterranean rooms."

A subterranean room, for the purposes of this book, is a hybrid of the natural cave and the interior courtyard or classical *peristyle* garden. Like the grotto, subterranean rooms were constructed specifically to create cool spaces; where the cavelike grotto adapts the mystery and spiritual ambience of being underground, the subterranean room relies on illusionistic effects, like painting, to reconnect with nature and the outdoors. Hence the grotto and the subterranean room diverge in both aesthetic treatment and in context.

The following five examples of subterranean rooms (three from the classical age and two from the Renaissance) illustrate how the natural cooling properties of the earth are combined with the design of social spaces (like dining rooms), recreational spaces (like swimming and fishing pools), and psychological and metaphysical spaces (like a simulated "mine-shaft").

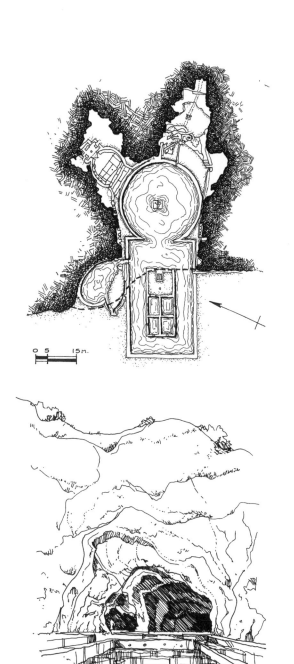

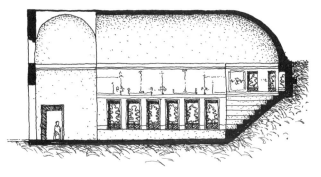

The evolution of natural caves into more architectural spaces can best be understood by describing subterranean rooms found at Sperlonga in Italy, built for the Roman emperor Tiberius during the first century BC. This series of three adjoining caves opens to the west and takes advantage of the breezes from the Tyrrhenian Sea (Figure I-20a). A spring-fed circular pool, about 33 feet in diameter, sits in the central subterranean room beside a long rectangular basin. The natural cooling properties of these subterranean rooms, combined with the use of water, produced a naturally air-conditioned complex. An island-like *triclinium*, or dining room, was constructed amid the water features, with low, slanted stone couches typical of the period. While food arrived by small boats, diners reclined on the "island" with their backs to the setting sun (Figure I-20b). Mosaic decoration and sculpture with heroic and maritime themes completed the scene.

Life in Roman cities obviously precluded the use of natural caves; to achieve the same thermal effects, subterranean rooms were built directly below urban developments. Built late in the first century BC, the subterranean room at the Auditorium of Maecenas complemented the gardens covering the Esquiline Hill in Rome. Half submerged into the earth, it contained a subterranean semi-circular exedra, a classical architectural feature forming an apselike recess or niche (Figure I-21). The flow of space through this architectural element combined with the garden scenes painted on the surrounding walls to provide the visitor with a desirable feeling of expansiveness and the sense of being outside and unseasonably cool (Figure I-22).

A second Roman subterranean room that portrays the idea of being in a garden is the House of Livia on the Palatine Hill. Livia's subterranean room was sunk 9 feet into the earth, and its four uninterrupted walls were filled with paintings of plants and garden elements.

Figure I-22
Auditorium of Maecenas, Rome, Italy.

Illusionistic painting of garden scene.

(Photo: Author)

The ideas of the Romans greatly influenced Renaissance culture and were reflected in the architectural devices of the time. Renaissance thought turned away from the introspective focus of medieval life and sought a broader understanding of the world and the role of the individual human being on earth, much like the classical scholars had centuries before. This line of reasoning, based on observations of nature and the role of the individual designer in shaping space, led to the increasing complexity of the subterranean room as a passive microclimatic and social and sculptural device.

The Villa di Papa Giulio in Rome serves perhaps as the archetype for the Renaissance use of the subterranean room, with its intricate manipulation of space for theatrical and climatic effect (Figure I-23). Pope Julius III commissioned the villa between 1550 and 1555 from the leading architect of the day, Giacomo Barozzi da Vignola, who was assisted by the equally renowned Bartolommeo Ammannati and Giorgio Vasari. The villa's purpose was strictly for entertaining; it was used as a cool daytime retreat in the hot summer months and contained no permanent living quarters.

A complex progression of vertical and horizontal planes unfolded to delight and surprise the visitor. Entering the garden through a horseshoe-shaped courtyard, the solid mass of building transforms into a semicircular vaulted loggia, and a colonnaded screen frames a central perspective of a similarly styled space beyond. The architectural elements create a mirror-like play of views from one space into another. Unexpectedly, the colonnaded portico directly opposite the entrance courtyard drops before the visitor's view, revealing a series of subterranean rooms (Figure I-24a). A pair of stairs lead to a lower mezzanine-level courtyard surrounded by a balustrade, and two rooms used for dining on its north and south sides. Tucked away to the sides of the northern dining room are two passageways with stairs that lead to

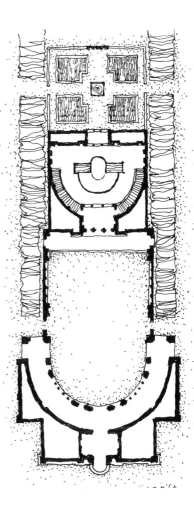

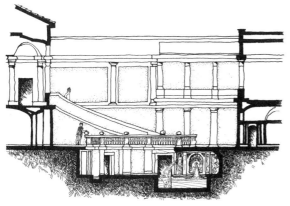

Figure I-23 *(above left)*
Villa di Papa Giulio, Rome, Italy.
Sunken court, subterranean rooms, and nymphaeum.
(Photo: Marc Treib)

Figure I-24a *(above right)*
Villa di Papa Giulio, Rome, Italy. Plan.
Villa, nymphaeum, and parterre.

Figure I-24b *(left)*
Villa di Papa Giulio, Rome, Italy. Section.
Relationship of subterranean elements.

the lowest level and the cool seclusion of the space called the *nymphaeum*: a cavelike pool or fountain whose name stems from its pagan use as a shrine to the water deities (Figure I-24b). The use of the nymphaeum itself as a passive microclimatic device will be presented in Book IV.

The lowest subterranean level at the Villa di Papa Giulio is an odd combination of cave, nymphaeum, and swimming pool. Here, the nymphaeum is embellished with ferns, mosses, caryatids, jets of water, and decorative rockery, almost like those of a stage set. Georgina Masson states that the nymphaeum of the Villa di Papa Giulio is a perfect example of "the old classical relationship between theater and garden design."[7] Two rectangular pools, commonly referred to as bathing pools, lie on both sides of the nymphaeum and continue into hidden rooms where one can swim in the cool darkness. A small narrow channel runs along the edge of the entire court, completely enclosing it in water. The mezzanine above shades the pools and water elements, creating a cool and deeply relaxing place to withdraw from the hot midday or late afternoon sun.

The Villa di Papa Giulio displays a complicated choreography of circulation and perspective; a more fanciful and figurative example of the climatic effects of a subterranean room can be seen at the Villa Medici in Pratolino, outside Florence (Figure I-25). Built for the Grand Duke Francesco I de Medici, the garden occupies a steep and rugged site at the foot of the Apennine mountains, and serves as the setting for a bizarre sculptural mass aptly named the "Apennino." A large pool containing several very unusual subterranean rooms surrounds the gigantic figure—almost 40 feet high—designed by Giovanni da Bologna in 1579 (Figure I-26a). A rock cave once enclosed the back and head of the Apennino, but the cave disappeared in the seventeenth century with almost all of its waterworks, sculpture, paintings, and mechanical automata.

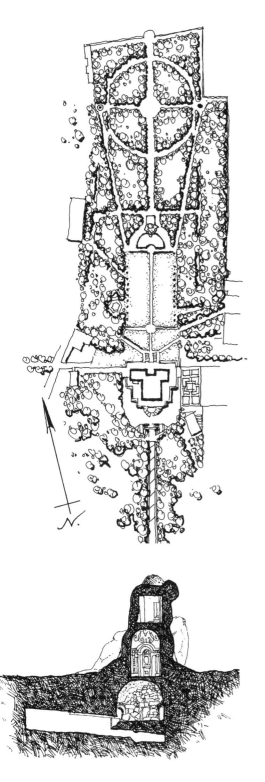

One of the few remaining original elements at the Villa Medici, the Apennino is "both a mountain carved into a man, and a man half transformed into a mountain."[8] Below the giant's head are a series of vertical spaces that open deep into the earth. The lowest of these, "the mine shaft," intended metaphorically—through its form and ornamentation—to create the illusion of geological exploration, mining, and metallurgy—processes relating to the extraction of natural elements in the earth (Figure I-26b).

The most amusing space in the once-subterranean structure is the uppermost room. Directly above the mine shaft are a domed room with rusticated walls and a hidden staircase leading to an ornamented room above it. Spiraling up to what is essentially the Apennino's "brain," small niches lead to openings equivalent to the giant's eyes; these allow the visitor to see through the eyes of the giant. According to legend, Duke Francesco would steal away inside the Apennino and spend the day fishing from its eyes. He enjoyed this creation so much he could disappear for weeks at a time! The journey inside the Apennino, from the depths of the earth to a vantage point high above the garden's central axis, takes place within a managed microclimate — insulated by the earth and the thick stone body of the sculptural figure.

We have examined a variety of subterranean rooms that have been used as devices for passive cooling through some type of visual or physical connection with the landscape. The next microclimatic device we will explore is the underground passage or *cryptoporticus*, which was used as a cool circulation space.

Subterranean Rooms
Contemporary Applications

1. Build the subterranean room at least 6 feet below ground if possible, using the earth as insulation.

2. Use illusionistic effects, like those created by trompe l'oeil painting of garden scenes, to represent the outdoors and disguise the fact of being underground.

3. Excavate the subterranean room into the foundation of a dwelling to create additional space for daytime retreats and summer dining.

4. Rooms can be built above ground and covered with thick layers of earth, with interior walls and ceilings built with concrete. Wire mesh coated with a concrete finish can retain an insulating layer of earth 2 to 6 feet thick. This passive cooling device can be sculpted into many geometric and anthropomorphic forms.

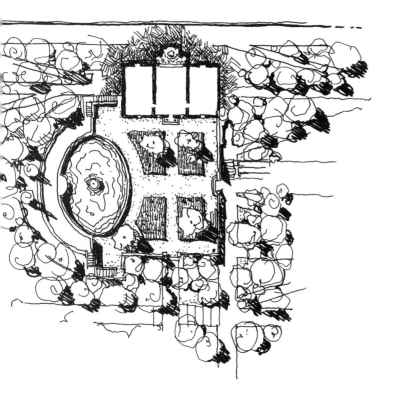

Figure I-27a *(above)*
Villa d'Este, Tivoli, Italy.
1550–72, designed by Pirro Ligorio. Section.

Cardinal Ippolito II d'Este of Ferrara had a series of isolated subterranean chambers built into the hillside, below his suburban estate, that used principles of microclimatics and "cool" imagery to create comfortable summer living spaces.

Figure I-27b *(opposite below)*
Villa d'Este, Tivoli, Italy. Plan.

Two smaller rooms flank the grotto's central room. They once contained beds on which people could nap after dining in the adjacent courtyard, or perhaps could spend the night when the heat was oppressive. The rooms might also have been used to change clothes for swimming in the adjoining Ovato Pool, or for bathing in the Fountain of Venus, also referred to as the "Bathing Rooms."

Figure I-28a
Villa Madama, Rome, Italy. 1516.
Plan by Raphael.

The Medici Pope Clement VII built the Villa Madama in 1516, on Monte Mario on the northern outskirts of Rome. Several artists designed the complex, although most people associate it with Raphael, who died during the initial phase of the project. Raphael's contemporaries — Antonio Sangallo, Giovanni da Udine, and Giulio Romano — strongly influenced the final design. The sack of Rome interrupted its construction in 1527, but speculative plans record the intended design.

Figure I-28b
Villa Madama, Rome, Italy. Section.

Three subterranean rooms, with arched recesses approximately 18 feet in height, depth, and width create a retaining wall for the terrace above. Narrow passageways interconnect these recesses. The floors of the three subterranean rooms are just a few feet above the surface of a pool, making it easy to dive from their edge. Jets of water from the terrace above arcs over the rooms and splashes into the pool. An early engraving shows arcs of water coming from small niches between vaulted openings. The high angle of the summer sun shades these rooms, and because they are insulated by the earth they remain comfortably cool even in the warmest weather. Deep in the shade of the recesses, the cool air from the pool floats inward and the vaults reverberate with the sound of splashing water.

Postulate IV: **Cryptoportici**

● The cryptoporticus is a narrow, underground corridor that connects a site's major architectural elements, and allows access and circulation removed from direct sunlight. As a subterranean space, the cryptoporticus uses the earth's natural ability to insulate; as a microclimatic device it profits from its position in the landscape. Its architectural form as a linear structure with high, vaulted ceilings stimulates the movement of air (Figure I-29).

Our ancestors would employ many methods to counter the heat: among them I am delighted by their underground porticoes and vaults which receive light only from the top. They also delighted in halls with large windows (provided they did not face south) which received shady air from covered places.[9]
Leon Battista Alberti

● Figure I-29
The cryptoporticus as a passive cooling device.

Figure I-30 *(opposite)*
Various architectural forms of the cryptoporticus.
Top:
As a long and narrow underground hallway with tall, arched ceilings
Center:
With openings in the roof to admit light
Bottom:
As an open loggia to capture prevailing breezes

The cryptoporticus was a truly marvelous invention. First developed by the Romans, and later refined by Renaissance architects, these ingenious spaces not only provided comfortable passage through a garden in summer, but also directed cool air into the adjacent rooms of a dwelling. Simply explained, by manipulating architectural form through openings and orientation, the cryptoporticus funnels and accelerates the cool air pockets within subterranean structures. The cool air that lies close to the earth's surface remains in constant flux with the warmer air currents above; the natural movement of air in itself refreshes and cools the skin. This simple form of air conditioning, when combined with other types of earthen rooms, creates a pleasant atmosphere during the scorching Italian summer season.

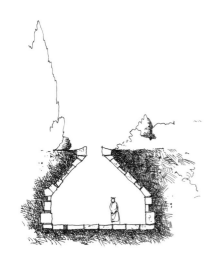

In Roman architecture the *Cryptoporticus subterranea* was an enclosed underground passage or portico (Figure I-30). It was typically a long, narrow room designed as a retreat from the summer sun that utilized the density of the earth to insulate and cool the space. Built as a single feature or sometimes forming a network of subterranean corridors, they were used by servants and family to move about the dwelling.

While very few written descriptions of these devices survive, early writings suggest that Pliny the Younger's Villa Tusci, near Citta di Castello in Umbria, included several cryptoportici that connected the various parts of the villa and its outlying structures (Figure I-31). Pliny had written about the cooling properties of this feature which "in the midst of summer heats, retains its pent-up chilliness, and enjoys its own atmosphere."[10] According to his writings, and confirmed by archeological evidence, Pliny was so impressed by the cooling capacity of his cryptoporticus that he included a variation of the device in his other villa in Laurentina (Figure I-32).

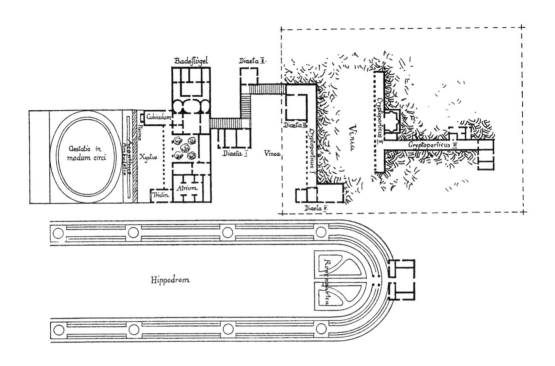

Hippodrom

Figure I-31
Pliny the Younger's villa, Umbria, Italy. Plan.

The cryptoporticus connects the villa to outlying garden structures.

Figure I-32
Pliny the Younger's Laurentine villa, Italy.

Section of cryptoporticus used to capture cool air.

Figure I-33 *(opposite)*
Hadrian's Villa, Tivoli, Italy.

Plan of the complex of buildings and gardens.

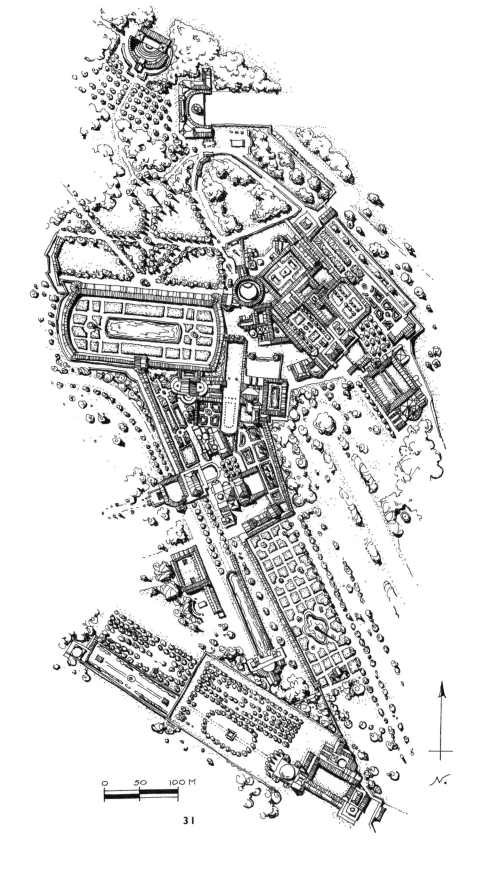

0   50   100 M

N.

31

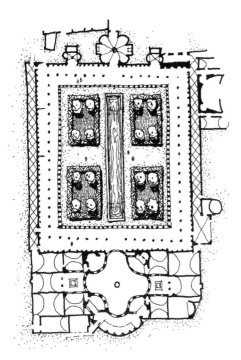

Though only scattered ruins of most cryptoportici remain, excavations of several sites—including the Imperial villas around Lake Albano—indicate how extensively the Romans used this device. While it is difficult to form a complete picture of the configuration of these forms, Hadrian's Villa at Tivoli contains the most outstanding examples of extant Roman cryptoportici.

Built between AD 118 and 138 at the base of the Tivoli hills east of Rome, the remains of Hadrian's Villa reveal the interrelationship of the underground structures to the villa. One of the largest archeological complexes from the Roman empire, the villa covers an area of roughly 740 acres and has a perimeter of three miles (Figure I-33). Hadrian's cryptoportici are believed to have once been so extensive that people could move from one part of the estate to another, completely underground, without ever being in direct sunlight. The vestiges of one cryptoporticus can be seen today along the east wall of the *ninfeo*, or nymphaeum, while the remains of two additional cryptoportici are located along the east and west sides of a large, rectangular courtyard known as the Piazza d'Oro. These parallel passageways are almost 200 feet long, and were designed so that occupants could walk comfortably and leisurely between buildings in the sweltering heat of summer (Figure I-34).

In addition to its use as a cool passageway for human circulation, the cryptoporticus also functioned as a circulation device for cool air. The cryptoporticus under the Peschiera section of Hadrian's Villa demonstrates the efficacy of this form as a sophisticated microclimatic device. The Peschiera was a rectangular pool, roughly 40 feet by 80 feet, once enclosed on all four sides by a continuous colonnaded portico or *quadriportico*. Directly beneath this ground-level portico was the long, vaulted, underground corridor of the cryptoporticus, also rectangular in plan (Figure I-35). Small openings

Figure I-34
Hadrian's Villa, Tivoli.
Plan of Piazza d'Oro showing parallel cryptoportici along the edge of the courtyard.

Figure I-35
Hadrian's Villa, Tivoli. *(opposite)*
Cryptoporticus with high opening to let in cool air from the pool's surface above.
(Photo: Marc Treib)

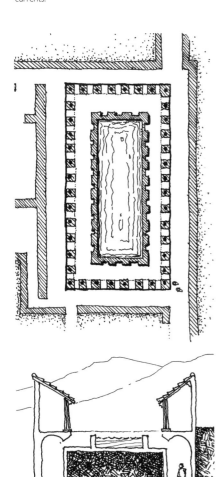

in the vault of the cryptoporticus, located slightly above the ground level of the pool outside, admitted daylight into the cryptoporticus and captured the cool air that would drift down from the surface of the pool (Figure I-36).

Originally, marble mosaics adorned the floors of these cryptoportici and paintings covered the walls and ceiling. The care and attention with which Hadrian directed the design of these spaces suggests that they were not merely passageways but discrete living places in their own right.

Italian Renaissance designers studied and elaborated upon the technology of the cryptoporticus as a microclimatic device handed down from the ancients. Historians believe that the cryptoporticus at Hadrian's Villa strongly influenced Pirro Ligorio's design for the Villa d'Este some 1500 years later (Figure I-37a). Located near Tivoli, in the same hills outside Rome, the connection to the cryptoporticus at Hadrian's Villa seems clear in both form and function. The relation was not missed by early visitors to the Villa d'Este: When Michel de Montaigne was there in 1580 or 1581, both the house and the garden were still unfinished but, with his perspicacious French eye for creature comforts, he noticed that an ingenious air-cooling system modeled no doubt on that of the Romans, was already working in the rooms of the lower floor.[11]

Built into the side of the steep hill forming the foundation of the villa was an air-cooling cryptoporticus (Figure I-37b). Oriented toward the west and insulated by the earth, the cryptoporticus was completely hidden from sunlight and remained an eternally cool passageway. A small opening at the southwestern end, situated at the edge of a cliff high above the valley below, caught the breeze rising up the side of the hill and directed it through the length of the 348-foot-long passageway. Consequently, the cool air in this 8-foot-

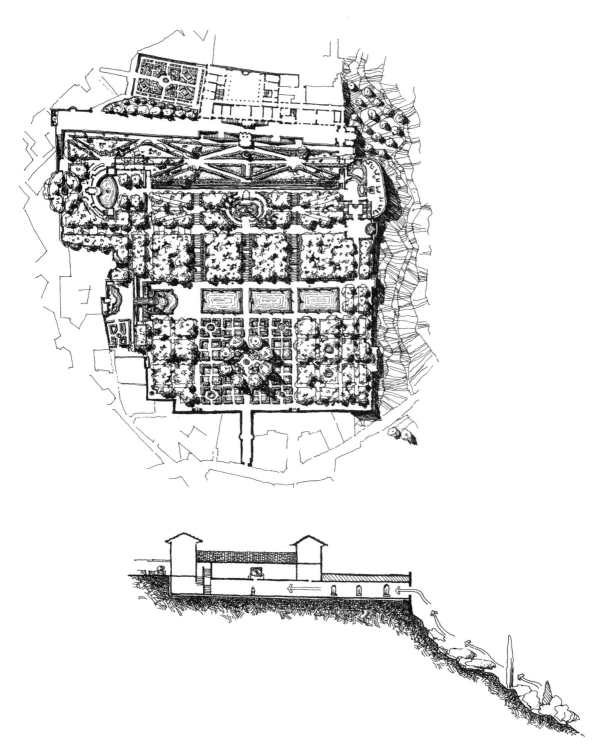

35   CRYPTOPORTICI

Figure I-38a *(left below)*

Villa Cicogna, Bisuschio, Piedmont, Italy.
Redesigned in the sixteenth century.
Gardens by Gianpietro Cicogna.

The building and gardens of Villa Cicogna are built into the hillside overlooking Lake Lugano. This illustration shows the cryptoporticus in a garden context, where it functions as a shaded passageway.

Figure I-38b *(left botom)*
Villa Cicogna, Bisuschio, Piedmont, Italy.

A high retaining wall bordering a long terrace contains the cryptoporticus in this garden. Approximately 8 feet wide, with an 18-foot vaulted ceiling, the cryptoporticus tunnels down the length of the entire garden, providing shade and insulated comfort in warm weather. The exterior of the cryptoporticus, covered with vines, has archways that lead inside to ferns.

wide tunnel was not only funneled into the adjacent rooms, but was also forced up the stairs at the end of the hallway into the upper level of the villa. By adjusting shutters at the opening, air flow was regulated. A series of small niches along the south wall of the cryptoporticus contained fountains which still cool the air today.

By examining the three examples described above, we have learned how the cryptoporticus created a microclimate by funneling chilled air while allowing comfortable access to different areas of a landscape. These subterranean elements also provided a framework for the landscape elements which helped modify the above-ground microclimate as well. These features, the bosco and the pinetum, are presented in the next two chapters.

Cryptoportici
Contemporary Applications

1. Combine the cryptoporticus with grottoes and subterranean rooms to form a network of earth-cooled spaces.

2. Use the cryptoporticus to funnel and accelerate cool air pockets created by other subterranean structures into above-ground dwellings.

3. Maximize the use of cryptoportici to walk comfortably between sections of above-ground structures.

4. Pools of water placed adjacent to small openings in the ceiling of a crypto-porticus will capture the cool air drifting down from the pool's surface.

5. Orient the narrow opening of the cryptoporticus toward the prevailing winds to funnel the air through the cool passageways and into adjacent rooms.

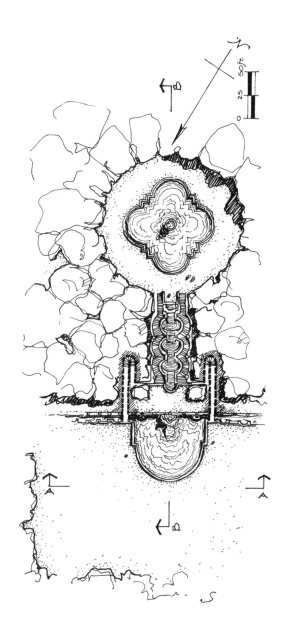

Figure I-39a *(opposite right, above & below)*
Villa Torlonia, Frascati, Italy.
Date unknown (Renaissance). Designer unknown.

Two parallel cryptoportici built into either side of the retaining wall defined the central water cascade. From a large clearing in front of the lower pool, one enters the cryptoportici through either of two arched doorways.

Figure I-39b *(right)*
Villa Torlonia, Frascati, Italy.

The darkness of these two tunnels contrasts with the sunlit plaza and provides a comfortable transition between the two levels: climbing from one garden terrace to the next, leaving the lower pool behind, passing deep inside the hill, up a winding stairwell, and exiting through a tunnel next to a splashing cascade.

Postulate V: **Boscoes**

● A bosco is an outdoor room, composed of densely planted trees, used to moderate the sun's heat and to create a unique passive microclimate. Large, wooded areas maximize oxygen production, air filtration, and the noise-abatement capabilities of broad masses of trees while creating agreeable environments. Boscos are normally sited on the north side of a garden or structure to block the cold north winds. They can be laid out in geometrical grids or planted informally to create a spreading canopy. Evergreen oaks are excellent species because their broad crowns produce abundant shade. Pathways provide suitable surfaces for strolling and Arcadian cavorting in the deep shade of the bosco (Figure I-40).

Plant many, many trees in good order and in rows...[12]
Leon Battista Alberti
The Family in Renaissance Florence

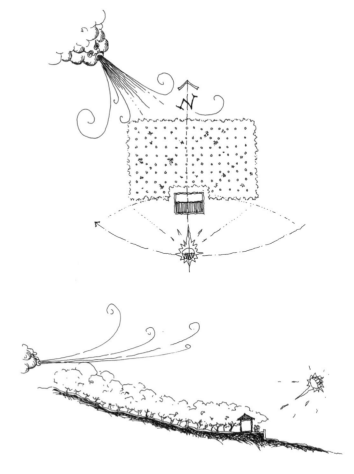

● Figure I-40
The Bosco.

Almost all plants grow from the earth; as such, the bosco is both a natural, earth-dependent structure and a self-sufficient system, in that it gives back to the earth as much as it takes. Compared to a building, which also mines elements from the earth for its energy supply to provide places for human activity, a bosco returns oxygen to the atmosphere, deposits additional nutrients in the soil, and provides habitat for many other forms of life. In this chapter we will examine how the bosco functions as a microclimatic device and how it was used as a favored landscape feature by the garden architects of the Renaissance.

The bosco inevitably evolved as a climatic modulating device from the first walled orchards of the Middle Ages, where fruit trees were planted in a system of grids for efficient irrigation and maintenance. Symmetrical planting also maximized each tree's surface area for capturing sunlight. These functional orchards eventually led to the development of the formal wooded grove, which became a prevalent feature of the Italian Renaissance villa.

According to C.L. Franck, in *The Villas of Frascati*, there existed a Renaissance "Canon of Horticultural Rule" which presented a format for placing landscape elements in villas and gardens (Figure I-41). As outlined in the canon, which Franck traces to ancient Rome, the bosco was an integral element of the site plan. As a result, even the smallest Renaissance garden usually had this manicured nucleus within its larger unordered landscape (Figure I-42). The bosco remained popular throughout the Renaissance, owing in part to Alberti's advocacy of the bosco as an important garden feature.

The purposes served by the planting of a bosco were many. Boscos not only provided ornamentation, but also created a wooded zone in which "humans could interact with the

Figure I-41 *(opposite)*
The "Canon of Horticultural Rule," showing the bosco
as an integral part of site planning.

Figure I-42
Villa Mondragone, Frascati, Italy.

The edge of the bosco.
(Photo: Marc Treib)

larger forces of nature in the microcosm. They also served more mundane functions, providing coolness and escape from sun or a private space for dining, music and other recreation."[13]

In addition to their social contributions, boscos played an important ecological role in the environment. The combined effect of planting trees in a landscape produces abundant vegetative mass for photosynthesis, from which the major benefit is the generation of oxygen. Masses of trees recycle oxygen; a tree, as dynamic and beautiful as it is, is also a unique chemical factory working constantly to insure that the earth will remain livable. Aloys Bernatzky's research involving beech groves revealed that a single tree with

> 1600 square meters of exterior leaf surface will produce 1.07 grams of oxygen per hour in favorable conditions. We can view the large blocks of trees in these gardens as green lungs. The amount of water transpiration of these wooded areas also has a positive effect on the microclimate. Trees modify the microclimate by lowering temperatures and raising humidity levels. When leaves release water into the heated atmosphere through evapotranspiration, the temperature is cooled and stabilized. For example a free-standing beech tree transpires 100 gallons of water on a hot summer day. [14]

The reduction of heat levels is another important climatic benefit of the bosco; the plantation mass effectively blocks the sun, thus reducing ground-level temperatures. Robinette states: "trees, shrubs, ground cover, and turf, or even a combination of these, are effective in reducing direct as well as reflected solar radiation... Thus plants provide insulation for buildings and the earth, not only from the intense heat of solar radiation, but also from abrupt temperature changes. Plants absorb more of the sun's heat during the day and release it slowly in the evening—not only cooling the daytime temperature, but also warming the evening temperature and moderating it."[15]

The mass of the typical bosco provides ample opportunity for photosynthesis, respiration, and water transpiration. Perhaps one of the most attractive qualities of the bosco is its balance between structure and vegetation. Almost every Italian Renaissance garden included a bosco as a main feature; generally, the vegetative mass of the bosco equaled or exceeded the architectural mass of the villa itself. This formula was followed perfectly by the Renaissance architect and sculptor Francesco Borromini in his redesign of the Villa Falconieri in 1548. On the south side of the villa lay a sunny, open area, 48 feet deep by 85 feet wide. Directly beyond this flat expanse stood the pleasant dark-green backdrop of the bosco (Figure I-43a). A central north-south axis intersected the villa and divided the bosco into two equal blocks of trees. Beyond the southern boundary of the bosco, formal plantings fanned out as they climbed the hillside and faded into the woodland edge.

The shady bosco offers a cool place for walking and resting near the dwelling; and through careful planning, a balance of shadow and light filled the bosco. The contrast of light and dark becomes even more stunning as the sun hits the facade of the villa, animating its architectural detail with deep shadows (Figure I-43b).

The formal geometry of the bosco is apparent in more architectural contexts as well, where the trunk of a tree can be interpreted as a column and the tree's canopy a ceiling or roof. The design of the Villa Torlonia features the bosco as a more architectonic landscape element. Steps and ramps on the northwest border of the garden lead to a sprawling terrace that forms the foundation of a 5-acre bosco, 660 feet wide by 340 feet deep (Figure I-44a). Here, the bosco is a mysterious place, its trees grown together so tightly that hardly any sunlight penetrates within. Pathways and benches occupy the shadows; the compressed planting spaces open

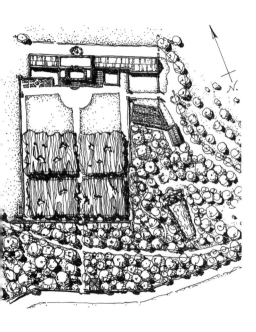

Figure I-43a

Villa Falconieri, Frascati, Lazio, Italy.

Plan showing relationship of bosco to villa.

Boscoes
Contemporary Applications

1. Plant the bosco in a symmetrical grid to maximize the amount of sunlight for each tree. A regularized grid system is an efficient layout for maintenance and irrigation.

2. Large plantations of trees produce significant quantities of oxygen. For cleaner air, plant large-growing evergreen trees to increase photosynthesis and oxygen production.

3. The vegetative mass of the bosco should be three times the structural mass of the architecture.

4. Large areas of evergreen trees with broad canopies will reduce ambient temperatures in summer.

5. Plant the bosco on the north side of a building or dwelling to block the cold northern winds in winter.

to circular outdoor rooms containing small fountains. The bosco continues southward until it meets a large pool and cascade at the base of the hill; here, the bosco forms the edge of a large clearing around the cascade's lower pool. Shade and tranquility are the prime qualities of this ordered woodland setting (Figure I-44b).

Renaissance designers viewed the bosco as a form of architecture and used it as an adjunct structure integral to the balancing of built form and landscape. As a highly ordered landscape feature, the bosco accented the contrast between the cultivated and the wild. This balance of structure to vegetation could also be a basic guideline for current planning, not only to encourage a dialogue with nature, but to encourage the beneficial ecological effects that result from an integrated landscape plan. The final postulate of Book I reviews the microclimatic and aesthetic impact of a different type of natural woodland ecosystem, the Pinetum.

Figure I-43b

Villa Falconieri, Frascati, Lazio, Italy.

View from shady bosco to villa facade illuminated by sunlight.

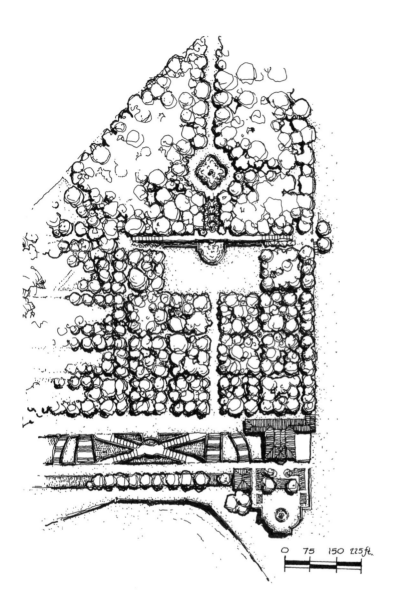

0   75   150 225 ft.

Figure I-44a
Villa Torlonia, Frascati, Lazio, Italy.
Plan of the bosco.

Figure I-44b
Villa Torlonia, Frascati, Lazio, Italy.
The interior of the shady bosco.

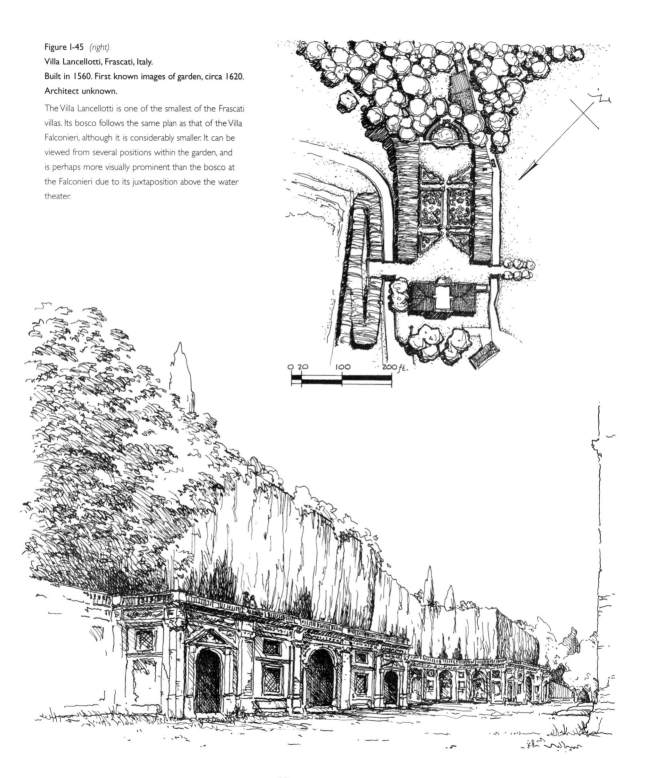

Figure I-45 *(right)*

Villa Lancellotti, Frascati, Italy.

Built in 1560. First known images of garden, circa 1620.
Architect unknown.

The Villa Lancellotti is one of the smallest of the Frascati
villas. Its bosco follows the same plan as that of the Villa
Falconieri, although it is considerably smaller. It can be
viewed from several positions within the garden, and
is perhaps more visually prominent than the bosco at
the Falconieri due to its juxtaposition above the water
theater.

0 20   100   200 ft.

Figure I-46 (opposite below)
Villa Aldobrandini, Frascati, Italy.
Late seventeenth century. Designed by Giacomo
della Porta, and completed after his death by Carlo
Maderna and Giovanni Fontana.

Where the bosco meets the edges of the central axis
above the theater, the trees have been sheared into a
tall sharp hedge, behind which, the bosco becomes
more natural—the clipped edge contains the wilder-
ness. The large scale of the bosco is an effective
counterpoint to the mass of the villa.

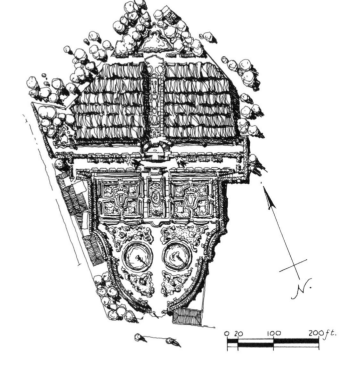

Figure I-47a (above right)
Villa Garzoni, Collodi, Italy.
Date and designer unknown.

The bosco at the Villa Garzoni combines a curious mix
of formal planting and hidden pathways. An unkempt
canopy of leaves tops a formally clipped corridor of
ilex beneath it. The bosco invites the visitor into a
tunnel of green, with its dappled sunlight providing a
striking relief from the lower sun-filled parterre.

Figure I-47b (below right)
Villa Garzoni, Collodi, Italy.

Cut into this massive block of ilex trees, and perpendicular to the central water cascade, five shaded walks
follow the contours of the precipitous slope. Although
comparable to the hillside wood of the Villa Aldobrandini, the interior pathways of the Villa Garzoni
more dramatically organize their bosco. The plan allows
excellent opportunities to stroll at length in abundant
shade; the central axis choreographs a series of parallel
weaving paths that alternately guide the visitor toward
the axis and then out into the countryside.

Figure 1-47c
Villa Garzoni, Collodi, Italy.

From the decorative parterre above, the central axis
of the garden ascends northward through five terraces
dominated by staircases and a cascade. The hillside
cascade divides the gigantic block of ilex trees into two
parts; the total area of the bosco adds up to a little
more than 1 acre.

Postulate VI: **Pineta**

● A pinetum is a stand of pine trees planted in geometrical grids, spaced very closely together. The pine trunks are trimmed high to shape the upper canopies into an umbrella-like form. A pinetum is sited on the south side of a property so that it can catch prevailing summer breezes. Although historically used to drain wetlands and produce a timber crop, the ultimate objective of the pinetum in the design of microclimates is to create a light and airy space, full of the scent of pine, and graced with soft, filtered light from above (Figure I-48).

The stone pines lift their dense clumps upon slender length of stem, so high that they look like green islands in the air flinging down a shadow on the turf so far off that you scarcely know which tree has made it.[16]
Hildegarde Hawthorn

● Figure I-48
The Pinetum.

A *pinetum* (pl. *pineta*) is essentially a bosco planted with Italian stone pines, or *Pinus pinea*. Usually set out in a very tight grid, their lower limbs are trimmed annually to give the tree an umbrella-like shape; hence, the other common name of the species, *umbrella pine*.

This practice of pruning might have developed from the tradition of harvesting only the lower limbs for firewood, but it promotes a vastly different feeling than does the typical bosco of ilex. The bosco's low, evergreen oak canopy creates a dark enclosed space of muffled silence and dense shadows. In contrast, the pinetum's slender, towering trunks, and light-green canopy effect a different, cathedral-like atmosphere. In the summer, the sun warms the pine needles and sap, and fills the air with a sweet aroma. When the wind blows, even softly, the pine needles whisper musical sounds.

Historical records indicate that pine plantations existed in the Italian city of Ravenna during the Roman empire. The Romans used the pinetum as a method to drain swampland and reduce the risk of disease. What we now understand as insect-caused malaria, was then thought of as emanating from the bad air (*mal* + *aria*) associated with the marshes. Remnants of these early pineta can still be seen in low-lying regions of Italy. The pinetum might also have evolved from an agricultural use: the harvesting of the tasty pine nuts (*pignoli*) that are a staple of many Italian dishes.

The Roman tradition of planting pineta continued well into the eighteenth century. Many of the large villas had imposing ilex boscos, as well as vast pineta. Today, large plantations of pine still dot the hills of Rome, silhouetted against the sky (Figure I-49). One of the most famous of these is located on the Janiculum Hill in Rome, in the gardens of the Villa Doria Pamphili. Alessandro Algardi and Giovanni Francesco Grimaldi designed and built the villa for Camillo

Figure I-49
Umbrella pines dot the hills of Rome.

Figure I-50 *(opposite above)*
Villa Doria Pamphili, Rome.
Area of the original pinetum.
(G.B. Falda, Giardini di Roma, *seventeenth century)*

Figure I-51 *(opposite below)*
Villa Doria Pamphili, Rome.
Ordered space of the pinetum's immense grid.
(Photo: Marc Treib)

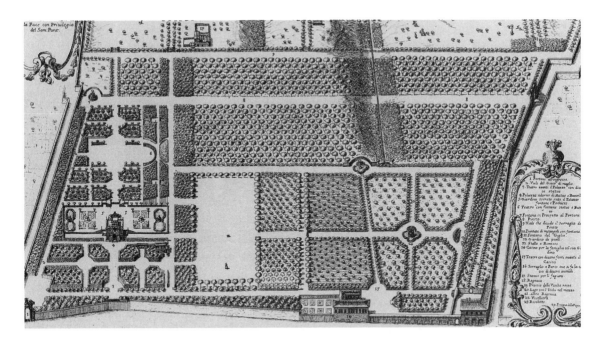

Pamphili in 1650. With grounds that measure 6 miles in circumference, it is one of the largest parks in Rome. The original pinetum once covered an area of 150 acres, a large portion of which still exists (Figure I-50). Inside the pinetum, vistas of pine extend in every direction in seemingly infinite rows, overwhelming the visitor with feelings of awe. Spaced on an ordered grid of 32 feet by 26 feet, the pinetum rolls over a grassy dale, and quietly works its aromatic magic on the visitor (Figure I-51).

On a visit to the gardens in the 1920s, author André Gide relied on the words of composer Gabriel Fauré to beautifully describe the comfortable and cool experience of wandering through the airy depths of filtered sunlight:

> I could see the sun: but the air shone, the light was everywhere, as if the azure of the sky had become liquid and was pouring down like rain. Yes! Light came in waves, in eddies: light sparkled on the moss like drops of water; light filled all that great alley like a river, tipping all the branches with golden foam.[17]

The experience of being within a spacious pinetum in summer is unforgettable, where a high canopy of pines creates a green barrier from the heat of the sun. The unique form and height of the canopy produces a very uplifting yet secure feeling. As a result, the architecture of this landscape type leaves its mark from an emotional and spiritual perspective.

In summary, the bosco and the pinetum were places to retreat from the sun and linger within the mystery of a grove. They allowed a communion with the fecund and fertile, the beautiful, and the sublime.

In Book I we have reviewed how designers in past centuries utilized the earth for shelter, protection, and nourishment for body and soul. These builders, whether architects, artists, or monarchs, understood the meaning and power of the

Pineta

Contemporary Applications

1. Select slender, tall pine trees indigenous to the region.

2. Plant the pine trees in a tight grid 10 to 30 feet on center. The pines should be planted so closely that their canopies touch.

3. The pinetum should be at least 1 acre in size to be spatially effective.

4. Trim the pine trees' lower limbs to produce a green umbrella-like canopy.

5. The pinetum works best climatically when planted on the northern or western portion of a site.

earth. In the design of microclimates they created landscapes that balanced the physical and spiritual needs of people with the intrinsic course of nature.

Using forms of earth and plants as architecture we too can build a landscape of comfort and wonder. Such a landscape is proposed in the Garden of Bacchus, the prototypical garden that summarizes the techniques of climate modification outlined in Book I.

In Book II, we will explore the power of the sun as a source of energy, heat, and light, in the further development of the garden as a climatic landscape.

Figure I-52 *(opposite)*
Casino Corsini dei Quattro Venti, Rome, Italy.
Late seventeenth century.
Design attributed to Simone Salvi.

Known as the Quattro Venti, or Four Winds, the Casino Corsini primarily housed an art collection and was used by the Pope only for ceremonial purposes. A wonderful pinetum still exists on top of a slight rise. These pine trees are planted so close together, sometimes as close as 10 feet, that their trunks twist outwards in every direction, and appear very random when compared to the orderly pinetum next door.

A painting by Fragonard, who visited the gardens in the mid-eighteenth century, reveals how the shade of the pinetum was filled with people dining and relaxing. Even today, this scene is enacted during the Italian holiday of Pasquetta, when hundreds of families sit under the pines picnicking and frolicking, just as it must have been 200 years ago.

(Jean-Honoré Fragonard, The Umbrella Pines at the Villa Pamphili, *1773–1774. Rijksmuseum, Amsterdam)*

Figure 1-53
Villa Borghese, Rome, Italy.

Plans and descriptions from the eighteenth century
indicate that around 10 acres of stone pines were
planted in a grid formation, though less than half of
that original grove remains. Even in its reduced state,
the pinetum still feels quite vast and provides the
visitor with long shadows and dappled light. This
extensive pinetum follows the graceful curve of the
hippodrome.

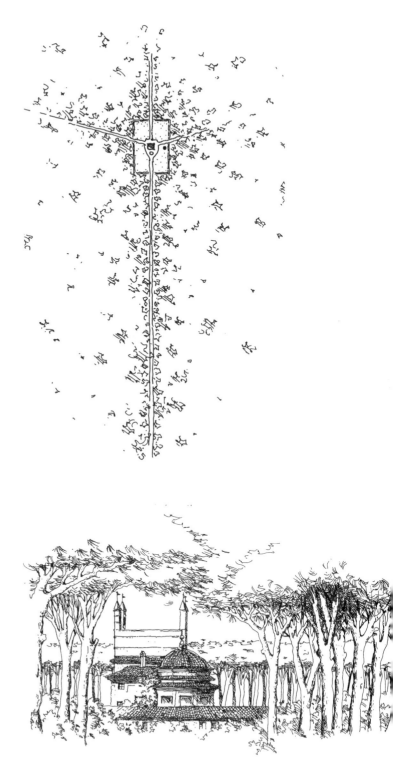

Figure I-54

Villa Sacchetti, Lazio, Italy.

Pinetum planted in 1710, following a design by Pietro da Cortona.

In the first half of the seventeenth century Cardinal Sacchetti started renovations to the existing grounds of this villa which had been used primarily for hunting and fishing. Da Cortona, who was inspired by Borromini's design for the Villa Pamphili, developed a site plan that related the villa to the pine forest. The villa sits in the center of a vast rectangle of lawn amid an enormous plantation of pine. Thrust into this wild green pinetum, an allée of pines over a mile long leads to the villa. The flat grassy opening, surrounded in every direction by walls of pine, contrasts dramatically with the void.

Figure I-55

Villa Sacchetti, Lazio, Italy.

Great care was taken by the architect to plant the pines just the right distance from the villa so that they would create the illusion of a gigantic green backdrop. The magnificence of this huge pinetum still overwhelms the visitor today.

Garden Prototype I:

The Garden of Bacchus

The Garden of Bacchus has been designed for a site in
the vineyards of Napa Valley, an hour's drive north of San
Francisco, California. Framed by small mountain ranges to
the east and west, beautiful rolling vineyards run north and
south and nestle in this fertile landscape. In summer, the
temperatures are normally high, at times reaching over 100°
Fahrenheit. Periods of drought can last years, so water
conservation is very important. While the summers are dry,
the winters tend to be wet and cold with freezing weather
on rare occasion.

The valley's excellent growing season is attributed to this
climate, and its picturesque landscape makes it an ideal
place to live. Turning west off Highway 101 and onto a gravel
road, a beautiful view opens to the north. Just a short
distance ahead, around a curve, the site becomes visible in
the woodlands. The whole site rises northward on a gentle
slope. An oak woodland crests the top of a hill, with pines
planted to the west. A broad panorama of grapes, with an
occasional plot for fruit trees or vegetables, patterns the
foreground view with agriculture. One passes through farm
fields along the southern boundary of the site, then
through an ordered plantation of pines, and parks one's
vehicle in a small lot shaded by pines. From here, terraces
of vines are visible, climbing up the hillside to the north.

The Garden of Bacchus integrates all of the microclimatic
devices we have explored in Book I. In this garden design,
the earth has been manipulated, not only to provide a
comfortable shelter, but also for the growing and harvesting of the fruits of the vine. Studying the historical examples set forth in Book I, we can integrate them to create a
new garden form.

The god Bacchus embodied the power of the cool earth;
he symbolized fertility and the underworld, the duality of
life and death. During his festivals the dead rise to join the
drunken rampage and dance through the gardens of the
living. The dual nature of Bacchus, and his ability to restore
life through the power of the earth, provides a powerful

parable for climatic design. The first garden prototype
revives the earth-based passive microclimatic devices used
in historic gardens and proposes a new garden form
inspired by ideas of earth as fertile ground.

The Garden of Bacchus:

A Description of Passive Landscape Elements

A. Pinetum

The pinetum planted on the western corner of the site
blocks the late afternoon sun in summer. The pine trees
are trimmed up very high, creating a canopy of shade, but
at the same time allowing air to flow freely beneath. The
pines are planted on a tight formal grid of 20 on center to
maximize shade. The rhythm of their long shadows plays
on the sandy earth, and the light filtering down through
the pine needles casts a golden hue. The needles that
cover the ground emit a pleasant fragrance that fills the
pinetum. In addition, the pine needles rustling in the wind
recall the peaceful sound of waves crashing on a beach.
The grid of the pinetum merges with the ordered rows of
the adjacent vine arbors. From the lower, southeastern
edge of the pinetum we find the entrance to the western
cryptoporticus.

B. Cryptoporticus

After parking in the pinetum, one enters the garden
through one of the cryptoportici that radiate southward
from the subterranean room near the center of the garden.
The main cryptoporticus aligns with the central north-
south axis of the site. On either side of the axis, two
additional cryptoportici reach out to the southeast and
the southwest. Intentionally sited in these three directions,
they catch the prevailing summer winds from the south. In
addition, their openings splay out slightly to funnel the
breezes inward.

The flared openings, constructed of cast concrete, direct
the visitor into the narrow tunnels with high vaulted ceilings.
This design produces dark, cool spaces that facilitate the
movement of summer breezes, and funnel the air upward.

Figure I-56
Garden plan.

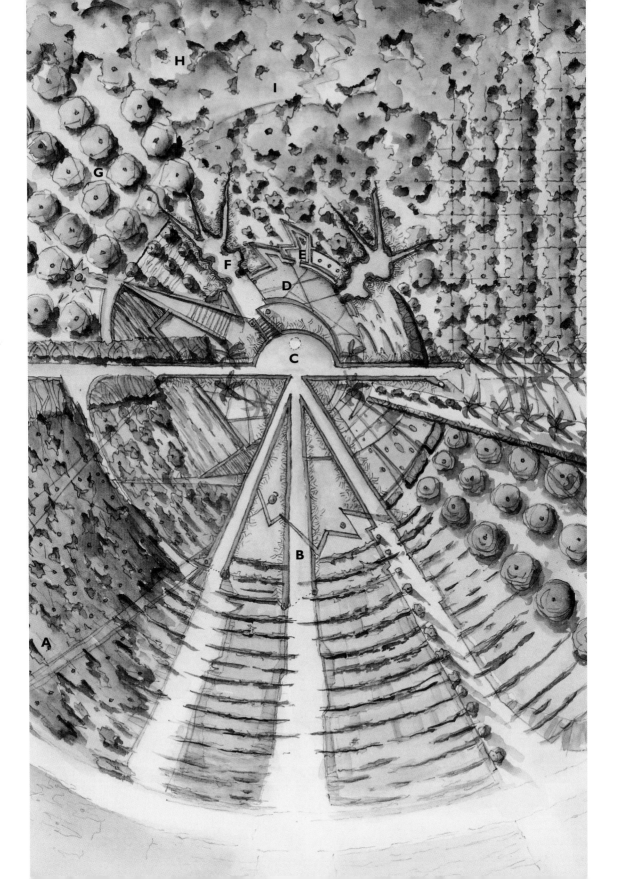

into the rooms of the dwellings on the higher terraces. The walls and vaulted ceilings are smooth concrete, dyed a deep Victorian blue. These tunnels provide immediate relief from the hot Napa climate: A gentle breeze flows past, and the blue walls refresh the eyes from the glare of the valley.

C. Subterranean Room

Once the eyes have adjusted from the exterior brilliance to the cool blackness of the cryptoporticus, one makes the passage into the earth toward a patch of shimmering sunlight at the end of the hall. After reaching this patch of inviting light, one finds the subterranean room directly ahead. Here, in a delightful underground chamber, one is surrounded by trompe l'oeil paintings of mountains and valley, and madrone, oak, and manzanita — all species native to the Napa woodlands. An oculus provides the curious, compelling light, and evenly illuminates the paintings. The insulation of the earth keeps this room very cool in the summer and stores heat in the winter. Along the north wall of the subterranean room shafts force the cool air from the cryptoportici into the dwelling above. In the rear of the room are curving steps that lead to a patio on the next level.

D. Turf Seat

Climbing upward on the gently curving steps, one rises into the light of an open patio that faces south. The patio is composed of cubist-like forms with surreal sculpture bursting through the broken grid of colorful paving. To the rear of the patio, a semicircular concrete wall retains the hill above. A brick-faced turf seat forms the base of the retaining wall. Planted with grass, Sonoma sage, and woolly thyme, the turf seat remains cool throughout the day, shaded by the oaks on the terrace above. Sitting on this curving seat of cool, green grass one can view the panorama of vineyards, pinetum, and agricultural lands to the south.

E. Earth Seat

At the eastern end of the earth seat mentioned above, one finds a passage into a small, sunken court with other earth seats along the edges and a table in the center. Carved from the earth, the walls and seats glow with the reddish hue of the Napa soil. The space provides a cool place for seclusion, an earthen room with a canopy of green leaves as its roof. On the opposite side of the earth seat, a cavelike opening accents the edge of the patio.

F. Grotto

At the western end of the patio, one finds a mysterious cavernous portal built from rough hewn stone. Inside, one slowly begins to make out the details of the surrounding space. The craggy walls are made out of soft stone covered in moss. The grotto is composed of three rooms, each progressively smaller, their vaulted ceilings descending in height. The walls of these chambers are lined with stone seats, and the last room has three small tunnels burrowing deep into the hillside, bringing cool air into the grotto — a cool retreat on even the hottest of Napa days.

G. Bosco

From the patio, a series of irregular stone steps curve up and around the entrance to the grotto. Here, the hillside becomes steeper, wooded, and shady. From the top of the patio's retaining wall, a formal bosco of oak trees planted on a 35-foot grid casts an expanse of cool shade. Scattered through the bosco are tree seats at the base of several oaks. The formal bosco also provides protection for the main living units that are just above the retaining wall of the patio.

Figure I-57 *(opposite)*
Section through garden.

Figure I-58a *(right)*
View toward pinetum from the terrace.

H. Woodland

As the formal planting progresses northward, and the hillside becomes steeper still, the planting of oaks gradually turns more random, and the bosco softly dissolves into a wild woodland mosaic. This plantation blocks the cold northern winds that can be fierce during the winter season. The bosco and woodland also provide a haven for wildlife, and act as an additional layer of protection to the earth-sheltered dwelling below its surface.

I. Earth-Sheltered Dwellings

Built into the southern edge of the hillside bosco are two dwellings, side by side. These dwellings are entered from either the subterranean room, or from doors along the southern edge of the dwellings. A small terrace follows the curve of the dwelling's south face. This slightly curving facade provides shade in the summer, but conversely follows the sun in the winter. Nine-foot-high, operable windows form the southern facade. The structure burrows north into the earth, its deep soil layer acting as an insulating barrier keeping the interiors cool in summer and warm in winter.

Operable vents and doors accept the cool air from the cryptoportici and the subterranean room, and allow air to flow freely into the dwelling. The structures use the earth as their main building material, which provides protection from the elements and naturally conserves energy.

Figure I-58b
Section showing earth seat and grotto entrance.

Summary

In Book I, Earth, we discovered how designers throughout history were able to maximize the inherent qualities of the earth for summer comfort. The great gardens of the Romans and the Italian Renaissance molded the earth and enhanced its fecund properties to produce microclimates that still function today. These designs were also great artistic achievements possessing an eternal beauty. They contained the power to transform the climate, and at the same time move the spirit. The Garden of Bacchus links the earth and the mythological god of the vine, while establishing a blueprint for translating previously known climatic techniques. The occupants of Garden Prototype I are fully integrated into a union with earth and climate.

Through the exploration of the climatic fundamentals of earth, we have established some basic postulates that illustrate the great potential of the earth as a means of energy conservation. The Garden of Bacchus investigated how historical devices could be given a contemporary form. From the surface of the earth, we will now look up to the sun, to study the element of Fire in Book II. Observation of the sun's skyward movement guided the garden designers of the past as they learned of its alchemical power to turn cold into warmth. Watching the sunlit patterns change as the earth revolves will allow us to grasp how ancient designers carved out niches for winter warmth.

Notes

1. Clemens Steenberger and Wouter Reh, *Architecture and Landscape: The Design Experiment of the Great European Gardens and Landscapes*. Munich: Prestel-Verlag, 1996, p. 35.

2. W. Lawson, *The Country Housewife's Garden*. London, 1626, p.16.

3. Georgina Masson, *Italian Gardens*. New York: Harry Abrams, Inc., 1961, p. 50.

4. Naomi Miller, *Heavenly Caves, Reflections on the Garden Grotto*. New York: George Braziller, Inc., 1982, p. 14.

5. Ibid., p 10.

6. Giovanni d'Vincenzo Scamozzi, *L'idea della architettura universale*. Venice, 1714, p. 328.

7. Masson, *Italian Gardens*, p. 149.

8. Claudio Lazzaro, *The Italian Renaissance Garden*. New Haven, CT: Yale University Press, 1990, p. 149.

9. Leon Battista Alberti, *On the Art of Building in Ten Books*. Translated by Joseph Rykert and Robert Tavernor, Cambridge, MA: MIT Press, [1550] 1988, p. 354.

10. Maria Luise Gothein, *A History of Garden Art*. Vol. I. Translated by Archer-Hind. Edited by W. Wright, London: J. M. Dent & Sons Ltd, 1928, p. 116.

11. Masson, *Italian Gardens*, p. 156.

12. Leon Battista Alberti, *The Family in Renaissance Florence*. Translated by R.N. Watkins, Columbia, SC, [1433–1439] 1969, p. 191.

13. Lazzaro, *The Italian Renaissance Garden*, p. 47.

14. Gary Robinette, *Plants/People/and Environmental Control—A Study of Plants and Their Environmental Functions*. Washington, DC: National Park Service and American Society of Landscape Architects Foundation, 1972, p. 53.

15. Robinette, *Plants/People/and Environmental Control*, p. 72.

16. Hildegarde Hawthorn, *The Lure of the Garden*. New York: The Century Co., 1911, p. 63.

17. Gabriel Fauré, *The Gardens of Rome*. Translated by F. Kemp, New York: Brentano's Inc., 1924, p. 5.

Book II: **Fire**

The sun is the source of energy for almost every organic substance. All living material can trace its origins to the heavenly fire: The sun's light is the basis for the photosynthetic production of all foodstuffs; its heat provides correct temperatures for growth and development. Sunlight is necessary not only for most physiological processes, but also for emotional health and well-being. Without the sun we cannot thrive; our souls seek to be en*light*ened.

Early philosophers acknowledged the distinct temperament of the sun, and believed it to be one of the four basic elements that constituted physical reality. With all sides similar, the tetrahedron — fire's Platonic solid — can be mathematically reconfigured into the geometries of the other three elements, reflecting the power and capacity of fire to transmute other substances and affect our lives.

In the "Dark" Ages, such alchemy and heliocentric thinking was avant-garde and often politically dangerous; but we may still be in the dark ages when it comes to solar energy. As a direct source of electric power, solar technology still lags behind the nonrenewable alternatives. Yet, there are passive ways to use the sun's radiant energy for making pleasant environments; these will be promoted in this section.

The Romans recognized the sun's powerful climatic impact and observed how villa inhabitants sought shade, or at times, absorbed the sun's warmth. As early as 36 BC, Varro identified the southeast-facing hillside as the ideal location for a villa. His tenets on the placement of buildings, paired with the later writings of Pliny the Younger, formed the basis of site design for Renaissance architects and theorists Leon Battista Alberti and Andrea Palladio, who adopted their predecessor's approach to solar orientation as one of the basic principles of microclimatic design (Figure II-1).

The choice of site for a villa was accorded the greatest importance by the Romans, not only for aesthetic consideration such as the view, but also for practical considerations of health and comfort, for which exposure to sun and wind were carefully studied. [1]
Georgina Masson

WINTER

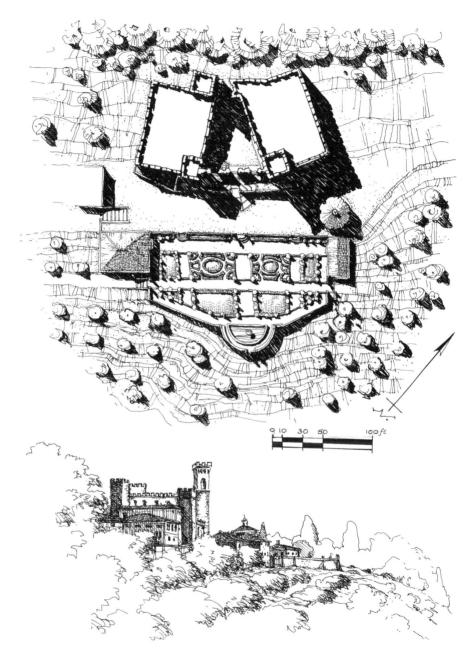

Figure II-I

Castello di Celsa, near Siena, Italy

Plan and view showing the proper siting of villa and
garden as recommended by Varro in 36 BC.

Thus, in the past, solar orientation was a guiding principle in laying out garden and dwelling. Warmth was needed during the cold and windy winter months, coolness in the searing heat of Mediterranean summers. These climatic variations led the Romans to study carefully the effects of sunlight, prevailing breezes, and the lay of the land on the siting and design of villas and gardens. The sun's energy was critical for success: During the winter months, when temperatures were low, the villa and garden still provided comfort. Likewise, adequate shade and ventilation during summer months offered cool places of retreat. The Romans, and their Renaissance successors, understood that comfort derived from the proper orientation of villa and garden, but also that solar alignment alone was not enough; additional techniques were needed to warm the body in winter and cool it in summer — all the while maintaining the order and harmony of the villa.

Stone or masonry spaces designed to face the sun in winter received direct radiant heat on clear days. The sun's energy was stored as heat and then re-radiated, warming the immediate area throughout the day. Southern or western exposures guaranteed greater solar collection during the winter months.

In this section, we look at techniques developed to resolve the challenges of solar orientation. We will examine proper orientation for warmth and its creative opportunities for designers today. These examples will demonstrate the insistence by each of these cultures that beauty and comfort go hand-in-hand in the layout and design of garden spaces and dwellings.

Postulate I: **Hot Seats**

● Hot seats gently and thoroughly warm the body with the sun's heat. Facing the winter sun, these thick stone seats capture the warmth of the sun and radiate it outward. Seatbacks are high enough to shield the body from winter winds and provide a sheltered niche. A view toward a prospect, a small intimate garden, or other focal point compounds the pleasure of warmth outside on a brisk day (Figure II-2).

Then you sit down on that southern slope, out of the wind, and there it is warm, whether it be January or February, tramontana or not. [2]
D. H. Lawrence

● Figure II-2
The hot seat.

The "hot seat" does not refer to being put on the spot, but to a passive garden device that retains the sun's energy to warm a seating niche or bench. These seats, typically of stone, are sheltered from the cold winter wind and oriented to maximize solar exposure. Social functions might also occur in these comfortable and pleasant spaces (Figure II-3).

The Villa Medici in Fiesole, long considered to be the first true Renaissance villa, includes in its garden a perfect example of the hot seat. The architect Michelozzo designed the villa between 1458 and 1461 for Cosimo de Medici's second son, Giovanni. However, Giovanni died before its completion. Consequently, Lorenzo de Medici (Lorenzo the Magnificent) became the original occupant of the villa; and it is he who is most closely associated with the events of the early Renaissance at Fiesole. Michelozzo intentionally integrated a hot seat into the construction of the villa's western facade. Its location allowed for a year-round forum for intellectual discussion and influenced the development of the villa concept for subsequent Renaissance designers.

On the west side of the villa, a small parterre occupies a platform well above the surrounding landscape overlooking Florence (Figure II-4). A 75-foot bench extends along the western base of the villa; a high row of cypress trees along a wall on the northern edge of the property blocks the winter wind (Figure II-5). This seat was seamlessly integrated into the architecture of the house at the time of construction, respectful of the principles for proper solar orientation described by Varro and Pliny (Figure II-6). The hot seat effectively catches the winter sun's warmth, creating a comfortable space for relaxing and conversing on a clear winter afternoon or early evening.

Renaissance architects and designers rarely sacrificed beauty when designing for comfort. The design of this area is no exception.

Figure II-3

Social gathering in a sun-warmed urban space in Vernazza, Italy.

(Photo: Elizabeth Boults)

Figure II-4 *(opposite above)*
Villa Medici, Fiesole, Italy.

The western parterre garden.

Figure II-5 *(opposite below)*
Villa Medici, Fiesole, Italy.

Section of the western parterre garden with the villa's built-in hot seat.

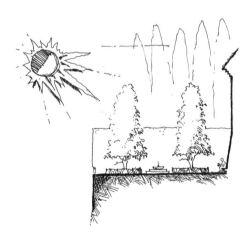

Although only a few paces square and laid out in the simplest Renaissance style, with a circle opening and a fountain at the crossings of the paths, this little garden was perfectly designed for talk or contemplation, with stone seats placed along the wall of the house for daytime shade and to catch the low evening sun, while at the corner the boundary wall is replaced by stone balusters so that the beautiful view out over the Arno, that also inspired one of Politian's poems, can be glimpsed through them. [3]

Simple solar design for comfort combined with a sophisticated aesthetic vocabulary enhanced the environment for intellectual discussion and arguably contributed to Villa Medici's becoming an important literary center. An atmosphere conducive to contemplation and discussion resulting from Michelozzo's design inspired Lorenzo de Medici to assemble the members of his Neo-Platonic Academy, Marsilio Ficino, Poliziano, Pico della Mirandola, and Landini, heralding the revival of classical antiquities that was to play such a critical role in the Italian Renaissance.[4]

The Villa Pia, a secluded outdoor retreat in the Vatican gardens, contains another fine example of the hot seat. Pirro Ligorio, architect of the Villa d'Este in Tivoli, designed Villa Pia (also known as the Casino of Pius IV) for Pope Pius IV in 1560. The classical Roman architecture that Ligorio had studied and recorded, particularly the Maritime Theatre at Hadrian's Villa, inspired his design for the Casino.

Built on a gentle slope and surrounded by a shady bosco, the villa possesses the aura of a woodland retreat (Figure II-7). In the court of the villa, a sophisticated adaptation of the hot seat virtually defines the form of the space as it borders the casino's oval courtyard (Figure II-8). This thick bench is made of stone and capped with marble vases that presently hold spiny agaves spaced 8 feet apart (Figure II-9). The entire bench sits on a subtle base elevated about 8 inches above the courtyard, while the intricate geometric stone patterns of the courtyard's paving further accentuate

the raised seating wall. The centerline of the oval court extends 84 feet in an approximately north-south direction, with a 55-foot-long cross-axis. In a raised stone basin at the center of the space, putti ride dolphins and spray water into a pool. At the north and south ends of the court, small, deep, but well-proportioned porticos create a marvelous transition. On the east side of the court, an open pavilion overlooks a water tank with cascades; along the opposite side lies the entrance loggia to the casino. Lavishly ornamented sculptures and bas-reliefs adorn the facades of both these structures.

With its oval configuration, this enclosed court creates a natural solar trap. The high seatbacks deflect winter winds from all directions while the bench collects and retains the sun's heat. On a cold December day the temperature may be as low as 45° F, yet one can sit in complete comfort even after the sun has dipped below the stone pines. Moreover, the orientation and shape of the oval court allow it to act as a solar clock and offers the opportunity to migrate to the seat that is receiving the most direct sun at any time of day. Conversely, in the summer time, one can follow the shifting shadow as the sun moves across the sky. Such an organization of space provides a comfortable seat no matter what the season.

Pope Leo X also made this casino a center for artistic and literary life. Leo X would hold banquets and give concerts and poetry recitals while the audience reclined on the benches surrounded by a backdrop of pines and ilexes. Today, even with the omnipresent bustle of the Vatican nearby, the courtyard still provides an isolated retreat for contemplation and reflection.

The next postulate, Warm Walks, advances the solar trap as a circulation device.

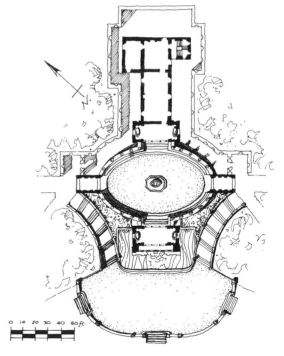

Figure II-7
Villa Pia, Vatican Gardens, Rome, Italy.

The hot seat in winter.
(Photo: Marc Treib)

Figure II-8
Villa Pia, Rome, Italy.

Oval court with its continuous hot seat.

Hot Seats
Contemporary Applications

1. Hot seats must face the winter sun to maximize solar exposure.

2. Place the hot seat in a sheltered location where it is protected from the northern winter winds.

3. The back of the hot seat should be at least 4 feet above the seat bottom to block the cold winds. The seatbacks should be solid and at least 6 inches thick.

4. Oval-shaped seating areas with high, solid seat backs can divert the winter winds to either side of the protected benches.

5. In new construction the hot seat can join with the southern and western facades of a building. The mass of the structure will naturally block the winter winds and the south and west facades will store the sun's heat.

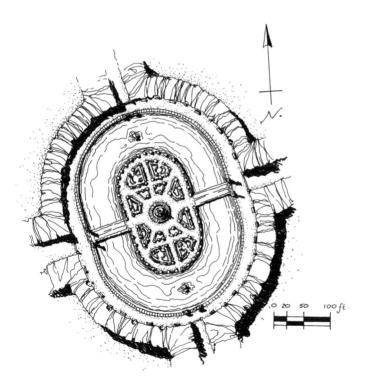

Figure II-9
Villa Pia, Rome, Italy.
Section of the stone hot seat.

Figure II-10a
Boboli Gardens, Florence, Italy. 1567–76.
Redesigned by Alfonso Parigi, 1618. Plan.

More than twice the size, yet oriented in almost the same direction as the Casino of Pius IV, the Piazzale dell'Isolotto of the Boboli Gardens measures roughly 210 feet by 110 feet. Constructed entirely out of sculpted vegetation, this green oval contrasts sharply with the hard architectural forms of Pope Pius's casino. Its tall planted walls inscribe a wide gravel path, embracing the visitor.

Figure II-10b
Boboli Gardens, Florence, Italy.

The pathway of the Isolotto shelters benches set in niches cut into the 20-foot-thick ilex wall. The closely spaced trees form a green room with a broad overhang that runs the length of the enclosure. The arrangement of twenty stone benches along the ilex wall suggests a solar clock, where people can always find a warm, sunlit seat at any time of the day.

On the following page:
Figure II-11 *(above)*
Alcazar Gardens, Seville, Spain. 1350. Designer unknown. Built by Moorish craftsmen.

Built for Peter the Cruel, the Hispano-Moorish gardens of the Alcazar contain a variety of hot seats. Peter the Cruel's Walk encloses the southwest corner of the patio area called, in English, the Tiled Plaissance (A *plaissance* usually refers to an enclosed "paradise" garden or park.). Unglazed tiles laid in a herringbone pattern completely cover the ground plane.

Figure II-12 *(center)*
Alcazar Gardens, Seville, Spain.

The Pavilion's single 100-foot-long bench faces the winter sun; its high back collects, stores, and radiates solar heat. These seats also provide protection from the cool ground air and its continuous surface, completely covered with decorative tiles, retains the sun's energy. In the summer, people can move into the shade and follow the shadows as they move across the garden.

Figure II-13 *(below)*
Alcazar Gardens, Seville, Spain.

The sixteenth-century Pavilion of Charles V stands in the center of the Tiled Plaissance, adjacent to a grid of orange trees planted in circular openings edged with colorful tiles. Long, high-backed benches surround the pavilion, displaying a stunning panoply of color, every inch covered in a variety of warm-hued colors.
(Photo: Author)

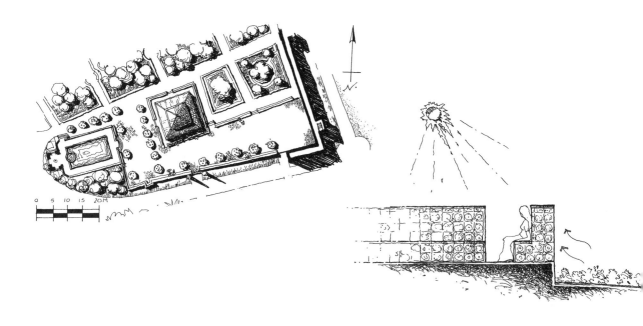

Postulate II: **Warm Walks**

● Warm walks provide pathways for strolling during winter. Usually set
in south-facing terraces and constructed of stone, these pathways
absorb the sun's heat and radiate it outward. In order to provide
maximum comfort and protection, narrow paths (about 4 feet wide)
keep pedestrians close to the warm rear wall, which, at a height of
at least twice the width of the path, blocks cold winter winds
(Figure II-14).

Socrates:
*Dear Phaedrus, whither away, and where do you
come from?*
Phaedrus:
*From Lysias, Socrates . . . and I am going for a walk
outside the wall. For I spent a long time there with
Lysias, sitting since early morning; and on the advice
of your friend and mine, Acumenus, I am taking my
walk on the roads . . .*[5]
Plato, *Phaedrus*

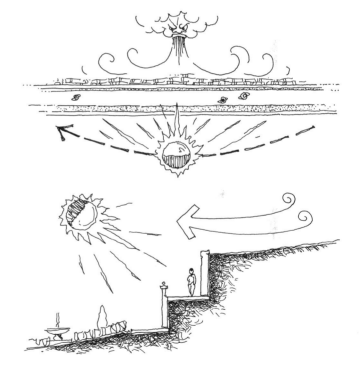

● Figure II-14
The warm walk as a passive microclimatic device.

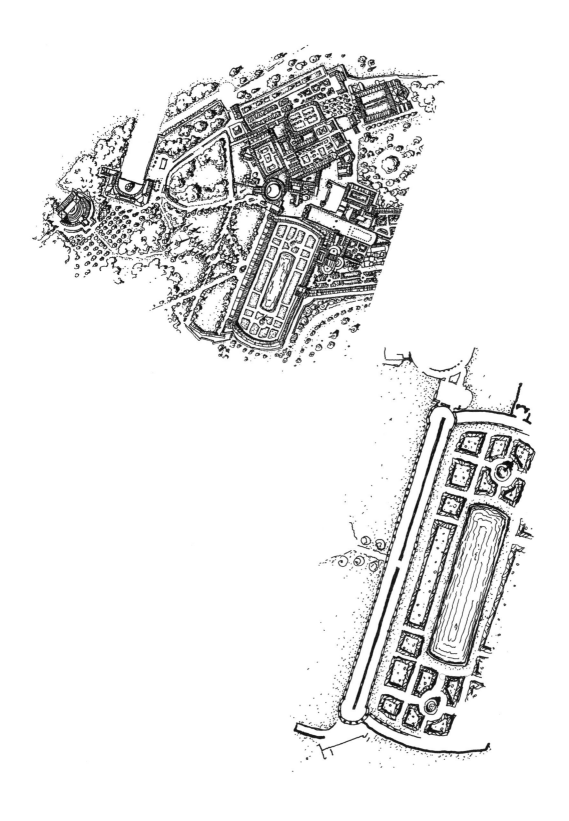

While many Italian Renaissance gardens include walks designed for strolling on the chilly days of winter, the origins of the warm walk date to ancient Greece. At the Platonic Academy in Athens, teacher and student would stroll and engage in Socratic dialog along the tree-lined allees and loggias of the Philosopher's Walk. Aristotle taught his students while walking beneath porticoes or lanes of trees, hence the term "peripatetic" walk. Later in Italy, Pliny the Younger described rising with the sun and working until eleven, then taking the airs on his terrace. After lunch, a long walk would aid digestion, and after dinner, the entire household would walk through the garden while conversing. Markers inscribed in some Roman garden promenades informed strollers of the distance they had covered. The walk, also known as "taking the airs" or the "constitutional" became part of a daily health routine.

This routine evolved into what is presently known in Italy as the *passeggiata*. The connection between walking and health led the Italians to design specific spaces for walking in the garden at all times of the year. Vitruvius, writing in the first century BC, states that:

> Walking in the open air is very healthy, particularly for the eyes, since the refined and rarefied air that comes from green things, finding its way in because of physical exercise, gives a clean-cut image, and, by clearing away the gross humors of the eyes, leaves the sight keen and the image distinct. Besides, as the body gets warm with exercise in walking, this air, by sucking out the humors from the frame, diminishes their superabundance, and disperses and thus reduces that superfluity which is more than the body can bear.[6]

Romans of this era followed Vitruvius' advice and constructed several promenades specifically designed for expelling bodily humors. Perhaps best known among these was the Great Palaestra at Pompeii, built during the reign of Augustus. Three lengthy porticoes enclosed the space on the

Figure II-15a *(opposite above)*
Hadrian's Villa, Tivoli, Italy.

The Athenian Poekile or Stoa Poekile.

Figure II-15b *(opposite below)*
Hadrian's Villa, Tivoli, Italy.
(Detail of Figure II-15a)
The walk with its unique cul-de-sac.

Figure II-15c
Hadrian's Villa, Tivoli, Italy.

Section of the 30-foot-tall covered walk with tiled

south, west, and north sides; there is a wall to the east and a large swimming pool at its center. The warm walk along the eastern wall of the large *palaestra*, or exercise field, furnished an environment for walking, conversation, gymnastic exercises and games. Such walkways became institutionalized in Roman architecture and would continue to be a part of architectural and garden design for hundreds of years to come.

Hadrian's Villa at Tivoli, constructed around AD 120, contains such an example (Figure II-15a). The walk, designed so that the emperor could take his constitutional every day of the year, consisted of a huge, freestanding wall along the northern edge of an immense enclosed courtyard that contained formal gardens. Called the Athenian Poekile or Stoa Poekile, the wall, once covered with frescoes of lively sea monsters, stretched east to west for almost 600 feet and rose approximately three stories into the air (Figure II-15b). This solid wall effectively blocked the northern winds from slicing through the rest of the Poekile. At each end of the walk, a semicircular colonnade acted as a cul-de-sac for reversing directions so that Hadrian could continue his walk without interruption (Figure II-15c). The tiled roof and colonnade of Hadrian's Walk illustrate a unique example: a single structure that offers both a covered pathway on the south side of the wall, and a cool walk for summer strolling on the north side. Although the tiled roof and colonnade have vanished, its northern side still allows shady promenades, and its southern face, exposed to the sun, warms the winter ambler (Figure II-16).

Roman-style warm walks can be found throughout the Mediterranean. The Iberian peninsula had been the site of many Roman villas, and at the time of the eighth-century conquest of the Moors, the warm walk had survived in the form of covered walks, like at the palaestra. The Moors probably adapted warm walks from their Roman predeces-

sors. The gardens of the Alcazar in Seville, first occupied by the Moorish kings in the twelfth century, employ a variety of ingenious winter walks. The original building was destroyed, and rebuilt in the fourteenth century by Moorish craftsmen for Peter the Cruel and his court. These gardens contain some of the finest Western examples of the Islamic paradise garden. Along the great white walls of the Alcazar, one also finds the most inventive promenades. "Those contiguous to the palace extend up to the second-story terrace, and their tops are turned into promenades and provided with a contiguous parapet seat. Thus the inmates might step out and walk through the garden at the second level."[7]

Three distinct walled areas define the gardens of the Alcazar in Seville. The first, at the very northeastern corner of the garden, is called the Estanque de Mercurio. A fortified wall along the east border contains Peter the Cruel's Walk. Directly to the west and down a set of stairs are a series of walled gardens called the Gardens of Maria Padilla. This first set of walled gardens squeezes between the palace to the north and the thick parapet wall that encloses their southern edge. Passing through this parapet wall, one enters the second walled area, the Jardin de las Damas which is subdivided into eight planted, rectangular plots. The final section spreads to the south of the Jardin de las Damas and is the setting for the Pavilion of Charles V and the Pool of Joan the Mad.

Figure II-16 *(opposite)*
Hadrian's Villa, Tivoli, Italy.

The freestanding wall is all that remains today of Hadrian's walk.
(Photo: Catherine Harris)

Figure II-17
Alcazar Gardens, Seville, Spain.

A unique system of warm walks with their built-in benches.
(Photo: Author)

A sumptuous warm walk extends along the top of the thick wall that separates the Gardens of Maria Padilla and the Jardin de las Damas. Beginning at the southwest corner of the Estanque de Mercurio, this 6-foot-wide aerial walk traverses a length of 1,000 feet, and with waist-high parapet walls, receives the sun's full exposure (Figure II-17). Elevated above the winter dampness and chill of the lower garden, the thick wall traps and stores a great deal of heat that slowly radiates outward. Several built-in seats facing the sun are found along the walk. Three narrower elevated walks meet at right angles and connect to the interior of the palace to the north. These perpendicular walks also subdivide the gardens of Maria Padilla into three smaller, enclosed patios (Figure II-18a). Isolated from the world outside the garden walls, these particular walks allow one to focus upon the gardens below and contemplate the earthly paradise juxtaposed against the heavenly realm above (Figure II-18b).

Peter the Cruel's Walk, so named because it was his favorite place to stroll, is built within the wall. Its white-painted walls and ceiling reflect the light of the sun, illuminating the narrow walk (Figure II-19). Byne and Byne describe the climatic effects of this practical and decorative feature as:

> Open on the south side overlooking the garden, this arcade is penetrated by the sun on its lower winter arc and is at the same time shielded against the north wind; while in the summer it is an equally agreeable promenade because it is always in shadow.[8]

A thick two-story-high wall that was once part of the fortress's boundary, encloses the garden on its eastern edge. This massive wall runs 875 feet in length and has two distinct promenades built into it: an open walk along the top and a protected walk built into the wall below (Figure II-20). Each type of walk utilizes the climate to its best advantage and demonstrates the potential for creating thermal comfort and places of spiritual inspiration. (Stairs connect both walks to the Estanque de Mercurio.) The upper promenade opens to the sky and readily collects sunshine, producing a warm walk on winter days. Much higher than the other elevated walks previously mentioned, this promenade offers broad views not only of the fortress garden, with its geometric parterres and fountains, but also out to the city and landscape beyond. From this privileged vantage point, one can view the microcosm of the paradise garden below against the reality of the world beyond its walls.

Figure II-18a *(opposite left above)*
Alcazar Gardens, Seville, Spain.
The aerial walks with their garden views.

Figure II-18b *(opposite left center)*
Alcazar Gardens, Seville, Spain.
Section through aerial walks

Figure II-19 *(opposite right)*
Alcazar Gardens, Seville, Spain.
Sun-filled interior of Peter the Cruel's Walk in winter.
(Photo: Author)

Figure II-20 *(opposite left below)*
Alcazar Gardens, Seville, Spain.
Promenade of Peter the Cruel, built into the fortress wall.

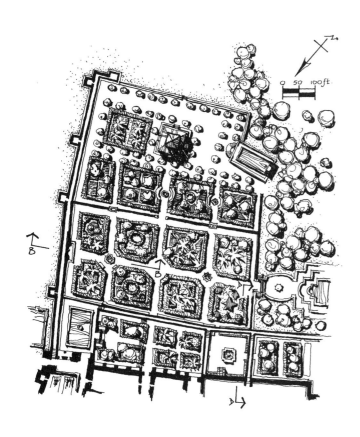

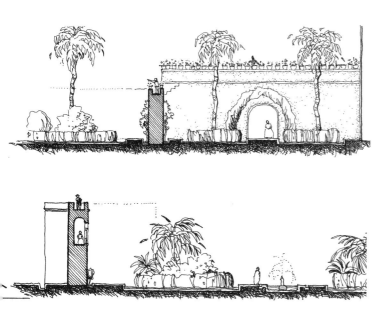

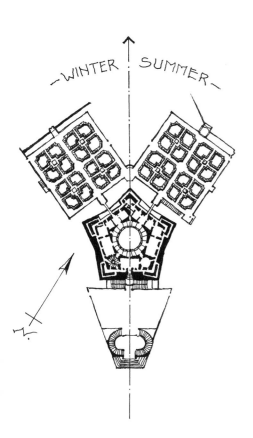

WINTER | SUMMER

N.

Figure II-21

Villa Farnese, Caprarola, Italy.

Designed by Giacomo Barozzi da Vignola.

Plan of villa showing winter and summer gardens.

Warm walks continued to enjoy popularity throughout the Italian Renaissance. For example, the Palazzo Farnese, built for Cardinal Alessandro Farnese, grandson of Pope Paul III, contains numerous climatic architectural elements, including a warm walk. The villa took three decades to complete and stands as one of the most magnificent villas ever built in Italy. Surrounded by the beautiful Cimini hills in the small town of Caprarola, the palazzo sits atop a prominent hill overlooking the village. Giacomo Barozzi da Vignola, the villa's architect, cut a perfectly straight axis through the town in order to heighten the drama of the approach. Ascending the hill to the palazzo from the east, the perspectives of the villa's central facade constantly change.

A continuation of this axis through the pentagonal-shaped structure would essentially divide the villa into two climatic halves: the winter apartments facing south and west, and the summer apartments facing north and east. Given the difficult shape of a pentagon, Vignola designed two rectangular gardens, the summer garden to the north, and to the west, the winter garden (Figure II-21). A bosco separated the two gardens while a series of bridges, spanning a deep moat, connect the gardens to the villa. Each of the garden's enclosed parterres related to the rear facades of the villa and, like the interior of the villa, used design characteristics based on specific climatic conditions.

In the winter garden, a warm walk ran the complete length of the garden (Figure II-22). Reached by a pathway between the two gardens, this narrow terrace, about 8 feet in width, opened to the rays of the sun, encouraging the massive rear stone wall to store solar heat; the adjacent bosco deflected the winter winds which might dissipate this thermal advantage (Figure II-23). A stroll along this walk afforded views to the large garden and villa below, as well as the greater landscape beyond. Among its winter sights was a garden

Figure II-22
Villa Farnese, Caprarola, Italy.
Warm walk built into hillside overlooking parterre.

Figure II-23
Villa Farnese, Caprarola, Italy.
Warm walk opened to the rays of the sun.
(Photo: Author)

dedicated to Bacchus, where the bare limbs of the dormant grapevines might conjure thoughts of springtime renewal and fecundity (Figure II-24).

Within the villa, Vignola also designed four northwest-facing rooms for summer use, and four southwestern rooms for winter use. Zuccaro decorated the summer apartments with frescos representing each of the four seasons, such that each room created a unique sensory and psychological experience associated with the season depicted. For instance, in the summer room, a fresco depicted the fable of Phaeton, child of Apollo, who, having received his father's permission to command one of his chariots, drove his four horses off their regular course and too close to the sun, resulting in the world being burned by heat. Jove indignantly turned the sky into summer lightning illuminating the clouds on hot nights. Conversely, the winter and autumn rooms contain woodland and agricultural scenes with nymphs painted in cool colors. In these seasonal rooms, the atmospheric images of these incredible paintings effectively reinforce the emotional and psychological sense of warmth or of coolness.

The simple connection between walking and health in ancient Greece, and a persistent cultural conviction that walking not only enhances health but also stimulates the intellect, prompted the development of warm walks into an architectural feature of significance. The simplicity of their design and construction allowed the warm walk to serve a variety of purposes, whether as an enclosure, a terrace, an axis, or a spatial connector, each having valid applications in contemporary design. Warm walks act as one of the fundamental building blocks of passive environmental design. Other devices, such as loggias, courtyards, and, to some extent, limonaias, build on the climatic principles of warm walks to create increasingly complex and sophisticated intersections of architecture and nature, as we shall explore in subsequent chapters.

Figure II-24
Villa Farnese, Caprarola, Italy.

Section through a warm walk.

Figure II-25a *(opposite)*
Villa Bombicci, Colazzi, Tuscany, Italy. Circa 1560.
Designed by Santi di Tito. Plan.

Located in the rolling farmlands of Colazzi, the Villa Bombicci stands on a rise that commands a panoramic view of the Tuscan countryside.

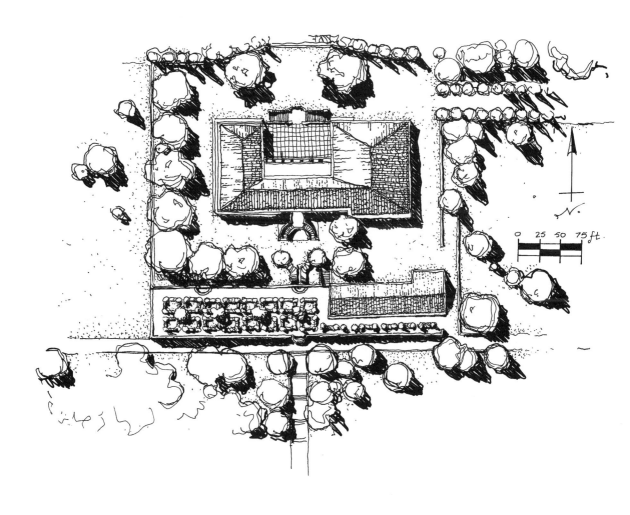

Warm Walks
Contemporary Applications

1. Create climatic environments conducive to seasonal walking, as exercise has been proven to be one aspect of a healthy lifestyle.

2. Build long promenades open to the sun along the southern edge of a site, with walls at least 8 feet high along the northern edge to protect from cold, northern winds.

3. The tops of garden walls can be constructed sufficiently wide to produce elevated sky walks. Even rooftops can be utilized for similar purposes.

4. Where possible, build seats into sky walks.

5. Rooms for winter occupancy should occupy the southern and western zones of a dwelling. Conversely, summer living areas should be located on the north side, out of direct sunlight.

6. Landscape paintings with subjects reinforcing the psychological sense of warmth or coolness can enhance the natural seasonal effects of climatically zoned interior spaces.

Figure II-25b
Villa Bombicci, Colazzi, Tuscany, Italy.

A great sheltered walk follows the southern exposure of a 22-foot-high stucco wall, just below the lawn before the villa's south facade. The walk is 192 feet long and completely exposed to the sun, making it an excellent location for winter strolls. Sixteen low-clipped boxwood parterres fill the 40-foot-wide terrace, acting as a decorative foreground to the agricultural backdrop.

Figure II-26

Villa Medici, Rome, Italy.

Begun in 1540; later work by the architect Nanni di Banco Bigi and his son Annibale Lippi. Section.

Along the northern edge of this garden, under the tall stone pines, the hot walk employs a freestanding wall to block the winter winds and to reflect the sun's rays. This wall played an essential role in the design of the villa, since the site was on a promontory rather than a true hillside.

Figure II-27

Villa Medici, Rome, Italy. Plan.

The garden is divided into three major parts: an open area with six parterres directly in front of the villa; an extensively wooded bosco of shade trees to the east of the par-terres; and sixteen rectangular spaces in the western third of the garden enclosed by high evergreen hedges that create garden rooms.

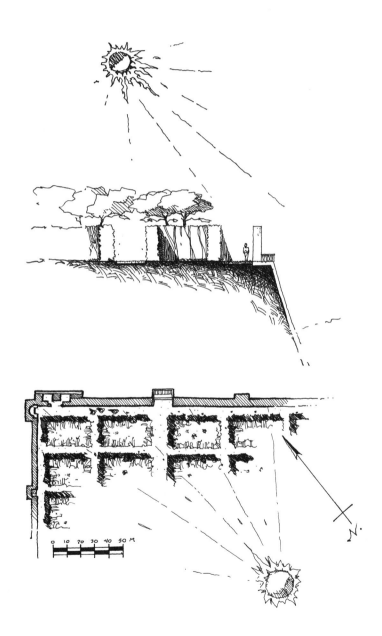

Figure II-28a
Collegio Rosa, Spello, Italy.
Circa 1800. Attributed to Piermarini.

The warm walk on the terrace of the Collegio Rosa
began as a simple vegetable garden attached to a
monastic school. During the Renaissance, Piermarini
refined its design, although the basic layout remained
the same. A higher terrace serves as a platform for a
double row of thickly planted cypress trees which, in
addition to creating an excellent avenue, act as an
efficient wind break. A second terrace, 50 feet wide
and built into the hillside below, forms a 400-foot-
long warm walk. The lower terrace itself contains
four narrow parterres with vegetation clipped into
various shapes.

Figure II-28b
Collegio Rosa, Spello, Italy.

On the north side of the terrace is a finely detailed
composition of alternating rectangular and arched
niches set between engaged columns. The solid parapet
atop this wall acts as a railing for the terrace above, its
rectangular surface animated by sunlight moving across
its face. Four semicircular fountains set along the wall
demarcate each of the four cross axes of the parterres
opposite. Cypress trees, sculpted into rectangles and
clipped at right angles to align with the top of the
upper terrace, border both sides of a pool. This simple
but elegant walk satisfies all needs and desires: panoramic views, subtle architectural detailing, the playful
sounds of water, a lofty canopy of sun-drenched
cypress trees, and a sunlit garden.

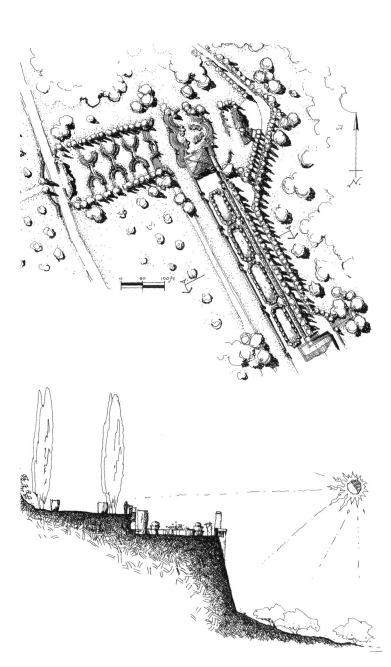

Postulate III: **Sunlit Terraces**

● A sunlit terrace usually faces south, enclosed on three sides by architectural elements. Exposed to the sun while protected from the wind, sunlit terraces create a solar heat trap that encourages use and enjoyment during winter months (Figure II-29).

The glorious sun
Stays in his course and plays the alchemist
Turning with splendor of his precious eye
The meager cloddy earth to glittering gold. [9]
William Shakespeare

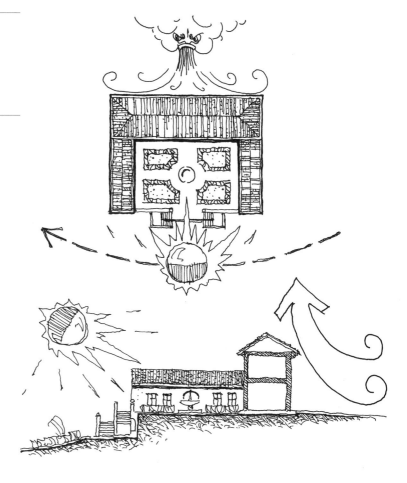

● Figure II-29
The sunlit terrace.

The Romans were the first to conceptualize the idea of the terrace as a place to view the countryside and to take the airs. Renaissance designers continued to refine the use of terraces as architectural bases for splendid villas and gardens, creating a distinct symbiotic relationship between design and climate. Most importantly, the terrace provided a defined architectural edge for sitting in a comfortable microclimate while contemplating the harmony of the immediate and distant views. Sunlit terraces demonstrate how integrating houses and gardens can create places where people can extend the warm seasons and pursue the love of outdoor living. In this way, many outdoor activities became part of the daily experience; distinctions between dwelling and garden began to lessen and become part of the same climatic totality.

Numerous Italian gardens employ sunlit terraces to trap sunlight during the winter and catch cool breezes in the summer. Following the recommendations of Varro and Pliny the Younger, Renaissance designers typically located a villa and its gardens on south-facing hillsides to maximize solar exposure. Probably originally designed as agricultural terraces for winter crops, these small terraces reflected a uniform architectural vocabulary between the villa and its garden. The dwelling and its adjacent structures usually enclosed three sides of the space, while the open southern flank exposed the terrace to the sun's heat. The villa's residents could spend pleasant winter afternoons in these warm spaces, conversing, dining *al fresco*, or cultivating winter plants.

The early seventeenth-century hillside villa of Castello di Celsa, near Siena, utilizes one such terrace. Overlooking the hills facing the city, the villa's olive trees and oaks remain essentially unchanged from their seventeenth-century form. Originally designed as a fortress in the thirteenth century, it was converted by Baldassare Peruzzi from a collection of somber towers into a peculiar villa garden complex for the Celsi family.

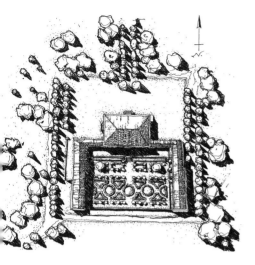

The crenellated villa, sitting atop the hill, splays outward, creating an unusual triangular courtyard. From this courtyard, a narrow terrace with a circular chapel (also attributed to Peruzzi) at the eastern terminus leads to an iron gateway where steps descend to the lower terrace. A 175-foot-long stone wall bounds the north side of the lower garden while garden buildings enclose the west and east sides of this C-shaped terrace. Eight parterres of clipped boxwood and grass embroider the garden into intricate designs. A small, semicircular pool, 36 feet across with a raised basin in its center, terminates the central axis.

The elevated southern edge of the terrace is not a straight retaining wall like so many other gardens of this style, but projects dynamically as a semicircle into the landscape beyond. Parapet walls radiate from the two buildings on the east and west sides of this terrace toward the center, where they meet the edge of a semicircular pool. This configuration results, again, in an enclosed garden cut into a hillside on its southern face, protected by garden structures on its east and west edge, and open to the winter sun and summer breezes from its elevated southern terrace. The oblique composition at the Castello di Celsa represents an unusual variation of the formulae described by Pliny and Alberti, but is nonetheless based on the same principles. The intricate parterres provide a complex composition of order when viewed against the woodland backdrop. The semicircular walk protrudes into this woodland and affords a 180-degree prospect of the Tuscan hills.

A very short distance from Florence, another example of the sunlit terrace can be found in the seventeenth-century Villa Poggio Torselli. Nestled in the rolling hills of Tuscany, this unfinished villa sits on the ridge of a hill near a bygone agricultural center, overlooking richly cultivated farmlands. At the base of the villa, a terrace remains hidden from sight.

Sunlit Terraces
Contemporary Applications

1. Sunlit terraces should be sited on south-facing hillsides to maximize solar exposure.

2. The sunlit terrace provides excellent opportunities to integrate the architecture and the garden for outdoor living.

3. The sunlit terrace should be enclosed on three sides. The southern edge of the terrace should remain open to capture and retain the sun's heat.

4. Structures should be massed on the north, east, and west sides to protect the sunlit terrace from winter winds and create a solar trap. Building mass should be high enough to block the winter winds.

5. Shade trees should not be planted on the sunlit terrace since they will block valuable winter sun.

From the cypress-lined approach to the villa, an imposing three-story northern facade hides the enclosed garden terrace beyond. Passing through the villa, one enters the delicately proportioned garden previously invisible (Figure II-30a).

The villa structure embraces a rectangular terrace garden on the north, east, and west sides. The southern side, once again, remains unbounded. The villa itself forms the walls of a terrace with its compact parterre garden of clipped hedges. This configuration harmoniously unifies the house and the garden. The spacious garden terrace is 185 feet long by 135 feet deep. Shade trees have been omitted in order to gain full exposure to the sun. A parapet wall about 12 feet high borders the southern edge of the garden, while two-story garden buildings on the east and west sides shelter the enclosed space. The three-story villa of ample mass protects the garden from the north winds. The distinct relationship of villa to garden thus produces a microclimate that can be especially pleasant in winter (Figure II-30b).

Further examples of the unity between architecture and landscape in producing effective microclimates are discussed in the next postulate, Warm Loggias.

Figure II-31
Villa Medici, Fiesole, Italy. 1458–61.
Designed by Michelozzo Michelozzi.

Michelozzi oriented this long, rectangular terrace at
the Villa Medici to the south, with the north face
enclosed by a massive, 30-foot-high retaining wall. The
garden sits between two high, retaining walls deeply
cut into the hillside, thus providing a magnificent
panorama of the Arno Valley and distant Florence.
(Photo: Marc Treib)

Figure II-32

Villa Medici, Fiesole, Italy. Section.

The artistic handling of the problematic slope offers an excellent example of the classic balance between hillside and garden terrace. The mass of the stuccoed masonry wall stores the sun's heat, and releases it slowly, well into the evening hours.

Figure II-33

Villa Medici, Fiesole, Italy. Plan.

This very simple garden is 160 feet long and a little more than 50 feet wide and enclosed on the east and west by service buildings. A combination of elements works to create a solar pocket that provides an almost perfect winter microclimate. Its tall, rear retaining wall shelters the garden from the north winds while the 20-foot-high buildings at its edges also help deflect unwanted winter winds. The absence of large shade trees in the garden allows full penetration of the sun. The fusing of architecture and nature in this garden for the creation of microclimate makes it one of the great achievements of the Renaissance.

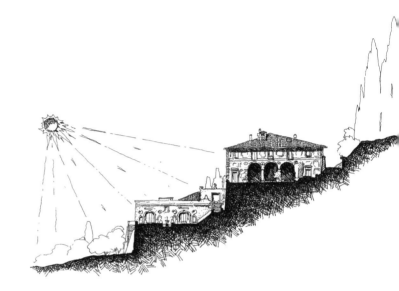

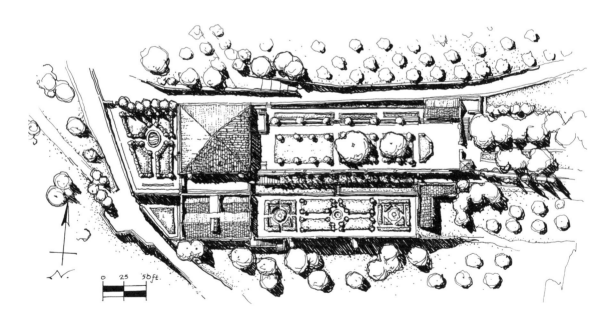

Postulate IV: **Warm Loggias**

● Loggias extend the architecture of the dwelling into the garden. A loggia is a covered space with at least one solid wall and an arcade, usually open to the south, that can be set into a garden terrace, hillside, or building. Their roofs are high enough to allow the winter sun to penetrate and heat the loggia's floor and rear wall, yet low enough to block the high summer sun. They can have built-in seating along the rear wall, and ideally, open to a garden, view, or other pleasant prospect (Figure II-34).

We ought to make our houses conform to the physical qualities of nations, with due regard to the course of the sun and climate.[10]
Vitruvius

● Figure II-34
The warm loggia.

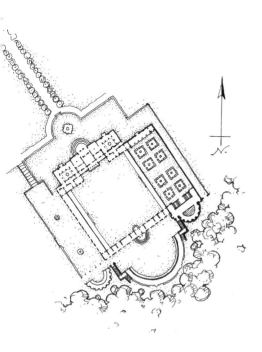

Leon Battista Alberti promoted the common-sense use of passive solar design as long ago as 1482. In his rules for building, *De re aedificatori*, he recommended that porticoes and loggias be made integral elements in planning a villa. Most of all they should absolutely welcome the winter sun by facing south, "so that in summer when the sun traces a higher orbit, its rays should not enter, whereas in winter they should enter." Alberti also stated that during the site planning stage "... every consideration must be given to region, weather, use and comfort ... [in] keeping out the biting boreas and chill from air and ground in cold climates."[11] He believed that the loggia should be designed not only to capture a beautiful view, but also to provide year-round comfort by admitting sun or breezes, depending on the season. Alberti even proposed the use of glass to keep out the winter wind and let in the clear sun and undefiled daylight.

An excellent example of a sun-filled loggia can be found in the enclosed garden at the Villa Mondragone in Frascati, outside of Rome. Martino Lunghi first designed this villa around 1567; later, Cardinal Borghese enlarged and modified it with the help of Vasanzio and Rainaldo. The enclosed garden lies directly east of a large quadrangle in front of the villa; it is framed on the east and west by high, corniced walls interspersed with circular niches (Figure II-35). On a raised terrace across the southern end of this court, a hemicycle, or semicircular theatre, looks out across two foursquare gardens. An 1809 print by Percier and Fontaine depicts four rectangular box parterres with a pair of circular fountains in the crosswalks. But, original planting of this court, once called the Flower Garden, has completely disappeared, leaving only grass and dust. The center of the surviving hemicycle contains an elaborate, balustraded semicircular pool and fountain, backed with niches and trompe l'oeil perspectives.

Along the north face of this enclosed garden is the type of winter loggia proposed by Alberti and enjoyed by Pliny. Vignola reputedly designed this magnificently proportioned loggia, sometimes referred to as a portico. Measuring 98 feet long and 11 feet wide, with a high, cross-vaulted ceiling, the loggia consists of five great arches made from brown tufa rock, a soft, indigenous volcanic stone. Ionic columns rise from a solid parapet and support an unbroken entablature and roof. Carved dragons of the Mondragone family crest animate the spandrels. The careful design and orientation of this loggia allows the sun to fill the south-facing space with warmth in the winter (Figure II-36). The flower parterre and the ornate hemicycle can be enjoyed throughout the winter months as the sun pierces the interior loggia. In contrast, during the hot summer months, the roof shields the space from the sun. The heavy doors covering window-like openings on the rear wall can be opened in the summer to welcome the breezes blowing up the valley.

The Italians were not the only people to take advantage of the warm loggia. The Alhambra gardens, high above the city of Granada, Spain, also contain examples of this passive device. Originally designed as a fortress, the Alhambra sits on a red plateau, with the snow-capped Sierra Nevada as a stunning backdrop. Although Mohammed I began construction around 1240, Yusuf I and Mohammed V commissioned the major work on this magnificent garden complex between 1333 and 1391. The intricate Hispano-Moorish gardens within the Alhambra contain a number of passive devices including a complex variety of courtyards. Unlike the loggia at Villa Mondragone, which lies adjacent to an exterior wall of the villa, the loggias at the Alhambra intimately weave themselves into the fabric of the building complex.

The Torre de Combres looms above the north end of the

Figure II-36
Villa Mondragone, Frascati, Italy.

Sunlit interior of loggia on a winter day.

serene rectangular Court of the Myrtles, linked by a long, rectangular pool. Framed by clipped myrtle hedges, the pool's tranquil surface reflects both the tower and the sky. Delicate, slender marble columns support lofty arches and a red-tiled roof. The entire surface between the arches and the eaves of the roof teems with intricately carved patterns that come to life in the Mediterranean sun. This loggia receives exceptional exposure to the sun in winter due to the shape and orientation of the space, reinforced by the protective stillness of an enclosed court (Figure II-37). The long, rectangular court faces south, its arches letting in the winter sunlight. White stucco walls reflect the light and intensify the illumination. Thick doors along the north side of the loggia can be closed to block the winds and to keep in the heat generated by the sunlight. Conversely, as at the Villa Mondragone, the door can be opened during the summer to allow a cooling breeze (Figure II-38). In addition, the smooth surface of the water reflects sunlight into the arcade, adding to the sense of thermal comfort.

The next postulate explains how the courtyard is similarly used as a passive garden device to promote pleasantly

Figure II-37 *(above)*
Alhambra, Granada, Spain.

Warm loggia in the Court of the Myrtles.

Figure II-38 *(right)*
Alhambra, Granada, Spain.

The lower angle of winter sun penetrates the south-facing loggia.

Warm Loggias
Contemporary Applications

1. Warm loggias have tall arcades facing south and thick walls facing north to repel the cold winds. The loggia's roof should be high enough to let the winter sun fill the space with light.

2. The loggia can serve a dual-season function when openings are built into the north wall with thick doors. Closed in the winter, these doors can be opened in summer to allow cool cross-ventilation.

3. The warm loggia can be freestanding in the garden or integrated into the structure to allow for an intimate relationship with interior spaces.

4. White stucco walls will reflect light and increase the sensation of warmth.

5. When pools of still water are placed along the south side of the loggia, the smooth surface of the water will reflect sunlight into the arcade and psychologically increase the feeling of warmth.

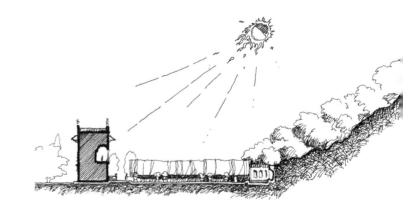

Figure II-39 *(above)*
Villa Lancellotti, Frascati, Italy.
First known images of garden, c. 1620.
Designer unknown. Originally owned by the Piccolomini family.

The Villa Lancellotti also has a south-facing loggia, although diminutive in comparison to the Villa Mondragone. The relationship between the garden and the structure is nonetheless exceptional. A small, but high loggia, acting as an outdoor garden room, is inserted into the center of the second story of the villa.

Figure II-40 *(below)*
Villa Lancellotti, Frascati, Italy.

This warm room, roughly 10 feet wide by 30 feet long, has three arched openings almost 20 feet high that admit abundant winter sunlight. In addition, its elevated position affords an excellent view over the garden.

Figure II-41
Court of the Oranges, Cordoba, Spain.
AD 976, built by Al-Mansur.

A continuous loggia encloses the north side of
the Court of the Oranges, a lush garden filled with
orange trees and the sound of water flowing from
fountains. This south-facing loggia glows with the
warmth of the low, winter sun and provides a comfortable environment.

(Photo: Author)

Posulate V: **Courtyards**

● Courtyards integrate the landscape into the architecture of a
  dwelling. Enclosed on all four sides by structure, this ancient and
  flexible architectural space can incorporate other passive devices
  into its design to provide seasonal outdoor comfort. The size and
  scale of a courtyard can vary from very intimate to quite spacious.
  In every case, the courtyard creates a wonderful frame for light
  and air (Figure II-42).

Hot-seared by desert glare find healing
In its velvet shade. Splashing fountains and
rippling pools
In cool retreats sore-wearied limbs restore,
And tired hearts awake with joy once more. [12]
Unknown Sufi Poet

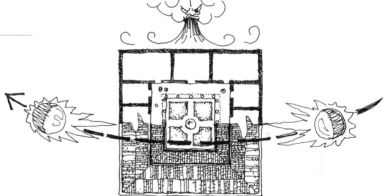

● Figure II-42
  The courtyard.

Some theorists believe that the courtyard was an Egyptian or north African concept, or that the Moroccan *riad*, a large room with a columned portico surrounding an open atrium, may have been one source of inspiration. A type of space that responds well to the harsh climatic extremes in much of the Arab world, the open-air courtyard is a much-used outdoor living space that also affords privacy. Capable of incorporating other passive devices such as the hot seat, warm walk, and loggia, the courtyard excels as a space for delightful thermal comfort. Considered an extension or an elaboration of the loggia, the courtyard most efficiently modifies a climate when enclosed on all four sides by loggias. Indeed, some traditional courtyards can be viewed as four-sided loggias.

The typical Pompeiian house was organized around a system of open-air rooms: The atrium was usually the first room, open to the sky, with a rectangular pool to catch the rainwater funneled from the roof. The next outdoor room, called the peristyle, was much larger and usually surrounded by a colonnaded, paved loggia. The main open space of the peristyle most closely resembles a garden, with plantings, fountains, and sculpture. Climatically, these protected outdoor spaces function quite well and accommodate year-round outdoor living.

During the Middle Ages, the peristyle evolved into the Italian *cortile* and monastic cloister. With the decline of the Roman empire, monastic orders began to inhabit derelict Roman structures and properties donated by Christian converts. Reportedly, St. Benedict was one among the first groups of monks to live in these free complexes. He and his fellow monks inhabited:

> the ruins of Roman buildings and there can be little doubt that the monastery cloister evolved from the colonnaded peristyle of the Roman country house, nor that without its shelter classical culture

Figure II-43

Typical Italian cloister garden, showing loggia with courtyard garden and well.

Figure II-44
The Great Cloister Garden,
Certosa di Pavia, Italy.

The typical cloister offers a comfortable climate for walking at any time of year.

and the art of the garden would have never survived the Middle Ages.[13]

Consequently, Benedictine monastery life typically revolved around a central, enclosed, four-sided space with a roofed walk about which the monks came to study and to meditate. The cloister was usually built in the form of a square, although the planting of the interior garden could vary greatly. Sometimes, there was a fountain or a well in the center; and the vegetation could vary from fruit trees to arrangements of medicinal herbs, to simple gardens for food and flowers (Figure II-43). It was a space very similar in form and use to the atrium and portico of the Roman dwelling. Every effort was made to make it a comfortable and pleasant climate in which to sit and reflect throughout the year. The cloister offers a sheltered, sunny walk or a seat in the winter, or a cool corner in the summer (Figure II-44).

The ambulatory, or the loggia encircling the cloister, allowed the monks to walk and meditate in a sheltered space, participating in the deeply rooted tradition of walking for physical and spiritual health. Jashemski describes the "benefits to be derived from walks in the open air. The green of the plantings was good for the eyes, and the Romans were notorious for their eye problems. The Romans appreciated the benefit of walking for general health."[14] The courtyard was the perfect year-round space for physical and mental health.

Florence is a city of great courtyards with a broad variety of pleasant and charming courtyards that exist within a short walking distance of one another in the historic city center. In 1419, the architect Brunelleschi rebuilt San Lorenzo, the parish church of the Medici family, in what would become a classic Renaissance style. Between 1457 and 1462, Antonio Manetti designed an exquisitely proportioned courtyard attached to the south side of the church. The courtyard, a perfect 100 feet square, still provides access to Michelangelo's

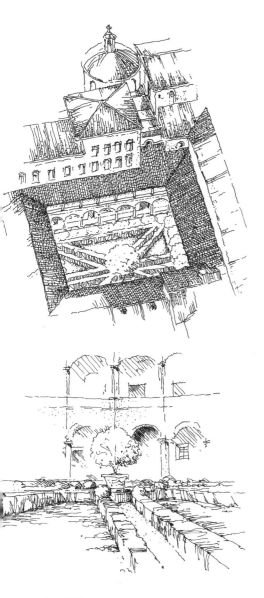

Laurentian Library (Figure II-45). A loggia, composed of graceful arches with Ionic capitals, surrounds the open court; a 2-foot-high wall forms a base for the columns. This horizontal band provides a comfortable ledge for sitting and contemplating the garden. The central formal garden is planted with clipped hedges, and pomegranate and orange trees, set within a lawn. Six gravel paths, bordered by hedges, radiate outward from a slightly raised circle where a single orange tree accentuates the center (Figure II-46). Above this loggia, the second-story loggia looks down on the geometric designs of the garden while offering a view of Brunelleschi's dome at the nearby Cathedral of Santa Maria de Fiore. In the summer, when masses of tourists throng the nearby streets, the serenity of this space still remains undisturbed amidst the urban bustle. The courtyard integrates a wide variety of passive devices into its design, each creating its own thermal environment.

Ideas of fire and earth join to create a warm microclimate in the next postulate on Secret Gardens.

Figure II-45
The cloister of San Lorenzo, Florence, Italy.
A two-story loggia encloses a central garden and orange trees.

Figure II-46
The cloister of San Lorenzo, Florence, Italy.
Clipped hedges radiate outward from a single orange tree in a terra-cotta pot.

Courtyards
Contemporary Applications

1. Many passive climatic devices such as the hot seat, warm walk, and loggia can be easily integrated into the courtyard form.

2. Courtyards in urban settings are ideal devices for climatic modification and privacy.

3. Built spaces can be planned around a sequence of courtyards.

4. Courtyard design can vary from simple four-square gardens with a central focal point to more complex forms.

5. An 18-inch-high wall between the columns surrounding a courtyard is a perfect place for sitting in the sun and contemplating the garden.

Figure II-47
Santa Maria Novella, Florence, Italy. 1279–1357. Designer unknown.

The Dominican monastic order also built the gothic church of Santa Maria Novella in Florence. On the west side of the church is the Chiostro Verde, which served as its convent. The courtyard's name derives from the green tinge of Uccello's fresco, Noah and the Flood, located in the loggia. The courtyard is approximately 130 square feet with a single-story, tile-roofed loggia surrounding a lawn. Four stone paths meet a raised basin in the central square; four gigantic cypress trees seem to fill the sky and create an oasis of peace and tranquility.

Postulate VI: **Giardini Segreti (Secret Gardens)**

● The giardino segreto is a walled garden usually located apart from main landscape features. Where possible the garden is sunken into the ground to take advantage of the added benefit of earthen insulation, and aligned with the arc of the passing winter sun. The walls, made of a material that can absorb the sun's heat, force the winter winds to pass overhead and not into the garden. Seats can be built along the walls so that visitors may enjoy the winter sun, protected from the cool gusts of winter wind (Figure II-48).

My proposal is to make walled inner space at the center. I see this as a kind of magic secret garden, which can enlarge the psychic dimension of your space.[15]
Babur, Mugal emperor

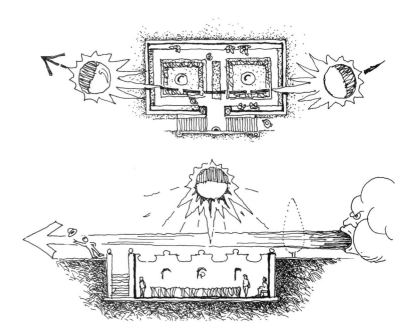

● Figure II-48
The passive microclimate of a sunken garden.

Secluded warm rooms, consciously designed as temperate microclimates, date back to Roman times. In a letter to his friend Galto, Pliny the Younger describes a solar room in his seaside Laurentine villa near Rome. In ruins today, this most famous of Pliny's villas had a garden:

> fragrant with sweet-scented violets, and warmed by the reflection of the sun from the portico, which while it retains its rays, keeps away the north-east wind; and it is as warm on this side as it is cool on the opposite; in the same way it is protected from the wind on the south-west, and thus, in short, by means of its several sides, breaks the force of the winds from whatever quarter they may blow. These are some of its winter advantages.[16]

Pliny's villa contained another unique type of garden device for passive solar heating: the *heliocaminus*, or heated sun bath, located in a garden room open to the sky to capture the sun's rays. Even on days when the cold winter winds would blow, the heliocaminus remained warm and comfortable. One of the first known examples of a giardino segreto, this particular space allowed Pliny to:

> lie and sunbathe in the brilliant sunshine, even on one of those brisk Italian winter days when the cold northern tramontana winds bring a crystal clearness to the air, with the fragrant spacious and well proportioned portico consisting of several members, particularly a porch built in the ancient manner.[17]

The heated heliocaminus of the Romans evolved into the ever-popular giardino segreto of Renaissance Italy. Usually a sunken space with decorative stone or stucco walls, the enclosed room deflected cold winds and collected heat from the sun. Two of the finest examples of the giardino segreto can be found just outside of Florence, on the grounds of the Villa Capponi, a small villa built in the second half of the sixteenth century by Gino Capponi (Figure II-49a). The first sunken garden is dug into the grass terrace in front of the villa. This rectangular space, 150 feet long by 30 feet wide, subtly connects to the villa by a single set of stairs, although

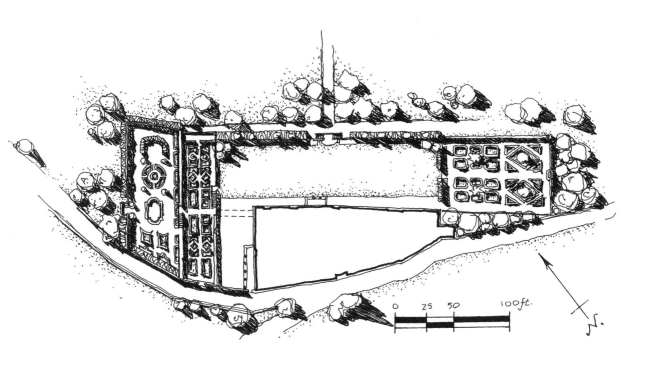

Figure II-49a
Villa Capponi, Florence, Italy. Plan.

The villa and its two beautiful sunken gardens.

Figure II-49b
Villa Capponi, Florence, Italy. Section.

Section of two sunken gardens and tunnel from adjacent villa.

108

the original entry into the garden from the villa passed through an underground tunnel (Figure II-49b).

Descending into the garden, the panorama of Florence gradually disappears from view as the walls of the giardino segreto frame the Mediterranean sky. The tops of the 12-foot-high walls are sculpted into battlements of small, flowing curves, with rounded insets and finials placed along its breadth. The garden itself is composed of geometric boxwood parterres enlivened by roses and other flowers. Tall shrubs and climbing vines grow along the surrounding walls. A small, semicircular fountain is incised into the eastern wall. Along the western wall, a high window, covered with heavy grillwork, admits the low winter sun (Figure II-50). Stairs at the western edge of the garden lead to the second, and much larger, giardino segreto. This lower garden, similar in size and character to the upper garden, displays high hedges whose tops are carved into playful shapes. Geometric parterres and gravel paths fill the garden and frame a low pool surrounded by a hedge at the center of the space.

Stepping into these two gardens is like stepping into another dimension: They create a unique reality, hidden, and filled with flowers, lemon trees, and pools. They are especially inviting as the perfect microclimate for winter use and enjoyment, protected from the wind and filled with the warmth of the sun.

The eighteenth-century addition to the Renaissance-style giardino segreto at the Villa Gamberaia in Settignano, north of Florence, also beautifully exemplifies passive solar design. Much smaller than that of the Villa Capponi, it functions nonetheless as an effective solar collector. Located directly across from the central entrance to the villa, an iron gate in a tall stucco wall leads to a narrow secret garden, hardly more than 20 feet across and almost 100 feet long. This

diminutive garden runs east to west ensuring exposure to the morning and afternoon sun, and has flanking stairs and terraces that lead to a lemon garden above. This long and narrow space produces a much different effect than the other larger, walled rooms of the Capponi (Figure II-51a). In the warm months, terra cotta pots brimming with flowers fill the garden with color. The walls, decorated with highly textured tufa set in geometric patterns, descend 17 feet into the earth (Figure II-51b). On its eastern wall, a semicircular niche with sculpture completes the garden composition. In front of this niche, a raised oval basin spills water over its sides and into a circular pool. A long, rectangular panel of grass surrounded by a pathway occupies the center of the garden.

Cardinal Alessandro Ruffino started construction on the Villa Falconieri in Frascati in 1548; it was later redesigned by Francesco Borromini. This, the youngest of the Frascati villas, contains one of the most unusual giardini segreti in Italy (Figure II-52a). A circuitous uphill route, which runs through a wooded enclosure with a fountain in its center, leads from the front of the villa to a natural plateau on a cliff edge and the secret garden (Figure II-52b). Beyond, a low wall adorned with sculptural niches contains a double staircase leading to the upper plateau, where a long, narrow pool is revealed (Figure II-53). Instead of stucco or stone walls, solid walls of cypress trees—architecture created from plant material—enclose this unique secret garden. Described as a stupendous sylvan hall by Charles Latham in *The Gardens of Italy*, the cypress trees that enclose this secret garden are planted extremely close together, forming a solid dark wall 50 feet high on all four sides (Figure II-54). This Hall of Cypresses insulates against the cold winter winds and creates a sun-filled pocket.

Figure II-50 *(opposite)*
Villa Capponi, Florence, Italy.
Decorative wall framing the parterres of the sunken garden.
(Photo: Marc Treib)

Figure II-51a
Villa Gamberaia, Settignano, Italy.
The diminutive sunken garden

Figure II-51b
Villa Gamberaia, Settignano, Italy. Section.
Relationship of sunken garden to villa.

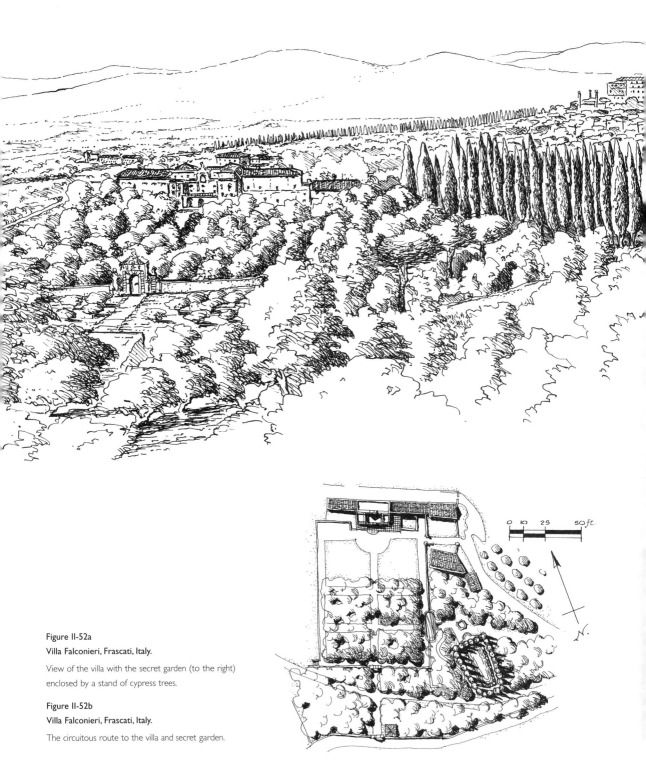

Figure II-52a

Villa Falconieri, Frascati, Italy.

View of the villa with the secret garden (to the right)
enclosed by a stand of cypress trees.

Figure II-52b

Villa Falconieri, Frascati, Italy.

The circuitous route to the villa and secret garden.

Figure II-53 *(below)*
Villa Falconieri, Frascati, Italy.

The dense cypress walls and central pool of still water.
(Photo: Marc Treib)

Figure II-54 *(right)*
Villa Falconieri, Frascati, Italy.

Staircases leading to the secret garden.

Giardini Segreti
Contemporary Applications

1. The sunken garden should be sited for full exposure to the sun's heat throughout the day.

2. As a passive energy device, the sunken garden should be excavated at least 8 feet into the earth, so that the cold winter winds will pass overhead.

3. Walled winter gardens should not be located in the shadow of adjacent structures or vegetation.

4. Dense plantations of evergreen trees along the northern border of the sunken garden will effectively block cold northern winds.

5. Variations of the giardino segreto can be constructed at ground level by planting evergreen trees tightly together to form dense walls.

One perceives the warmth of the sun immediately upon entering this space on a winter day. Sunlight reflecting off the surface of the pool further enhances this effect.

Perhaps so many Italian gardens contained giardini segreti because they were simply wonderful and intimate places that maximize the use of the garden. A basic, yet effective device for winter enjoyment, they created a setting for a sensual connection with the sun. Being aware of the movement of the sun also allowed Renaissance designers to develop garden elements for the growth of crops all year long. The energy of the sun was harnessed in the limonaia, an architectural garden structure that we will examine in the next postulate.

Figure II-55
Villa Imperiale, Pesaro, Italy.
New villa and gardens built between 1522–31.
Designed by Girolamo Genga.

The garden is laid out in a strictly formal pattern of low, clipped parterres, with no shade trees overhead to block the sunlight. The open, western side of the terrace allows for full penetration of midday and late afternoon sun.
(Photo: Marc Treib)

Figure II-56
Villa Imperiale, Pesaro, Italy.

The gardens of the Villa Imperiale became the model for many secret gardens during the Renaissance, and the modern designer can easily adapt its principles. The original designers extended the existing villa into the landscape with a series of large, deep courtyards and enclosed terraces. Built into the hillside, high walls covered with espaliered orange trees enclosed the uppermost terrace on the east, north, and south sides, creating a pleasant sun pocket—a three-sided version of the secret garden.

115   GIARDINI SEGRETI (SECRET GARDENS)

Figure II-57

Villa Torrigiani, Camigliano, Italy.

Seventeenth century. Designer unknown.

The Villa Torrigiani near Lucca contains a very large giardino segreto called the Garden of Flora.

Figure II-58a

Villa Cicogna, Bisuschio, Italy.

Gardens redesigned in sixteenth century.

Designed by Gian Pietro Cicogna.

The Villa Cicogna, built into a steep hillside near Lake Lugano in northern Italy, has a delightful sunken garden. The building's interior court forms an oblong space, enclosed on three sides, and continued on the fourth by a sunken garden. The sunken garden is such a perfect extension of the architecture that it is difficult to distinguish where the villa ends and the garden begins.

Figure II-58b

Villa Cicogna, Bisuschio, Italy.

Stone walls with niches frame grass panels and boxed parterres interlaced with gravel walks. In the center of the grass panels, small raised fountains fill the space with the sound of splashing water. Two rectangular pools with goldfish and enclosed by balustrades further enliven the space.

Postulate VII: **Limonaias (Warm Rooms)**

● The limonaia was one of the first solar-powered spaces developed in temperate climates for the winter storage of citrus plants. Similar in form to the loggia, limonaias face south and are enclosed with large plates of glass, like a greenhouse. These windows can be opened to regulate the interior heat. Plants are placed on tiered platforms at the base of the solid wall to receive plenty of sunlight (Figure II-59).

In our garden, an old secular priest looked after a number of lemon trees of medium height, planted in ornamental terracotta vases. In summer these enjoyed fresh air, but in winter they were kept in a greenhouse.[18]
Johann Wolfgang Goethe

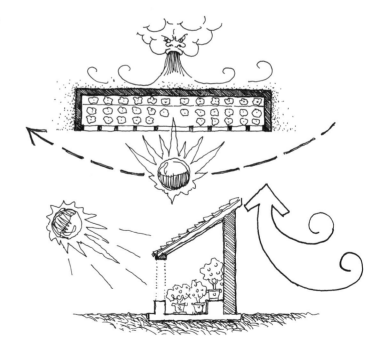

● Figure II-59
The passive microclimate of a limonaia.

The principles of solar gardening have been well understood for over two thousand years. The Romans had developed primitive greenhouses called *speculari*, structures designed with special frames to hold translucent sheets of mica, installed to provide winter protection. This type of solar growing house disappeared during the Dark Ages, but began to reappear in the thirteenth century and eventually evolved into the *limonaia*.

The Moors first brought citrus plants to southern Spain and Sicily in the twelfth or thirteenth century. Sometime later, citrus trees arrived in central Italy and became common garden elements during the late medieval period. Although these trees are susceptible to frost, the Italians' love of citrus inspired the development of a method to provide a favorable climate for fruit trees throughout the year.

The limonaia, or lemon house, was an important adjunct to many Italian gardens. Also called *stanzone*, these structures controlled solar energy in order to facilitate crop production. Similar to Alberti's concept of the sun-filled winter loggia, the limonaia was usually a narrow and tall structure, with a closed north side and a southern facade open to the sun. A major difference between the limonaia and the warm loggia is that the limonaia was not generally connected to the villa, and was enclosed by large windows that admitted the winter sun, to protect plants from cold frosts and inclement winter weather. Frequently, the potted citrus plants were placed on steps with the larger ones to the rear and the smaller ones along the front to maximize solar distribution.

Because citrus trees were moved outside to the garden during the warm months, craftsmen were called upon to create very handsome, and often ornate, terra-cotta pots to complement the garden's design. Some of the larger pots had handles on either side for wooden poles that were inserted to facilitate relocation. Terra-cotta pots had been an integral part of

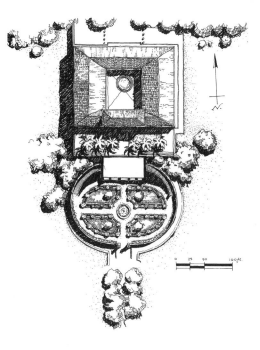

Italian gardens since the Middle Ages. During warm months, the pots were set on special decorative stone plinths in the garden, creating vertical accents along paths and around fountains and parterres. These plinths would take on a variety of forms, and were often numbered to correspond with specific trees so that the same perch was used year after year. The tradition of seasonal placement, harvest, and storage continues in formal Italian gardens to this day.

The Italians love not only the fruit of the various types of citrus trees, but also the fragrance of their blossoms. When masses of citrus trees bloom, their aromatic perfume fills the garden, creating an overwhelming olfactory experience. Boccaccio, in his Renaissance novel *The Decameron*, describes the focal point of a villa's garden where much of the story takes place:

> there was a lawn of exceedingly fine grass…surrounded by a line of flourishing bright green-orange and lemon trees, which, with their mature and unripe fruit and lingering shreds of blossom, offered agreeable shade to the eye and a delightful aroma to the nostrils.[19]

The limonaia is a versatile form, serving a variety of purposes. During summer months, the glass armor was removed and the limonaia transformed into a cool loggia. Here, the occupants of the dwelling entertained their guests, shaded from the summer sun and infused with the scent of the nearby trees.

Directly in front of the terrace on the south face of the Villa Palmieri, in Florence, lies a marvelously scaled enclosed oval, lemon garden (Figure II-60a). Laid out in 1697 by Palmiero Palmieri, Villa Palmieri has the distinction of being the setting of Boccaccio's *Decameron*, in which a small group of aristocrats take refuge from the plague ravaging Florence in 1348. The main terrace provides a lovely view down into the lemon garden and also forms the roof of the limonaia directly below. A set of gracefully curving staircases

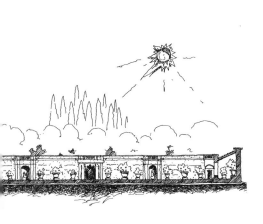

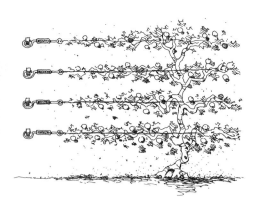

Figure II-61
Villa Medici, Castello, Italy.

The Orange Terrace.

Figure II-62
Villa Medici, Castello, Italy.

South-facing terrace wall with espaliered citrus plants.

Figure II-63 *(opposite)*
Villa Medici, Castello, Italy.

View of the citrus trees dotting the garden.
(Photo: Marc Treib)

descend from this level into the limonaia. The large glass windows of the limonaia face directly south and overlook the enclosed garden (Figure II-60b). The location of this limonaia provides direct access to the garden for easy transportation of the potted citrus trees. The oval garden measures 175 feet at its widest point. From the circular pool in the center, boxwood hedges divide the garden into four quadrants. The citrus trees rest on plinths around the pool and along the parterres. Palmieri masterfully integrated the architecture of the dwelling with that of the garden and limonaia. The result is a magnificently unified environment that not only allows for the cultivation of plants using solar energy, but also provides a flexible living area for the villa's inhabitants.

Gardeners at the Villa Medici at Castello, a few miles from Florence, also cultivated citrus trees using limonaias. This garden, a large walled, rectangular enclosure filled with geometric parterres, once boasted a collection of exotic plant species of horticultural importance, its varieties of oranges being one of the many plant curiosities. The villa forms the southern border of the site, while a high terrace wall runs along the northern edge (Figure II-61). Along the base of this grand terrace, the orange garden, which measures 340 feet long by 100 feet wide, comprises about one-fourth of the total area of the garden enclosure. Limonaias on the east and west sides open directly out onto this level. After the citrus trees are brought out from their winter shelter, they are placed not only on the orange terrace, but also throughout the garden. The feeling of the garden completely changes in spring, when these trees in their huge terra-cotta pots create a small verdant forest dotted with fruit, quite a contrast to the bare earth and naked branches of the winter garden (Figure II-63). Furthermore, espaliered citrus plants, tied onto horizontal wires with adjustable buckles, stretch across the face of the white stucco walls on the east, west, and north sides of the upper terrace (Figure II-62), while

below the orange garden glassed window boxes cling to the southern face of the terrace wall (Figure II-64).

Appended to this chapter is a brief description of the limonaias particular to the lake region of northern Italy. The ideas of this postulate and the others in Book II are synthesized in Garden Prototype II, which follows.

The Limonaias of Lake Garda

Along the shores of Lake Garda in northern Italy are the remains of extraordinary limonaias that warrant special mention, although little remains today of what must have been an incredible complex of lemon gardens. According to tradition, the brothers of the Franciscan monastery at Gardnano, founded in 1266, brought the first citrus seeds to the region. The lemon gardens themselves probably first appeared as extensions to a villa garden. They gradually evolved into a complex network of limonaias.

The tall mountains and hills to the north protect the lake from the cold winds that blow down from the Alps. The valley opens to the south, thus letting in the sun even in winter. The deep lake acts as a heat sink, storing up the summer heat and then releasing it throughout the winter. Almost all of the limonaias are perched on the western side of the lake, facing south for maximum exposure to the sun. These solar terraces took maximum advantage of the natural microclimate of Lake Garda in order to develop a near-perfect environment for the growing of citrus for profit. The stepped terraces were usually just wide enough to grow two rows of trees. High walls running along the steep hillsides acted as retaining walls for the terrace above (Figure II-65). The back wall usually stood 35 feet high and supported beams attached to columns rising from the terrace floor. Wood beams spanned the columns and supported wood or glass modular covers attached along the face of the structure during the winter. The columns framed a sheltered,

The terraces of the garden are held up to the sun, the sun falls upon them, they are like a vessel slanted up, to catch the superb, heavy light. Within the walls we are remote, perfect, moving in heavy spring sunshine.[20]

D. H. Lawrence

Figure II-64

Villa Medici, Castello, Italy.

Glassed-in window boxes at the base of the orange terrace.

Figure II-65 *(opposite)*

The Limonaias of Lake Garda, Italy.

The stepped terraces of the lemon structures.

(Photo: Marc Treib)

123   LIMONAIAS (WARM ROOMS)

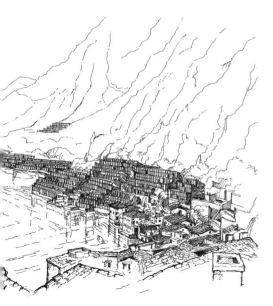

interior space, high enough to allow the lemon trees to grow to 25 or 30 feet and where air could circulate freely. In November, the limonaias would be covered with the panels, effectively keeping out the frost and retaining the solar heat. In April, the coverings would be removed. D.H. Lawrence gives us a first-hand account of this procedure:

> When the roofs were on they put in the fronts, blocked in between the white pillars with old dark wood, in roughly made panels. And here and there, at irregular intervals, was a panel of glass, pane overlapping pane in the long strip of narrow window.[21]

The orientation and interior configuration of the limonaias created a climatic system that maximized the thermal benefits of solar power and insulation (Figure II-66). The typical planting arrangement most likely consisted of low, clipped citrons along the south face of each terrace, behind which would be taller lemon trees with lower branches regularly pruned to encourage the trees to grow tall and narrow. Finally, along the rear wall, espaliered orange, lemon, and other citrons would take advantage of all usable space. Built into each terrace, a system of waterways allowed for the individual irrigation of each tree. When severe frost threatened, fires would be built on the first level to allow the hot air to circulate upward, thus stimulating air movement and heating the building. The irrigation system might also insulate the citrus trees with water so that they would not freeze, a technique still practiced by present-day citrus growers.

A number of circumstances led to the gradual cessation of production at the limonaias on Lake Garda. A root-rot disease in 1855 wiped out many of the trees. Then, in the late 1800s, the development of cheap rail transport virtually ended commercial citrus production in Lake Garda. The final blow was the severe freeze of 1928–29. Not even the limonaias' efficient climatic management could protect the remaining trees from such a harsh and sustained freeze.

Limonaias (Warm Rooms)

Contemporary Applications

1. Construct the modern limonaia as narrow, tall buildings with northern walls enclosed and southern walls open to sunlight. As a general rule, the south facade should be one and one-half times higher than the limonaia is deep.

2. Incorporate expansive floor-to-ceiling windows along the southern facade to admit as much sunlight as possible. Cultivation needs determine the length of the structure.

3. Design the limonaia with large removable glass windows. In the summer these shady interiors can be used as summer living spaces.

4. Traditionally developed as solar-powered greenhouses, limonaia can still be used for growing food in the winter.

5. Relevant today for its ability to capture and store the sun's heat, the limonaia can be an instrumental device for growing food as we move toward a sustainable future.

Unfortunately, only relics of this excellent example of solar heating have survived. Haunting ruins of the once astonishing columns and terraces remain as a small monument to solar ingenuity.

> I sat and looked at the lake. It was beautiful as paradise, as the first creation. On the shores were ruined lemon pillars standing out in Melancholy, the clumsy, enclosed lemon-houses seemed ramshackle, bulging among vine stocks and olive trees… They seemed to be lingering in bygone centuries.[22]

The ornate formal gardens of the Italian Renaissance, so often criticized as exercises in geometry imposed upon nature, continue to have relevance for designers and planners today. These gardens are filled with ingenious passive microclimates based on age-old allegories of climatic site planning. Moreover, these villas were agricultural centers that provided sustenance for not only their owners but for the families who cultivated and maintained them. Most of these farming villas produced cash crops and could be considered self-sustainable in many respects. For example, the Villa Medici in Castello had over 300 different varieties of fruit trees in cultivation. Even the smallest urban villa would produce a quantity of fruit. Like all of the passive devices mentioned in this book, the limonaia, integral to the Italian garden, can be retrofitted into new garden forms that will potentially serve as the foundation for sustainable communities in the future. The Renaissance designers have demonstrated that the garden can provide not only beauty, but also the ability to produce the food we eat, thus connecting us back to the earth in a subtle and nuanced way.

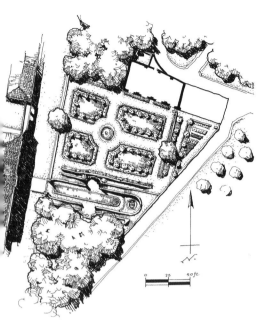

Figure II-67a *(above left)*
Villa Gamberaia, Settignano, Italy.
Begun in 1610, completed in the eighteenth century.
Designer unknown.

Unlike the Villa Medici at Castello, where orange and lemon trees completely fill the central garden space, the orange garden at the Villa Gamberaia occupies its own separate area. At Gamberaia, the limonaia is offset from the main axis of the garden and elevated 20 feet above the garden's main level. One reaches the lemon and orange garden by passing through the secret garden, and ascending two staircases.

Figure II-67b *(above right)*
Villa Gamberaia, Settignano, Italy.

The Gamberaia's limonaia has four tall, glass windows facing southward. "Here the lemon and orange trees, the camellias and other semi-tender shrubs are stored in the winter to be set out in their red earthen jars on stone slabs which border the walks…"[19] The piano nobile, the main living area on the second floor of the villa, shared the same level as the lemon garden.

Figure II-68 *(opposite right below)*
Villa Imperiale, Pesaro, Italy.
Built between 1522–31.
Designed by Girolamo Genga.

The Villa Imperiale in Pesaro also includes a similar type of moveable winter hot house for its citrus trees, built into the long and narrow second terrace of the secret garden. This terrace faces west and is sheltered by a tall brick wall along the east side. The walls of this garden are said to have had espaliers of lemons, oranges, and other fruits. Today, we can see the remains of the walls and terrace that once supported the glass structures used for winter protection.

Figure II-69 *(above right)*
Villa Imperiale, Pesaro, Italy. Section.

Citrus trees in terra-cotta pots accent a narrow parterre garden edged with boxwood. The high wall along the east side acts as a buffer from the prevailing winds that come off the Adriatic Sea.

Figure II-70 *(center right)*
Vicobello, Siena, Italy. Sixteenth century.
Attributed to Baldassare Peruzzi.

Vicobello, surrounded by other villas and agricultural lands, offers an outstanding view of Siena, 3 miles away. The gardens include a series of terraces that step down the southern face of the hillside. The largest of these terraces is the lemon garden, on the first terrace to the east of the villa, with a limonaia along the entire length of its northern edge.

Figure II-71 *(below right)*
Vicobello, Siena, Italy. Plan.

Tall hedges of cypress and laurel enclose three sides of the terrace, creating a secret garden of four square parterres, edged with low box hedges. The citrus trees sit on plinths that line the edges of each parterre. At the western edge of the east-west axis, cypress trees create a dark-green backdrop for a small garden house adorned with Ionic columns and a marble bench set within a semicircular niche. This small structure provides a focal point for the garden.

Garden Prototype II:
The Garden of the Phoenix

The Garden of the Phoenix has been proposed for a site near Taos, New Mexico, an area with excellent solar access, spectacular colors, and dramatic rock formations. With snow in the winter and extreme dry heat in the summer, the wonderful qualities of light and atmosphere have inspired artists for decades. This community is designed as an artist's colony of 30 people, a setting for creative endeavors. The site for this contemporary garden extends southward from the mesas and steep hillside. A road approaches the community from the east, terminating in a communal gravel parking lot. One enters the colony through the north facade, passing into a central courtyard that reveals a wide array of passive landscape elements. In this semiarid desert mesa, The Garden of the Phoenix emerges from the side of a cliff, much like the centuries-old dwellings of the Anasazi people. Where possible, the Anasazi built their dwelling complexes into south-facing cliffs to ensure solar-heat gain in the winter and to deflect winter winds. Similar to the Anasazi archetype, this design is sited at the base of a stone cliff that acts as a huge solar collector, providing insulation from the harsh winter climate of the desert.

The Garden of the Phoenix explores how each of the individual passive devices in Book II, Fire, can be retrofitted into a contemporary community. This new garden celebrates the movement of the sun and illustrates how its path can be used as an extraordinary source for new garden forms. In the past, many cultures believed that fire was sent from the heavens; today, the sun can still serve as a powerful generator of community design. This prototype offers an antidote to the suburban sprawl contaminating our countryside through the use of clustered multiuse buildings. Integrated with a series of passive gardens, the compact structural massing efficiently uses open space, while maximizing the potential of the adjacent land for productive gardens. The design philosophy of the Garden of the Phoenix proposes a strong connection to the landscape. This garden, manifested through an interlocking of building

and garden, blurs the distinction between interior and exterior space.

The Garden of the Phoenix:
A Description of Passive Landscape Elements

A. Central Courtyard
One enters the complex under the looming mesa cliff and rock outcroppings. Passing through a vestibule, one enters the central courtyard, with its enclosed loggia and buildings that house the administration offices, dining room, library, and galleries. The courtyard is the primary design feature and organizes all the other passive devices. The courtyard provides a strong visual and climatic transition from the surrounding desert to the oasis inside, with its lush green plantings and flowing water. The four sides of the court frame the sky, while creating a microclimate for year-round comfort. This interior space contains an interlocking zig-zag parterre garden, where, in the summer, jets of water leap from elevated basins.

B. Flanking Studios and Residences
Studio and living areas flank the west and east sides of the courtyard. South-facing loggias connect these spaces to the central space. The studios open onto the courtyard so that the residents can work in the sheltered loggias or on the sunlit terrace. The design allows for easy migration from interior to exterior space according to the weather. These flanking buildings have solid northern facades that block the winds and enclose the sunlit terraces.

C. Flanking Terraces
The studios and residential loggias enclose the south-facing terraces, capturing the winter sun. Activities on the terraces revolve around the gardens, which not only manage the microclimate of the terrace, but also act as the focal points of the adjacent studios and living spaces. In addition, they contain quite unusual sculptural features. From these terraces, one can move to the central staircase leading down to the viewing loggia.

Figure II-72
The Garden of the Phoenix. Illustrative plan.

D. The Viewing Loggia

Steps bring us down into the central east-west spine of the garden and into the viewing loggia. Built into the terrace wall, the loggia, with a solid north wall, opens southward to maximize solar insolation (incoming solar radiation). Seats built into the length of the rear wall of the loggia allow for protected strolling or sitting, as retained heat radiates from the walls and floors. On the east and west sides of this loggia, steps pass down to the Grand Warm Walk.

E. Grand Warm Walk

On the next level, one encounters the Grand Warm Walk. Open to the sun and protected from the cold northern winds by the terrace above, this gently curving, east-west walk totals a length of 1200 feet. Its great expanse allows for long and comfortable strolls, taking the airs while being warmed by the sun. One can stop and rest at the east or west terminus of the Grand Warm Walk at hot seat enclaves.

F. The Hot Seat Enclaves

At the east and west termini of the Grand Warm Walk are two cozy groupings of hot seats. These small benches are tucked into the solid, high walls of two spiraling oval staircases. The spiraling balustrades frame views into the central gardens below.

G. Sky Walk

From the central overlook of the Grand Warm Walk projects a semicircular sky walk affording views down into the three giardini segreti. The sky walk is composed of thick, waist-high parapet walls, barely wide enough for a single person to pass. The floor and parapet walls radiate warmth to the lower body, making the sky walk an ideal space for walking on clear windless days.

H. Giardini Segreti 1, 2 & 3

To reach the three giardini segreti, or secret gardens, one must descend the stairs located at the east or west terminus of the Grand Warm Walk, pass through the hot seat enclaves, and along the base of the lower terrace to a central rondel, or circular intersection. From this central point, paths radiate outward to three distinct variations of the giardino segreto, illustrating the diverse solutions available to the designer using historical precepts.

H-1 Sunken Giardino Segreto
One enters the central secret garden through a broad, sweeping staircase, gently curving and flowing into the garden. Sunken 12 feet into the earth, the solid concrete walls contain decorative niches. Like its Italian predecessors, this giardino segreto takes advantage of the earth's insulation and forces the winter winds to pass overhead, creating a solar trap. Entering this space, the view of the surrounding ground plane slowly disappears. Upon descending, the winds diminish and one begins to feel the radiant heat, becoming aware of the surrounding sky, rock outcroppings, and distant mountains. Hot seats encircle the enclosing, womblike walls, while, at the center, a low pool of water acts as a mirror, reflecting the sunlight and creating the illusion of a warm glow.

H-2 Secret Garden of Topiary
Plants, not earth, enclose this secret garden. Entering from the north, one finds an oval-shaped room created entirely from closely planted cypress trees. Here, the trees have been clipped into architectural walls, producing a work of true green architecture. A sculpted orb of reflecting glass, encased in fiberglass, acts as the central focal point. The muffled silence of the cypresses' thick branches and the wafting aroma of their sweet-smelling leaves slowly reward the discoverer of this secret garden.

H-3 Hedge-O-Rama Secret Garden
Hedges enclose the eastern secret garden, creating an ovoid space. However, unlike the architectural cypress trees, these plants have been allowed to take their natural form. This secret garden, also sited on the ground plane,

has lower hedges on the southern face for solar access that rise up along the northern edge to divert wind. An abstract gravel garden fills the central space, while stone benches punctuate its borders.

I. Limonaias
Built into the earth of the lowest terrace, the limonaias face southward to the agricultural terraces. These structures provide protection for the citrus and other trees during the desert's harsh winters. The southern facades have glass arches that, like those of the limonaias discussed above, can be opened to regulate the interior temperatures. Likewise, during the warm months the fruit trees are placed on elevated plinths located throughout the garden. This feature not only provides the community with an abundant supply of fresh fruit, but also an income. Of course, with the fruit trees in blossom, the sensual aroma of the nectar-filled air produces a delightful effect.

Figure II-73 (far left)
Cross-section of the site looking west.

Figure II-74a (left)
View from the Hot Seat Enclaves to the secret gardens.

Figure II-74b (right)
Inside the Hedge-O-Rama sculpture garden.

J. Agricultural Terrace

Agricultural terraces stretch southward from the secret gardens. Each of the terraces captures much of the rainwater runoff, directing and storing the water in underground cisterns. This water is then used to irrigate the crops during the dry growing season. These agricultural terraces demonstrate the necessity of integrating agriculture into community design, not only reclaiming lost agricultural opportunities, but also recycling the community's compost and other organic wastes.

Summary

In Book II, we have demonstrated how the sun can be used for thermal comfort, and how proper solar orientation and thoughtful site planning can achieve balanced microclimates. By examining some of the many methods that different cultures have used throughout history to capture the energy of the sun, we established a vocabulary of historical garden elements that acknowledged and understood the sun as the basic climatic element and discussed how these passive devices functioned in the landscape. These principles were applied in the contemporary design of a prototypical community where the residents of the Garden of the Phoenix, as full participants in the activities of the garden, benefit from the thermal delights of a designed and managed microclimate. The garden examples presented were works of art that elevated the human spirit, proving that climatic design can be beautiful, comfortable, and sustainable.

Onward now, from the divine realm of Fire, to the swift movement of Air. In the next book we discuss techniques that transform summer heat into cool, refreshing breezes. While we invited the winter sun into our gardens and homes for warmth and light, we now welcome the movable, active, and cooling qualities of the moist, flowing winds of summer.

Notes

1. Georgina Masson, *Italian Gardens*. New York: Harry Abrams, Inc., 1961, p. 17.

2. D. H. Lawrence, *Sketches of Etruscan Places and Other Italian Essays*. London: Penguin Books, 1994, p. 228.

3. Masson, *Italian Gardens*, p. 74.

4. Norman T. Newton, *Design on the Land: The Development of Landscape Architecture*. Cambridge, MA: Harvard University Press, 1971, p. 61.

5. Plato, *Phaedrus*. Edited by Harold North Fowler, Cambridge, MA: Harvard University Press, 1960, p. 413.

6. Vitruvius, *The Ten Books on Architecture*. New York: Dover Publications, [1914] 1960, p. 155.

7. Mildred Stapley Byne and Arthur Byne, *Spanish Gardens and Their Patios*. Philadelphia: J.B. Lippincott Company, New York, 1924, p. 193.

8. Byne and Byne, *Spanish Gardens and Their Patios*, p. 71.

9. William Shakespeare, *King John*. Edited by Clair McEachern, New York: Penguin Books, 1962, p. 44.

10. Vitruvius. *The Ten Books on Architecture*, p. 174.

11. Leon Battista Alberti, *On the Art of Building in Ten Books*. Cambridge, MA: MIT Press, [1550] 1988, p. 146.

12. Nader Ardalan and Laleh Bakhtiar, *The Sense Of Unity*. Chicago: University of Chicago Press, 1973, p. 134.

13. Masson, *Italian Gardens*, p. 46.

14. Wilhelmina F. Jashemski, *The Gardens of Pompeii, Herculaneum and the Villas Destroyed by Vesuvius*. New Rochelle, NY: Caratzas Brothers, 1979, p. 157.

15. Charles Moore et al, *The Poetics of Gardens*. Cambridge, MA: MIT Press, 1988, p. 220.

16. Inigio H. Triggs, *The Art of Garden Design in Italy*. London: Longmans, Green, and Co., 1906, p. 4.

17. Ronald King, *The Quest for Paradise*. New York: Mayflower Books, Inc., 1979, p. 35.

18. Johann Wolfgang Goethe, *Italian Journey*. London: Penguin Books, 1962, p. 488.

19. Giovanni Boccaccio, *The Decameron*. Translated by G. H. McWilliam, London: Penguin Books, 1972, p. 232.

20. D.H. Lawrence, *Twilight in Italy*. New York: The Viking Press, [1916] 1958, p. 60.

21. Ibid, p. 62.

22. Ibid, p. 67.

Book III: **Air**

Air, the ever-present ether, was one of the four basic elements of nature postulated by Empedocles and Plato, and one of the original substances thought to occupy "empty" space. In classical explanations of reality, water (graphically represented as an octahedron) was transformed by fire into air; air was condensed into water. This philosophy recognized the inter-relationship of ecological and natural systems, and is relevant today as we struggle to appreciate the value of clean air as a precious natural resource.

Garden designers have sculpted the movement of air and designed air-cooled spaces throughout history, particularly in Mediterranean climates. Alberti and Vitruvius both understood that solar orientation, as discussed in Book II, allowed for the development of warm places in winter. Both believed that a thorough understanding of the sun's position in the sky was also essential for providing cool, shady places in summer. These philosopher-architects grasped not only the importance of solar orientation, but also the role of seasonal environmental conditions as a basis for creating microclimates for summer use. They realized that "air"— wind that was to be avoided or thwarted in winter—was integral to the design of places for summer living. In their treatises, both emphasized the importance of air-cooling elements in combination with the correct orientation of buildings and grounds. Since the prevailing winds of summer are different than those of winter, during the hot summer months comfortable, air-cooled micro-climates can result from the proper manipulation of passive garden elements. Conversely, some garden forms that might create effective microclimates in the summer can create quite uncomfortable spaces in the winter. In the winter, shady spaces and areas of increased wind velocity must be avoided because they are simply too cold. In winter we block the wind, in summer we harness it.

Summers are extremely hot in the Mediterranean countries of Spain, Italy, and the Middle East. There is very little rain-

The Pleasant air and wind,
with sacred thoughts do
feed my serious mind.[1]
Rowland Watkyns, The Poet's Soliloquy

133

fall, and temperatures can often approach 100° F or more. In Iran, the annual precipitation can be less than 12 inches a year—a landscape and climate comparable to those of Arizona or New Mexico. Each of these cultures developed specific garden devices to deal with the scorching summer heat. Indeed, ancient gardens were ideal places to find refreshment amid cooling airs.

In a variety of ways, landscape design can exploit the cooling effects of moving air, thus reducing our dependence on mechanically produced air-conditioning systems. Avoiding artificial and expensive air conditioning reduces electrical and environmental costs. The proper manipulation of garden elements can easily achieve passive microclimates that take advantage of the cooling properties of air flow (Figure III-1). Air can be directed, funneled, and accelerated with simple landscape and architectonic forms such as seats, allées, arbors, pergolas, garden pavilions, and porches. Shady spaces can produce naturally cool air in the summer. Moving from glaring sunlight into the depths of a shady environment is physically and psychologically satisfying. This simple temperature differential produces quite a noticeable effect. In addition, air moving over perspiring skin also cools the body by accelerating evaporation. Almost any movement of air in the summer can be psychologically refreshing. Likewise, mechanical air conditioning of interior spaces makes the natural hot summer air outside feel even more uncomfortable. The colder the artificial air conditioning, the more drastic the effect will be.

Reducing our dependency on air conditioning by integrating passive landscape elements into our environments is a necessity for reducing energy consumption. Moreover, the spiritual benefit of a connection with the invisible yet tangible movement of this precious substance, the breath of life, must always be a basic tenet of design.

Figure III-1
Villa Medici, Fiesole, Italy.

Manipulating garden elements to take advantage of the cooling properties of air.
(Photo: Author)

Postulate I: **Cool Seats**

● Cool seats provide comfortable places to sit in the shade during hot summer days. Often open-backed to allow for ventilation, these benches are situated to catch the prevailing summer breezes, and are sometimes set above water features or grottos. Cool seats can also be built into walls or small enclosures. Small openings facing the prevailing breezes force the air to pass by the bench, thus gently cooling the seat's occupant (Figure III-2).

Certainly the air we breath and that plays such a vital role in maintaining and preserving life (as we can ourselves observe) when really pure, may have an extraordinary beneficial effect on health.[2]
Alberti, *On The Art of Building, Book I*

● Figure III-2
The cool seat.

Figure III-3 *(opposite above)*
Villa Gamberaia, Settignano, Italy.

The shady cool seat with its back open to the prevailing breeze.

Figure III-4 *(opposite below)*
Villa Gamberaia, Settignano, Italy.

A cool seat's intimate enclosure.

Hardly any garden exists without a simple bench, a place to pause, rest, and view one's surroundings. The sensitive garden designer of the past realized that in order to sit peacefully, one also had to be comfortable at all times of the year, especially during the hot months when the garden was the only respite from the oppressive heat of a building's interior. Thus, the cool seat can be considered any bench or seating arrangement that takes advantage of air currents by its position in the landscape.

As discussed in Book II, the Villa Gamberaia contains a number of passive garden devices for capturing the sun's energy in winter; but its designer also included devices to manage the microclimate during other seasons. For example, the villa's garden incorporates two different types of cool seats located on its terraces. The first takes the form of a low wall on the western terrace, 160 feet long, which furnishes occupants with a wide ledge for sitting. This seat wall, decorated with finials and animals mounted on arched pilasters, provides a comfortable, curved backrest as well as a place to sit. This bench tops a 15-foot-high terrace retaining wall with espaliered vines running the length of its surface. The moisture evaporating from the leaves of these vines filters and cools the air. This seat works best early in the day when shaded from the morning sun, where the dew evaporating off the adjacent lawn also lowers the air temperature. The placement of the bench on a terrace retaining wall catches the rising air from the valley below. As the sun rises overhead, one finds shade by moving along the length of the bench. On any point along this wall, one may sit and enjoy the valley breezes while looking over the tops of the orchard trees and down the hillside of the surrounding plantations. By the afternoon, however, this western garden facade will be in full sun and much too hot to be comfortable.

The second cool seat at the Villa Gamberaia is located at the southern base of a grand viale, where it catches the updraft from the valley below. Under a large, overhanging stone pine that casts a dark-green shadow throughout the day, this simple backless bench attaches to an open balustrade. The balustrade disperses and filters the air rising from the valley below and directs the cooling breezes toward the bench (Figure III-3). While the first terrace bench presents a place for contemplating the panoramic view of Florence below, this seat with its intimate enclosure creates a more introverted, reflective space (Figure III-4). Residents could begin their morning along the western terrace and, as the day became hotter, move to the shaded bench by the late afternoon. Here, the designer created two entirely different situations that responded to the daily and seasonal climatic variations, illustrating a sound understanding of local environmental conditions.

The Alcazar Gardens of Seville contain one of the cleverest air-cooled seats in garden history. This ingenious design produces a simple form of air conditioning that could easily be adapted into contemporary landscapes. We find this extraordinary bench in the Jardin de la Danza, a small garden room within a series of enclosed patios adjacent to the palace complex. Extremely thick walls enclose the garden on the east and west sides, while the southern wall addresses the prevailing summer breezes with an intimate niche. Between the two built-in benches, a small arched window with a decorative metal grille frames a picturesque view of the adjacent lower garden (Figure III-5).

The configuration of this unusual seating enclave modifies the microclimate and creates a cool seat. As the breeze flows, it is forced through the small window, thus increasing its velocity at its point of exit on the opposite side of the opening. This acceleration of air is known as the "Venturi

Effect," and was first noted in the late eighteenth century by the Italian physicist Giovanni Battista Venturi, who found that a drop in pressure corresponds to a suction action. In addition to this unique physical effect, the enclave remains cool in the summer because the thick wall that encloses it acts as an insulator, while the white walls reflect the heat produced from the intense rays of the sun. Because of its east-west orientation the entire enclave will remain in shade throughout the day in summer (Figure III-6). Furthermore, the clear-blue glazed tiles covering the top of the seat and wall feel cool to the touch. The bluish hues of the tiles create the psychological impression of a cooler space despite the extremely warm temperatures of the city of Seville, known as "the Frying Pan of Europe." Through such an intimate knowledge of climatic design, the unknown designer of this bench was able to realize an ingenious form of airconditioning that remains effective to this day.

This postulate described the form and function of the architectural "Cool Seat" as a basic passive design element. Like the bench, or cool seat, the allée is also an elemental building block for the garden and was used extensively as a passive landscape device. Postulate II endeavors to explain the modification of microclimate through the use of the allée.

Figure III-5 *(opposite)*
Alcazar Gardens, Seville, Spain.

The relationship of the cool seat to the patio gardens.
(Photo: Author)

Figure III-6
Alcazar Gardens, Seville, Spain.

The shady enclosure of the cool seat, looking out to the garden beyond.

Cool Seats

Contemporary Applications

1. Utilize a terrace or retaining wall as a base for a cool seat. Build retaining walls 18 inches above the adjacent garden level to provide a comfortable seat height.

2. Locate the cool seat perpendicular to the direction of the prevailing summer breezes.

3. Plant shade trees or vines next to the cool seat, to provide shade during the summer months.

4. Construct garden walls at least 4 feet thick so that a seating niche can be built inside the wall. Place a small opening approximately 2 feet square facing the prevailing summer breezes.

5. Cover the cool seat with glazed tiles in cool hues to create a physically inviting and psychologically cool surface.

Figure III-7 (opposite above)
Villa d'Este, Tivoli, Italy.
1550–72. Designed by Pirro Ligorio.

A simple air-cooled bench seemingly floats above a
grotto between the wall of One Hundred Fountains
and the Fountain of the Ovato. A white, stucco bench
rests in a 20- by 40-foot rectangle enclosed by a 3-
foot-high wall. This isolated, backless bench, shaded
throughout the day by a canopy of trees, looks toward
the massive waterworks of the Ovato. Carefully placed,
the bench catches the updraft of cool air generated
from the wall of One Hundred Fountains. The cooling
sound from the water of the grotto directly below,
the thunder of the waterworks of the Ovato, and the
splashing of the jets of the wall of One Hundred
Fountains contribute to this cooling sensation.

Figure III-8 (opposite below)
Villa Falconieri, Frascati, Italy.
1548, Redesigned by Francesco Borromini.

Another cool seat very similar to the bench at the
Villa d'Este can be found at the Villa Falconieri above
the northeast edge of the bosco. The cool air generated from the fountain and grotto drifts up to the seating area, where benches reside under the shade of a
dense tree canopy.

Figure III-9
Palazzo Farnese, Caprarola, Italy.
1557. Designed by Vignola.

Along the eastern border of the summer garden, a
wonderful structure projects out above the valley
below. Two seats are built into the base of the high
open arches of the structure, with their backs open to
iron railings that allow the breeze to penetrate.
(Photo: Author)

Figure III-10
Palazzo Farnese, Caprarola, Italy.

One can sit on the bench and lean out over the valley below and catch the updraft. In the summer afternoons, the space is in complete shade. Conversely, in the winter, if the sun is shining and the wind calm, this space will be comfortable (the lower sun will penetrate the arched opening, warming the seats).

Figure III-11
Casa de Pilatos, Seville, Spain.
Twelfth century. Designer unknown.

The opening of this cool seat is covered with a carved wooden grill, or *reja*. When condensation forms on the wooden grill, it cools the air that flows through into the interior. This opening also has wooden shutters that can be closed in the wintertime to block the cold winds and opened to allow the interior space to be warmed by the sun.

● Figure III-12 *(opposite)*
The cool walk.

142

Postulate II: **Cool Walks**

● A cool walk can be defined as a path or avenue edged with evenly spaced trees that are sufficiently close to create an avenue of shade. Cool walks often act as an organizing device or as connectors to major focal points in the garden. This path should be kept narrow to remain in shade throughout a summer day, and of a length that permits access to all parts of the garden (Figure III-12).

The paths along the edges of the garden were almost entirely hemmed in by white and red roses and jasmine, so that not only in the morning, but even when the sun was at its apex one could walk in pleasant-smelling shade, without ever being touched by the sun's rays.
Giovanni Boccaccio, *The Decameron.*[3]

Cool walks are parallel rows of evenly planted trees placed on either side of a path, avenue, or roadway, and are usually long enough to create a walk or promenade of some distance. The importance of cool walks as garden design elements cannot be overstated. They are commonly used to direct views, organize spaces, create vistas, and, in addition, they hold together various parts of a garden design. As avenues, they link the garden to the countryside, and frame views through enclosures. The common term for this type of garden device is the *alleé*. The allée first emerged as a major design element for spatial organization in Italian Renaissance gardens. In fact the allée was the backbone of the Italian Renaissance garden. However, many historians and other observers often overlook the passive design qualities of allées. This function of allées was not missed by Shepherd and Jellicoe, who described the importance of these cool, shady walks:

> The most practical need for the enjoyment of the garden was shade, and this was the reason for elaborating the treatment of trees and hedges. An avenue of cypresses, trees themselves that reciprocate the ideas of formality, make not only a shaded approach to a house but a magnificent one as well. Once inside the garden, the necessity of getting from one part to another in shade suggested pleached alleys...which enable one to make a complete circuit in shade.[4]

Figure III-13
Boboli Gardens, Florence, Italy.
The Viottolone dominates the eastern section of the garden.

Figure III-14 *(opposite)*
Boboli Gardens, Florence, Italy.
The optical illusion of the "infinite vista."

When designed and sited properly, the allée will also stimulate the movement of air, using the prevailing summer breezes to enhance the pedestrian's feeling of coolness. It can also be used to direct air currents into specific areas of the garden and garden structures. Placed along south-facing slopes, allées can benefit from naturally rising air currents that push air into the shade of the allée.

The Boboli Gardens in Florence are home to one of the longest cypress allées of the Renaissance. Cosimo de Medici employed Niccolo Tribolo to begin the garden's design, but after Tribolo's death, responsibility shifted to Bartolomeo Ammannati, and later to Bernardo Buontalenti. The garden was built in stages, the first half completed by 1595. Between 1630 and 1637, the villa's monumental cypress avenue (over 900 feet in length) was finished. This grand allée runs east-west, perpendicular to the palace, and dominates the eastern section of the garden. The dark-green avenue, called the Viottolone, begins at the crest of a steep hill above an amphitheater and descends a gentle slope, finally terminating in the Piazzale dell'Isolotto water garden. This "infinite vista," so termed by Claudia Lazzaro,[5] allows one to walk quite a distance in the air wafting around the cypress trees; it provides a refreshing contrast to the glaring sun that soaks the more open parts of the garden (Figure III-13). From the top of the hill looking down the length of the Viottolone, the Isolotto appears very far away. Conversely, from the bottom of the hill, looking at the allée from the Isolotto, the top of the hill looks extremely close (Figure III-14).

Very near the ancient hill town of Siena lies the small, but intriguing garden at Villa Geggiano. Begun as a fortified country farmhouse, it was remodeled into a villa in the seventeenth century to include a garden theater, sunken garden, and bosco. Approached on a gravel road along a ridge that passes through the vine-covered and olive-dotted Tuscan

landscape, glimpses of the villa appear on a distant hill. Before entering the garden, the road passes through a thick-ilex allée. On the exterior of this plantation, the ilex trees are permitted to take their natural form, rising upward to 40 feet and sweeping down to the ground in a broad fan-like arch (Figure III-15). In the deep shade of the allée, the trees on either side of the road have been pruned and trained to produce a cathedral-like space (Figure III-16). The road is slightly depressed into the earth and the trees are planted into an embankment bordering the road, giving the space a cool, earthy atmosphere. On one visit in June, the exterior temperature measured 105° F in the sun; in contrast, the interior temperature of the allée was a pleasant 72° F. This temperature differential illustrates the great effectiveness of allées in producing cooler zones in the summer.

The Palazzo Podesta in the shipping city of Genoa combines three different types of seasonal walks. It is located on an extremely steep site off Via Garibaldi, a street famous for its lavish palaces. Giovanni Battista Castello, also known as Il Bergamasco, designed the garden around 1567 for Niccolò Lomellini. The fact that this little urban garden sits in the middle of a bustling urban center makes it a particularly refreshing green oasis. One enters the palazzo through a foyer directly off the street. A narrow passageway opens to a sunny courtyard that contains a seventeenth-century fountain, attributed to Parodi. The main garden lies about 40 feet above the courtyard at the same level as the *piano nobile*, or second floor, of the house. Walls 30 feet in height enclose this narrow, rectangular garden, which is oriented toward the southwest (Figure III-17).

The harmony of landscape and architecture graces the garden level where:

> two wings of the piano nobile extend backwards to join the garden, whose promenades stretch out directly from the tall French win-

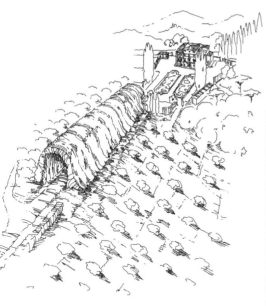

Figure III-15
Villa Geggiano, Tuscany, Italy.

Exterior fanlike shape of the ilex allée on the ridge of the hill.

Figure III-16
Villa Geggiano, Tuscany, Italy.

The deep shade of the cathedral-like interior of the allée.
(Photo: Author)

146

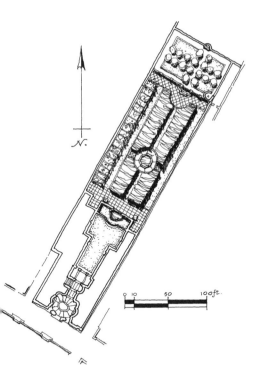

dows. These paths are carefully arranged to provide varying degrees of shade at different times of the day; on the western side there is both an open sunny walk and one partly shaded by an old fashioned rose pergola, which can be seen on the right hand side. While these are in the sun, the eastern promenade lies in the deep shade of the palms, the orange trees and a huge magnolia.[6]

On this principal living level, the garden is essentially a four-square garden with the traditional boxwood parterres, and crosswalks bordered with potted orange trees (Figure III-18). At the center of the cross axis, a 12-foot-diameter fountain with six benches placed around its perimeter allows one to sit in sun or shade as the seasons might dictate. At the rear of this level, the gurgling water of a small grotto refreshes both physically and psychologically. The cool walk along the eastern border of the garden remains in shade throughout the warm months and provides a respite from the urban summer heat. These ingenious cool walks function well throughout the year and illustrate a true understanding of seasonal variation in a garden. In this urban oasis one can find seclusion, comfort, and peace of mind; thus the Palazzo Podesta demonstrates the importance of creating passive microclimates in dense, urban areas.

The allée exists as such a marvelous and beautiful creation, that perhaps no landscape should be designed without one. But, even more so, their true attraction lies in their ability to so easily provide avenues of cool air and strong connections to the other passive devices in a garden. In the next postulate, Shady Tunnels and Pruned Walks, we will discover a radical type of allée, a walk similar in its basic form to the allée, but quite unusual.

Cool Walks

Contemporary Applications

1. To create a shady promenade, plant evenly spaced evergreen trees on either side of a path. To be effective the length of the walk should be at least 100 feet.

2. Orient the cool walk in the direction of prevailing summer breezes.

3. When possible, place the cool walk on a south-facing slope to take advantage of naturally rising air currents that will push air into the shade of the allée.

4. Excavate the path about 2 feet into the earth to form an elevated planting base along the edge of the walk. Plant closely spaced canopy trees along the walk at the edge of this embankment. Trim the interior branches into tall arches, forming a shady corridor.

5. Design cool walks that provide shade throughout the summer months. The ideal landscape provides an environment that allows one to linger or stroll in sun or shade as the season dictates.

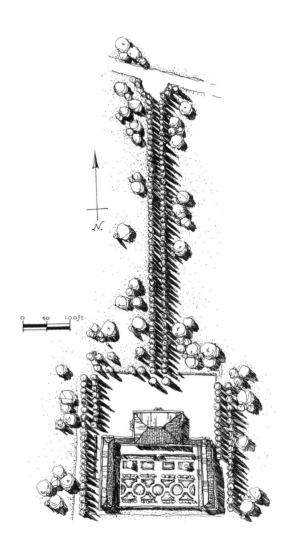

Figure III-19 *(above right)*
Villa Poggio Torcelli, near Florence, Italy.
Seventeenth century.
Designer unknown.

An avenue of cypress trees forms the central axis of this Tuscan mansion, functioning as both a major design element and a passive energy device. Through a semicircular gateway one enters into the deep shade of this 15-foot-wide allée of closely spaced cypress trees. The avenue runs 600 feet before it terminates in the courtyard at the base of the villa's north facade. The allée's north-south orientation and the narrowness of the passage insures shade for most of the day.

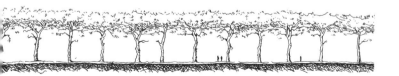

Figure III-20 *(opposite below)*
Villa Mondragone, Frascati, Italy.
Begun around 1567. Designed by Martino Lunghi, later modified by Vasanzi and Rainaldo.
A cypress avenue forms the main approach to the Villa Mondragone. This villa, perched on a broad, uniform terrace gives a sweeping panorama of the *campagna*, or flat landscape outside Rome, which is visible from the surrounding Alban Hills.

Figure III-21 *(left above)*
Villa Mondragone, Frascati, Italy.
Journeying up the complete length of the shady allée, the visitor suddenly emerges facing a grotto built into the north facade of the terrace. After walking in a broad sweep to the left or right of the grotto and reaching the upper terrace, the magnificent facade of the villa emerges dramatically. From this terrace one can see the long allée marching toward a distant Rome. Tradition has it that this was once to have been a grand avenue all the way to Rome.[7] Thus, the Pope could travel the distance from the Vatican to Frascati in complete shade.
(Photo: Marc Treib)

Figure III-22 *(left below)*
Villa Doria Pamphili, Rome.
Sixteenth century. Designed by Algardi and Grimaldi.
The Villa Doria Pamphili has two exceptionally long pine allées that transect the expansive gardens. Created from towering stone pines, these allées produce an entirely different effect than the typical cool walks of ilex trees or cypresses. The lower branches of the stone pines are pruned so that, as the tree grows, the top branches take on the shape of a spreading umbrella. When planted in allées, their thick trunks resemble columns supporting sprawling horizontal canopies.

The first allée begins at the eastern edge of the property above the sunken giardino segreto and proceeds west for 1400 feet. The second traverses the garden from north to south for well over 2000 feet, across the whole width of the western edge of the park.

Figure III-23 *(above)*
Villa Albani, Rome, Italy.
Eighteenth century. Gardens laid out by
Antonio Nolli.

The bosco sits several feet above the plaza in front of
the villa. One enters through a marble, neo-classical
temple facade, and finds not a building interior, but a
wooded ilex allée on the other side. After passing
through this threshold, one finds five parallel cool walks.
The main walk is lined on either side by statues and
marbles from Cardinal Albani's collection.

Figure III-24 *(above right)*
Villa Torlonia, Frascati, Italy.
Sixteenth century. Designer unknown.

The Villa Torlonia in Frascati contains another variation
of the standard cool walk, in the form of radial allées,
which issue from a circular focal point. Usually no less
than three allées but no more than five compose this
feature.

Figure III-25 *(right)*
Villa Torlonia, Frascati, Italy.

Five allées radiate from the clearing and extend to the
edge of the property, with the deep and mysterious
ilex woodland between. This system allows one to walk
almost endlessly through cool allées, with sunlight glistening off the fountain's jet as a dynamic, distant counterpoint to the shadowy path.

● **Figure III-26a** *(opposite)*
The pruned hedge.

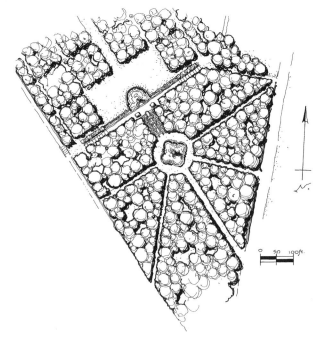

● Shady tunnels and pruned walks allow no sun to penetrate their interior. Ideally, plant forms are manipulated into architectural shapes that completely block out the sun with their green walls. The resulting deep shade provides pedestrians with a sheltered path away from the glare of the sun. Shady tunnels and pruned walks should be sited to allow a cool passage throughout as much of the garden and landscape as possible (Figures III-26a, b).

Those who have sojourned in the ardent climate of the south can appreciate the delights of an abode combining the breezy coolness of the mountain air with the freshness and verdure of the valley.[8]
Washington Irving

Shady tunnels are created by pruning or clipping allées into strong architectural shapes through a process called *pleaching*. Pleaching refers to the horticultural technique of interlacing or grafting together the flexible branches of parallel rows of trees so that they grow into a continuous green archway or other architectural form (Figure III-27). An ancient craft, pleaching was first developed by farmers to increase the yield from fruit trees by maximizing the branches' exposure to the sun. This practice eventually resulted in more decorative garden forms. Pleached allées are distinct from traditional allées because they are manipulated to create tunnels that are completely enveloped in deep shade (Figure III-28). Very popular in Italian gardens from the sixteenth century to the eighteenth century, the practice continues in many gardens to this day.

Pruned walks evolved from the ancient form of topiary design, which historians believe to have been practiced by the Greeks and Romans. Topiary refers to the pruning of shrubs or trees into ornamental, geometric, animal, or other shapes. Pruned walks can be created with shrubs or trees; often cypress or ilex trees are used, and planted so closely together that they can be sheared into vertical green walls.

Parallel rows of hedges can also be planted close enough and high enough so that the path between them will be in shade most of the day in summer (Figure III-29). Sometimes the tops of these hedges are shaped into decorative, architectural, or playful shapes. Unlike the pleached allée, whose tunnel form insures continuous shade, the planning and siting of the pruned walk must be well thought-out to remain in shade throughout most of the summer.

The seventeenth-century Villa Gori, built in the hills above Siena, has two of the world's most notable shady tunnels which create two lengthy axes in the villa's garden (Figure III-30a). Traversing the western slope, the first allée runs perpendicular to the spacious southern terrace and extends into a hillside clad with olive trees (Figure III-30b). The longer of the two, this allée runs an astonishing 840 feet before it terminates at a well-proportioned, open-air theater. The pathway, sunken slightly below the base of the trees, increases the effect of the overhead canopy. A 1904 Maxfield Parrish painting of these pleached walks illustrates how the exterior had been clipped into a symmetrical, rounded shape, resembling a green loaf of bread. The interior of this walk is also trimmed into a green vault of smooth ilex branches. The resultant mat of dense vegetation produces a very deep shade that insulates against solar loading caused by the buildup of heat from direct sunlight (Figure III-30c).

The second pleached allée extends 510 feet southward from the face of the villa down a slight hill, terminating in the remains of a circular landscape form called a *ragnaia*. A ragnaia was a bird blind, or camouflaged trap, that hunters would use to sight and shoot at the wild birds living in the adjacent woodlands.

These two allées created a unique cooling system, an "ancient tunnel of gnarled and interlocked trees, where a green twilight

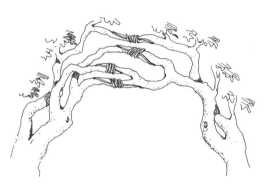

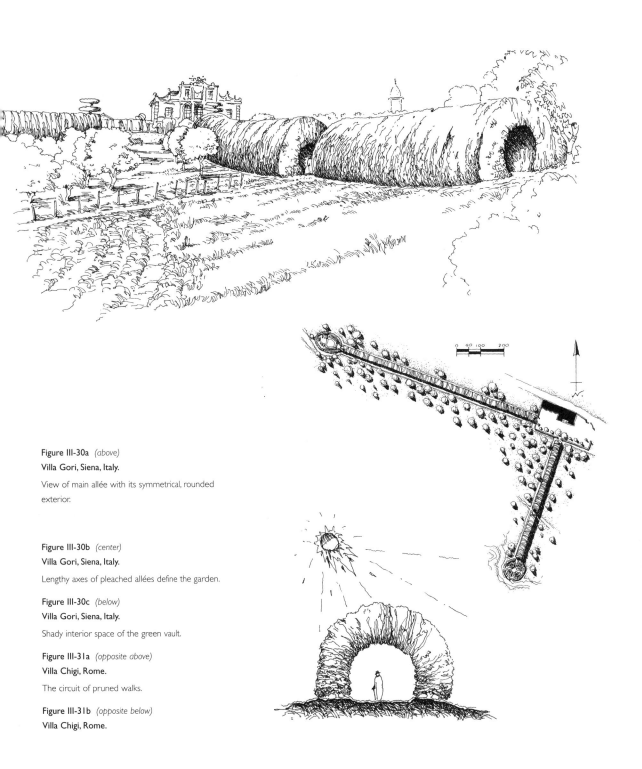

Figure III-30a *(above)*
Villa Gori, Siena, Italy.
View of main allée with its symmetrical, rounded exterior.

Figure III-30b *(center)*
Villa Gori, Siena, Italy.
Lengthy axes of pleached allées define the garden.

Figure III-30c *(below)*
Villa Gori, Siena, Italy.
Shady interior space of the green vault.

Figure III-31a *(opposite above)*
Villa Chigi, Rome.
The circuit of pruned walks.

Figure III-31b *(opposite below)*
Villa Chigi, Rome.

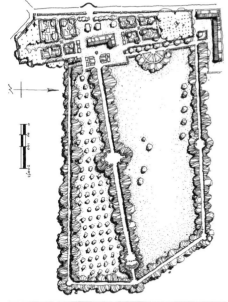

reigns in the hottest summer noon."[9] It is unfortunate that this landscape device, with its many wonderful aspects, has not made an appearance in contemporary gardens. Not only an outstanding example of landscape as architecture, the pleached allée has great potential for passive design applications.

The Villa Chigi in Rome also contains a variety of fabulously pruned walks. Built around 1760 for Cardinal Flavio Chigi on what was the outskirts of Rome, the urban sprawl of that great city now engulfs the villa. However, the villa's high walls still contain and isolate its unique grounds. An incredible circuit of pruned walks (laid out without the use of right angles or parallel rules) run around the perimeter of the property and down the central axis (Figure III-31a). These shady, pruned walks are created by parallel rows of trees planted tightly together like hedgerows. The walks consist of a thickly planted mixture of ilex, laurel, and box, neatly clipped only on the interior, while the exterior is allowed to take its natural form.

The central avenue at Villa Chigi, a cool, shady, pruned walk over 950 feet long, points eastward from the villa down a gentle grade, bisecting open agricultural fields (Figure III-31b). Halfway down this passage, a small opening allows sunlight to penetrate, accenting the space with a bright spot of light. The avenue continues to a shady pocket of clipped trees where a hidden stairway connects the western perimeter walk and the eastern walk, totally framing the farm fields. One can walk for hours through the interior of these avenues without exposure to the blistering Roman sun. An important effect of these shady lanes is that:

> they allow alternate routes of return for a visitor who has accepted the invitation of the plan to walk the Vale's length. All too often, even in plans of some magnitude and skill, the only way back from a distant point is a reversal of the way out, resulting in the monotony of mere repetition.[10]

Shady Tunnels and Pruned Walks

Contemporary Applications

1. Pleach the branches of parallel rows of evergreen trees into continuous green archways or tunnels.

2. Plant parallel rows of hedges sufficiently close together so that they may be sheared into green walls. The width of the path between them should be 3 to 5 feet. Train the hedges to grow high enough so that the pathway between them will remain in shade during the summer.

3. The thickness of the leaf canopy of the pleached allée should be no less than 4 feet to insulate against solar heat gain and produce a deep shade.

4. Ideally, pleached allées should be at least 100 feet long, or long enough to produce an easy, uninterrupted walk.

5. The pleached allée should face the prevailing summer breezes to capture and funnel this cool, shady air into building interiors.

The designers of these shady tunnels and pruned walks were not afraid to use their imagination to create architecture from plant forms. When we look at the incredible variety of forms springing from their wildest visions, we can see that there was no limitation to the sculpting of the landscape for passive design. The next postulate, Arbors and Pergolas, examines how trees and shrubs can be trained on structures to assist in moderating the climate.

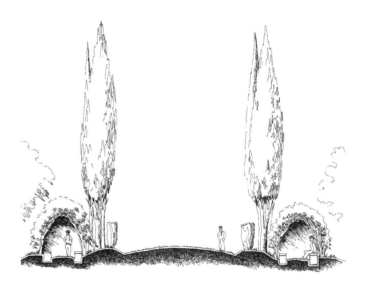

Figure III-32 *(opposite above)*
Boboli Gardens, Florence, Italy.
Sixteenth to seventeenth centuries.
Designed by Tribolo, Ammannati, and Buontalenti.

In addition to the grand cypress allée at the Boboli
Gardens, several dark and narrow tunnels wind their
way throughout the property. All the walks are paved
with gravel; some are also edged with stone. These
green tunnels connect the major features of the garden. Parallel tunnels of pleached trees flank the sides
of the Viottolone, the garden's monumental central
allée. These two walks extend the length of the
Viottolone, a total of 850 feet. A subtle, dappled light
penetrates the vegetation to reach the pathway itself.

Figure III-33 *(opposite below)*
Boboli Gardens, Florence, Italy.

Low parapet walls border some of these narrow,
tunneled walks, while the wider pleached allées have
benches placed periodically along the path so that the
visitor may rest in a cool place as well as walk in the
shade. Since these shady tunnels of the Boboli Gardens
are constructed with an extremely thick canopy of
leaves, the temperature inside is usually in the middle
70s, hardly ever exceeding 80° F throughout the
sweltering summer season.

Figure III-34
Villa Lancellotti, Frascati, Italy.
First known images of garden, c.1620.
Designer unknown.

Long parallel walls of clipped ilex also form a perfect
frame for the sensuous parterres on the south side of
the Villa Lancellotti in Frascati. The southern end of the
garden abuts a semicircular nymphaeum, a water feature
dedicated to the mythological nymphs, and filled with
grottoes, niches, and statuary. Two parallel rows of trees,
planted 20 feet apart, form a tunnel along the sides of
the central parterre garden. Their canopies are clipped
above eye level, allowing a view of the parterres while
walking in the cool shade.

Figure III-35a

Villa Carlotta, Cadenabbia, Lake Como, Italy. 1745. Designer unknown.

Contrasting with the single allées of the Villa Gori stands the tight network of shady tunnels that remain in the gardens of the Villa Carlotta in northern Italy. Oriented in a northwest-southeast direction, this romantic terrace garden sits on the western edge of Lake Como. On the lowest terrace, several steps above the water level, and on either side of the central axis, two pleached allées shelter multiple shaded tunnels. These massive, green blocks frame a sunlit square that opens onto the central axis. A circular pool with a fountain accents the center of this clearing. A central allée intersects these vegetative blocks, which are full of smaller tunnels that run parallel to the main allée.

Figure III-35b.

Villa Carlotta, Cadenabbia, Lake Como, Italy.

The exteriors of the pleached allées are clipped into right angles. Multiple pathways are carved from the dense green block, which produces a deep purple shade beneath, reinforced by the cooling effect of the air coming from the lake.

Figure III-36

Villa Garzoni, Collodi, Italy. 1652. Designer unknown.

The lower gardens of the baroque hillside gardens of the Villa Garzoni contain a pair of fantastically sculpted, shady, pruned walks. These parallel rows of hedges enclose and form the southern border of the garden's bottom terrace. Planted at 5-foot intervals, the tall trees (in some places reaching a height of 25 feet) provide dense shade along the entire length of this 800-foot passage. The two hedges that border these perimeter walks differ considerably. The first, which borders the outside of the garden, is 15 feet high and clipped into simple, straight lines. The opposite hedge, taller, is clipped into marvelous shapes of curlicues and ovoids. From this lower parterre, the garden ascends a hillside consisting of a series of terraces set against a large bosco that then merges into the wild, wooded hillside.

● **Figure III-37a**
The pergola.

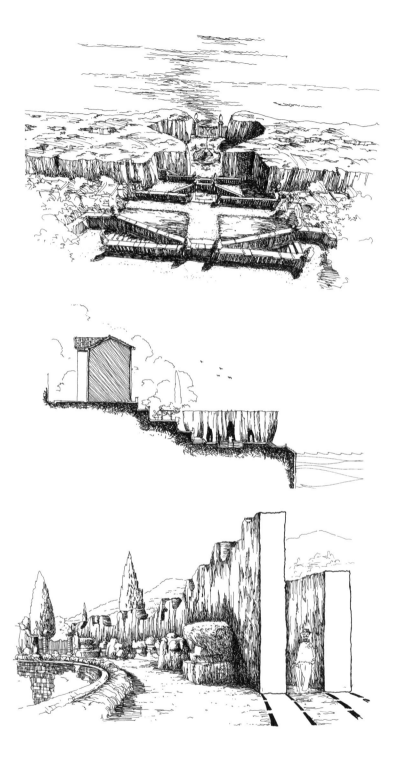

Postulate IV: **Arbors and Pergolas**

● Arbors and pergolas are freestanding structures, usually constructed of evenly spaced columns with wooden lintels to support vines. Ideal for maximizing the growth of vegetation above walks, arbors and pergolas provide a framework for abundant leafy screens of cool shade. The design of these structures can vary in complexity from very simple to extremely ornate. They may serve as organizational elements within a garden, and can be used for displaying a variety of vines or for growing grapes (Figure III-37).

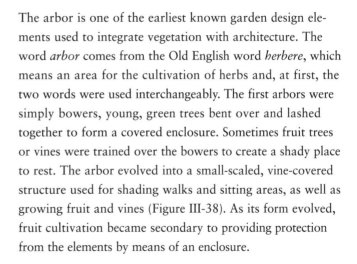

After this, they were shown into a walled garden alongside the palace, and since it seemed at first glance to be a thing of wondrous beauty, they began to explore it in detail. The garden was surrounded and criss-crossed by paths of unusual width, all straight as arrows and overhung by pergolas of vines which showed every sign of yielding an abundant crop of grapes later in the year. The vines were all in flower, drenching the garden with their aroma, which mingled with that of many other fragrant plants and herbs gave them the feeling that they were in the midst of all the spices ever grown in the east.[11]
Boccaccio, *The Decameron*

The arbor is one of the earliest known garden design elements used to integrate vegetation with architecture. The word *arbor* comes from the Old English word *herbere*, which means an area for the cultivation of herbs and, at first, the two words were used interchangeably. The first arbors were simply bowers, young, green trees bent over and lashed together to form a covered enclosure. Sometimes fruit trees or vines were trained over the bowers to create a shady place to rest. The arbor evolved into a small-scaled, vine-covered structure used for shading walks and sitting areas, as well as growing fruit and vines (Figure III-38). As its form evolved, fruit cultivation became secondary to providing protection from the elements by means of an enclosure.

The pergola has been an important part of garden design since the days of the Roman Empire, and it served as a major element in Italian Renaissance gardens. Pergolas evolved from arbors. Even though arbors and pergolas function essentially in the same fashion, the architectural and decorative features of the pergola's structure distinguish it from the more rustic arbor. The pergola's structure itself offers endless variations of possible designs of overhead elements to create shade. This structure consists of solid,

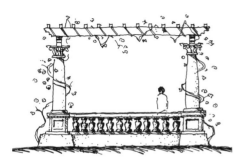

strong columns supporting an open roof of lintels and cross members in a decorative manner. At times lattice-work encloses the sides. Vines are often trained onto the base of the columns, but, unlike arbors, rarely dominate the structure, unless the vines are left unattended. Pergolas can cover garden paths or sitting areas, define areas of space, emphasize axes, and subdivide the garden.

The true beauty of the pergola and arbor lies in their countless design variations, from extremes of simplicity to intricacy, and their usefulness in creating a comfortable climate. Their form also provides an armature for growing plants vertically and horizontally in a small space. They increase our awareness of the changing seasons as the vines on them grow, flower, and fruit. Watching the shadows dancing on the ground makes one more aware of the movement of the air from even the most gentlest of breezes.

The excavations at Pompeii have revealed just how extensively the Romans utilized pergolas for air cooling purposes in their gardens. The pergola, which increased the livability of the courtyards and atriums so favored by the Romans, was an extension of the interior living spaces, giving the occupants a place to walk, or for growing fruiting vines. The open-air dining room of the House of the Ephebe includes one pergola typical of this era. In the center of the walled garden court, a vine-covered *triclinium*, or dining area, surrounds a rectangular opening where a statue of an *ephebe*, an adolescent male in training for citizenship in Ancient Greece, once stood. Sometimes fountains occupied the center of the triclinium instead of sculpture, adding to the delight of the dining experience. At the corners of the triclinium, stout round columns supported a wooden pergola overhead. Vines, planted at the base of each of the four columns, entwined with the overhead structure producing a pleasant shade (Figure III-38). This must have been a won-

● Figure III-37b
The arbor.

Figure III-38
Villa Cimbrone, Ravello, Italy.

A typical arbor.
(Photo: Author)

Figure III-39
House of the Ephebe, Pompeii, Italy.

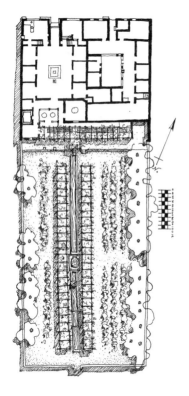

Figure III-40a
House of D. Octavius Quarto, Pompeii.

Section of arbor and dwelling.

Figure III-40b
House of D. Octavius Quarto, Pompeii.

The long pergola covering the central water channel.

derful space to eat in, sitting under the vines, listening to the play of water in the fountain. No wonder the Romans would linger in their vine-covered garden rooms, eating and drinking well into the night on their reclining couches.

A different type of pergola stands in the garden terrace of the House of D. Octavius Quartio. On the Via dell'Abbondanza on the eastern edge of Pompeii, a rather large, enclosed garden drops southward from a wide terrace off the back of the main house. On this terrace, a pergola, attached to the rear of the house, shades a deep-water channel running the complete east-west length of the dwelling. Interestingly, the channel runs along the base of the columns adjacent to the house, rather than down the center of the pergola as one might expect. The placement of the pergola along this edge of the dwelling extends the living area out into the garden, and acts as a transition to the outdoor space. This south-facing arbor helps block the summer sun, while the water humidifies the air (Figure III-40a). The columns along the dwelling side of the pergola are round and the columns along the garden side are square—a good example of the variation that a designer can give this form. Wooden lintels span the columns supporting the vines. Today, the pergola has been restored and replanted with grapevines that provide a luxurious shade in the summer.

A second watercourse continued through the center of the lower garden, ending before the southern wall. From the upper terrace, water cascaded down into a *nympheaum*, passing through two structures before finally terminating in yet another vine-covered pergola. Excavations along either side of the central canal have uncovered cavities believed to be structural supports for a long pergola that covered both sides of the water channel. These findings suggest that this garden made extensive and sophisticated use of the pergola for shade (Figure III-40b). The pergolas in this villa not only

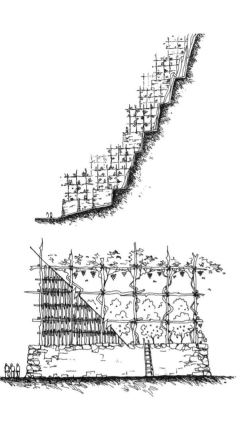

reduced the solar impact on the south facade, but also connected the house with the garden, and when integrated with a water channel, took advantage of the cooling properties of evaporating water. The widespread appearance of the pergola illustrates how the Romans used this device to reflect a way of life that was connected to the natural environment in a dense, urban setting.

South of Naples, from Sorrento to the Amalfi coast, the steep hillsides are lined with ancient stone terraces that climb the cliffs (Figure III-41a). Many of these terraces contain unique arbor structures that appear very old, but are still in use today. They are constructed out of thin cypress poles, crisscrossed to form scaffold-like structures that reach 20 to 30 feet above the terrace. Their purpose was to provide protection in the winter for the fruit trees planted in the interior. Although many have been replaced with fiberglass screens, in many places one can still see the wooden lattices that were used to screen the arbors in the winter (Figure III-41b). Inside, fruit trees were espaliered onto the arbor framework and grapevines were trained to grow on the wooden columns. The trunks of the vines rose up to the top of the structure and then fanned out horizontally across the top of the arbor as a green roof. Unfortunately, these examples of green architecture are disappearing quickly, but the arbors on the Amalfi coast illustrate the development of a particular passive energy form as a functional agricultural device.

Garden designers of the Italian Renaissance readily accepted the pergola into their design vocabulary and consistently included them in villa gardens for their aesthetic qualities and climatic benefits. "Relief from the burning sun on a sultry summer afternoon warranted their invention, but the dramatic effect [that] the pergolas created exceeded this stated aim."[12] Generally constructed of wood, they unfortunately deteriorated quickly, leaving few representatives of this era.

Figure III-41a

Typical arbors on the terraced hillsides along the Amalfi coast, Italy.

Figure III-41b

Structure of the hillside arbors with wooden lattice.

Figure III-41c

Interior of arbor with vines, forming a green roof.

Figure III-42
Villa Quaracchi, Florence, Italy. Fifteenth century.
Designed by Leon Battista Alberti.

An early example of the pergola, designed by Alberti, demonstrates his belief in the use of vine-covered arbors as an integral element of villa design. As he discussed in his treatise, *On the Art of Building in Ten Books*, walks in a garden should be covered by arbors supported by well-proportioned marble columns and trained with vines. Alberti felt that the arbor should not only provide shade, but also be sensitively designed.

At the Villa Quaracchi, a country villa for the Florentine merchant Giovanni Rucellai, Alberti followed these precepts, with pergolas so seamlessly integrated into the garden that they defined the pattern of the villa's exterior spaces. Climatically, they formed a circuit of cool air, integrated and designed with such pleasing proportions that the garden's owner bragged that they were the most impressive element of his villa.

Figure III-43 *(opposite above)*
Villa d'Este, Tivoli, Italy.
Begun in 1549. Designed by Pirro Ligorio.

Reconstructed from an engraving of the Villa d'Este by Étienne Dupérac from 1573, this figure shows an elaborate four-square pergola in the center of the lowest level of the garden. With its extreme length connecting all four corners of the garden, combined with its ornate construction and its voluminous proportions, this was one of the most monumental pergolas of its time. Although the d'Este pergola has disappeared, we can easily imagine its effectiveness as a wonderful shade-producing device for walking, resting, or garden viewing.

The top of the pergola was slightly rounded, and latticework enclosed those sides filled with doors and windows. A two-story, octagonal pavilion made of lathe accented the intersection, while arched doorways with carved wooden pediments marked the four entrances. This configuration allowed one to stroll or pause in shade and observe the terrace gardens above with their marvelous waterworks.

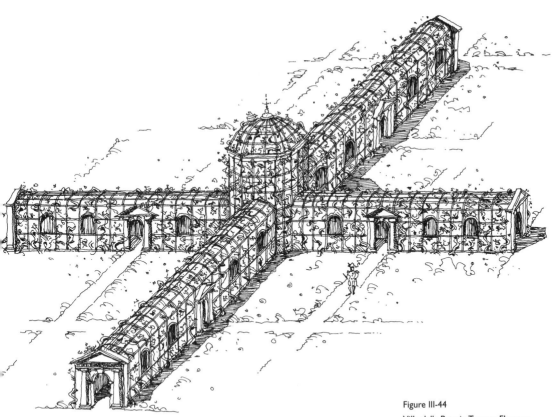

Figure III-44
Villa della Petraia, Tuscany, Florence.
Date unknown. Designer unknown.

This elevation interpreted from a lunette painting by
Utens depicts a pergola at the Villa della Petraia, just
outside of Florence. This garden follows a similar four-
square format, but the pergola takes on a very unusual circular form. Vaulted lattice pergolas inscribe circles
within the two large squares of the lower terrace.
Pathways further divide each of the two grass squares
into four smaller, symmetrical quadrangles. At the intersection of these pathways, a smaller pergola encloses
a circular opening, affording radial panoramic views of
the garden. Although long since disappeared, it is
believed that these tunnels had vines trained on their
sides. An enclosed plantation of holm oaks, planted in
circular patterns, echoed the vocabulary of the pergolas.
Because of the Duke of Tuscany's love of his pergolas,
they remained long after they fell out of fashion, and
there are references that indicate the structures were
still standing in 1773.

Arbors and Pergolas
Contemporary Applications

1. Use arbors and pergolas to create outdoor living spaces. Plant vigorous vines at the base of the columns and train their branches to cover the ceiling of the structure.

2. Arbors and pergolas can be the central feature of small, walled courts adjacent to structures.

3. When attached to the sides of buildings, arbors and pergolas can rise up many stories to provide shade from vines that also provide excellent insulation and oxygen production.

4. Build arbors and pergolas along the southern and western facades of buildings to reduce the solar impact of the summer sun.

5. Cover long water channels with leafy, green arbors and pergolas to shade and contain the evaporative cooling from the water.

Figure III-45
Cloister of Santa Chiara, Naples, Italy.
Eigtheenth century. Designed by Vaccaro.

At the Cloister of Santa Chiara, Vaccaro designed one of the most ornate structures ever built in Italy for supporting vines. Octagonal columns—faced with colorful tiles depicting landscapes, fruits, and flowers in a blaze of blues, reds, and gold—support a typical wooden pergola with benches placed between the columns. The shady walk is paved in brick, and the seats between the columns have high backs with curving baroque tops. Tiled like the columns, the backs of each bench depict a rustic landscape. The vines completely cover the wooden structure of the pergola, keeping the benches and walk in shade. In addition, the arbor encloses a courtyard filled with deciduous trees, greatly adding to the plush green setting. The refined architecture of the pergola, the integration of the benches with the columns, and the vivid colors results in a harmony of passive design and beauty. It is one of the supreme examples of the climatic, decorative, and architectural potentials of the pergola.

Garden Pavilions and Summerhouses

● The garden pavilion and the summerhouse are buildings designed to provide comfortable, cool living spaces during the year's hottest months. Constructed to benefit from the prevailing winds, they employ ceilings and large openings to permit the breezes to pass freely through the structure. Pavilions and summerhouses intentionally create deep recesses of cool shade, contrasting with the intense light and heat of summer. Often, these structures enrich the garden as its central feature, and when properly designed, can provide year-round living quarters (Figure III-46).

---

*And besides these shall be two gardens,
green, green pastures,
there in two fountains of gushing water,
there in maidens good and comely...
houris, cloistered in cool pavilions*[13]
Koran

● Figure III-46
Garden pavilion and summerhouse.

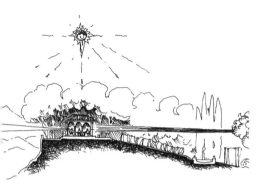

The Persian pavilion and the Italian summerhouse are both garden buildings designed for natural coolness. They represent intelligent passive devices, relevant footprints for reducing energy consumption in our built environment. At the center of the Persian garden, for example, one typically found an ornamental dwelling, quite open and airy, usually south-facing. In this pavilion, the boundaries between structure and garden melted away, and the landscape flowed right into and through the architecture.

Garden pavilions in desert climates commonly had an open platform on the south elevation, sometimes up to three stories high, which generally overlooked a central pool and provided deep shade to the interior spaces. The platform provided an airy retreat in hot weather, and often commanded the main axis of the garden. This space also served a dual function for year-round comfort: In winter, when the sun was lower in the sky, it could penetrate the space and warm the north wall that blocked the winter winds. The form of this garden element served as an ideal pattern for passive design: maximizing exposure to the summer breezes, capturing the sun's warmth in winter, and maintaining a sophisticated interrelationship of garden and dwelling (Figure III-47).

Italian Renaissance summerhouses, similar in function but very different in design, created the same passive environments. Whereas the form of the Persian pavilion remained constant, the form of the Italian summerhouse varied immensely, ranging in style from rustic to ornate, from diminutive to monumental. Unlike the Persian pavilion, the summerhouse was only occupied during the hot months as a retreat from the villa and for dining al fresco. These buildings were located in shaded areas of the garden, with large openings that faced the prevailing breezes. They might be focal points on the central organizing axis of the garden plan, or hidden deep in the woods as places for illicit assignation and viewing distant prospects (Figure III-48). Both the pavilion and the summerhouse are architectural forms that maximize the beneficial relationships between garden and dwelling.

Chehel Sutun, constructed toward the end of the sixteenth century, embodied the ideal of the Persian garden pavilion. Located within Shah Abbas's royal garden in Isfahan, Iran, the pavilion acted as the focal point for an enclosed garden (Figure III-49a). Its name, Chehel Sutun, means "Hall of Forty Columns," and refers to the mirror image produced by a pool that reflects the structure's 20 columns. Eugene Flandin, in his 1854 lithograph, *View from the Porch of the Chehel Sutun*, illustrates this effect well (Figure III-49b). The Chehel Sutun stands near the center of an enclosed garden, and has an extremely large platform on the southwest facade. The 20 slender cedar columns stand on stone bases and support a broad overhanging roof almost 30 feet high. This front platform, approximately 115 feet wide and 65 feet deep, rests upon a broad stone floor 2 feet above the ground plane of the garden. Open on three sides, the pavilion provides a prospect from which to view the garden, but, more important, allows for efficient cross-ventilation. In the hot, dry desert climate, this design traps the summertime breezes that pass beneath its broad, overhanging roof. The porch overlooks a rectangular pool that extends southwest into the garden. Tall trees border the pool, keeping it cool and shady. The prevailing winds blow the air cooled by this pool directly into the pavilion.

In the center of the porch, massive stone lions stand guard at the base of four columns that rise from the corners of the large, rectangular pool. Water froths from the mouths of the figures in a gentle arch, producing a fine mist as it splashes into the marble basin (Figure III-50a). In the center of the pavilion, another fountain features three stepped basins of

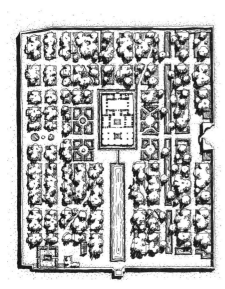

Figure III-49a
Chehel Sutun, Isfahan, Iran.

The garden pavilion is the central focal point of this enclosed garden.

Figure III-49b
Chehel Sutun, Isfahan, Iran.

View from interior of the pavilion looking outwards toward the garden.
(*Eugene Flandin,* View from the Porch of the Chehel Sutun, *1854*)

Figure III-50a (*opposite above*)
Chehel Sutun, Isfahan, Iran.

Stone lion fountains at the base of interior columns.

Figure III-50b (*opposite below*)
Chehel Sutun, Isfahan, Iran.

Shady outdoor room of the pavilion with its high and deep interior.

cascading water. Mirrors built into the ceiling reflect the shimmering water and further increase its psychologically cooling effect. The combined effects of these fountains misting the air in a shady outdoor room must have been a welcome comfort in the torrid desert summer (Figure III–50b).

Serving as a very efficient passive model, this template gave the Persian garden designer a basic format to which more sophisticated passive devices could easily be added, greatly increasing its climatic comfort. Likewise, the Italian summerhouse was also a sophisticated architectural model that encouraged its occupants to linger, away from the oppressive heat of summer.

The summerhouse in an Italian Renaissance garden was an open-air structure sometimes placed in a very secluded location. While not as ubiquitous as in the Persian garden pavilion, the Italian summerhouse could be used for dining in the hot summer months or as a place to escape the heat of the villa. A perfect example of this type of summerhouse is found in the gardens of the Villa Imperiale in Marlia, Italy. Built in the late seventeenth century for the Orsetti family, the villa included a tall, open-air building hidden away in the woods, possessing large windows and doors and a vaulted ceiling. Beneath each window, lovely built-in seats provided excellent views of the surrounding woodland. In the center of the room, a fountain set on a decorative pedestal helped to cool the air, while the floor was kept cool by hidden jets of water that occasionally wet the paving of stones and pebbles set in a variety of patterns (Figure III-51). The central door of the pavilion looked down a woodland allée where, "hidden away in the shadowy depths of the encircling woods, [this] cool loggia was undoubtedly designed for gay al fresco meals on summer days."[14] Set within the woods, the dark cool air of the interior, damp and languid from the occasional sprays of water and the gentle gurgling of the fountain, emoted a dreamy state.

Garden Pavilions and Summerhouses

Contemporary Applications

1. The garden pavilion should be placed on the central axis of the garden. Ideally, the open porch should face south, overlooking a pool at least the same width as the porch. Maximize the pavilion's openings facing the prevailing summer breezes.

2. Design the pavilion's overhang to keep the porch shaded in the summer, while allowing the winter sun to penetrate.

3. Build open-air retreats for summer occupation detached from the main structures. Place the retreats in the shade of oak boscoes. The summerhouse should have high ceilings with large openings on all sides to allow complete cross-ventilation.

4. The base of the pavilion should be 4 feet above the garden level to catch updrafts. The porch roof should be at least 25 feet high, supported by tall, slender columns. Keep the porch open on three sides to maximize cross-ventilation. The north elevation of the pavilion should be solid to block the northern winds.

5. Place simple pools of water in the center of the porch floor. Build mirrors into the ceiling to reflect the shimmering water, increasing its psychologically cooling effect.

Figure III-51
Villa Imperiale, Marlia, Italy.
The secluded summerhouse.
(Photo: Elizabeth Boults)

Figure III-52a *(opposite above)*
Divan Khaneh, Isfahan, Iran.
Date unknown. Designer unknown.

The Ayina Khaneh, also known as the Divan Khaneh, or Audience Hall, was another cool-air pavilion in Isfahan, very similar in design to the Chehel Sutun. Unfortunately this garden pavilion exists only in an engraving by Coste in the book, *Notes et Souvenirs des Voyages*. The platform was set three steps above the grassy lawn, with a fountain in its center to help cool the air. The square platform dominated the structure and supported a series of enclosed rooms to the rear. Although it shared the same footprint as the Chehel Sutun, the Ayina Khaneh pavilion did not stand within an enclosed garden, but rather in an informal, parklike setting on the grassy banks of the Zayandeh-Rud River. The impressive structure loomed over the river's banks and could be observed from some distance.
(Pascal Coste, *Pavillon Des Miroirs*, 1867)

172

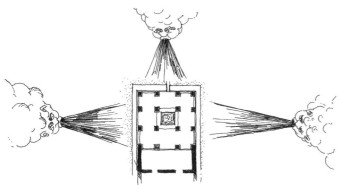

Figure III-52b *(middle)*
Divan Khaneh, Isfahan, Iran.

The open, three-sided platform of the Ayina Khaneh was planned to maximize ventilation. Well over three stories high, the Ayina Khaneh faced the river in order to capture the refreshing breezes from the valley and the river.

Figure III-53a *(below)*
Ali Qapu, Isfahan, Iran.
Seventh century. Designer unknown.

Commissioned by Shah Abbas, the Ali Qapu, or "Lofty Gateway," was elevated four stories above the surface of the garden, an unusually tall structure for Iran. This lofty perch arose at the center of the western side of the *maydan*, a large, open court used as a bazaar that was similar in scale to a parade ground. Through a gate in the enclosing courtyard wall, one passed through the formal entry and into the maydan and royal gardens. Once inside the courtyard, one found the entrance to the Ali Qapu through a two-story-high archway. Stairs ascended to the fourth floor where the platform floated above the city like a magic carpet. The fourth floor contained rooms reserved for the Shah, and it was often used for royal audiences. Open on three sides, this broad, covered platform faced east with the solid western facade at its back blocking the afternoon sun. Eighteen wooden columns supported the thin roof, making the structure appear nearly transparent, in marked contrast to the massiveness of the rear facade. Built into the floor was a pool filled with water jets, long since vanished.

On the following page:
Figure III-53b *(above)*
Ali Qapu, Isfahan, Iran.

The 20-foot-high roof, combined with its open sides and playing water fountain, made the porch exceptionally receptive to breezes, while providing inspiring views. Perched like a falcon's nest on the face of a sweeping cliff, the porch provided a panoramic vista of the urban fabric and encircling mountains. An exceptional outdoor room, the Ali Qapu allowed maximum exposure to any stirring summer breeze, with continuous summer shade.

Figure III-54 *(middle)*

Shalamar Bagh, Dal Lake, Kashmir.

1643. Designer unknown.

In 1643, Mughal ruler Jahangir built the Shalamar Bagh, or the Abode of Love, in honor of his wife. Located at the northeast end of Dal Lake in Kashmir, the imposing castle includes a series of pavilions placed along the perimeter walls of the complex. (The outer pavilions of the Mughal gardens of India tended to be much smaller than their Persian equivalents.) Six cool-air pavilions, one at each of four corners and two almost in the center of the eastern and western limits, rose above the enclosing garden walls. The pavilions most likely evolved from earlier defensive outlooks, as each projects beyond the wall, resembling a turret. Entered by climbing an interior stairway from the garden, the octagonal pavilions rose almost a story above the walls. Each pavilion had arched windows nestled under a broad, overhanging, tile roof. Elevated above the surrounding walls of the garden, these large openings afforded views of the world beyond the royal enclosure, and maximized ventilation. The octagonal shape of the pavilions accepted breezes from all directions. Seen from high above the garden, the landscape spanned a full 360 degrees, while the cool air drifted under the broad roof.

Figure III-55 *(below)*

Villa Rizzardi, Valpolicella, Italy.

1783. Designed by Luigi Trezza.

The Villa Rizzardi contains an unusual summerhouse set deep within a dense bosco. Its mock Roman ruin, with open ceiling and trick fountains, was used for dining on hot days. The walls of the structure were constructed of rough stone accented with decorative pebbles, in places creating niches for sculpture. The foundation contained benches. The deep shade of the bosco kept the summerhouse cool in its wooded isolation, a thermal pleasure reinforced by an occasional burst of water from the jets hidden beneath the floor. The charm of this villa was compounded by its pleached allées, unusually pruned cypress trees, garden theater, and open-air belvedere.

Postulate VI: **Interior Porches and Cool Rooms**

● Interior porches and cool rooms are architectural elements thoroughly integrated with the landscape, and blending seamlessly into the garden. They provide shade and capture the prevailing summer winds. Interior porches have high and deep ceilings that shade the space throughout the day. They are specific to Persian garden forms. Cool Rooms result from the movement of air instigated by the design of the openings in its walls. They are common features in Hispano-Moorish gardens. The air cooling properties of both elements can be enhanced by their adjacency to water features (Figure III-56).

While the city below pants with the noontide heat and the parched vega trembles to the eye, the delicate airs from the Sierra Nevada play through these lofty halls, bringing with them the sweetness of surrounding gardens.[15]
Washington Irving

● Figure III-56
The interior porch and cool room as passive devices.

175

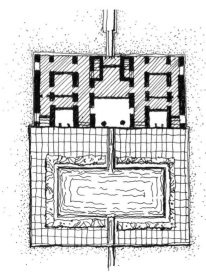

Interior porches and cool rooms reflect a design attitude that works with climate rather than against it. These elements truly embrace the air, accommodating architectural form to the natural climate. When combined with the other passive garden devices already noted, the interior porch and cool room complete the picture of the totally climatic and vital landscape.

The interior porch was generally integrated into the main living structure of the Persian dwelling. In the hot, arid summer of the desert, this porch was a necessity. Elevated above the garden, perched over a large pool with the gardens extending to the south, the porch made every attempt to catch even the softest breezes. Many variations were possible, but a connection to the garden was essential. The height of the porch was engineered so that the interior would be shaded in the summer, when the sun's angle was high. Conversely, during the winter, the lower sun could penetrate the porch and warm the space, much like an Italian loggia. Canvas awnings were cleverly designed to increase the shade both inside and outside the porch. The following paragraphs present three examples of interior porches found in Persian gardens.

Built in the nineteenth century, in northwest Shiraz, Iran, the Bagh-i Eram, or Garden of Paradise, includes a large pavilion on the north side of the expansive, enclosed garden. The Bagh-i Eram pavilion is almost three stories high, with its facade opening to a large, rectangular pool and the extensive gardens to the south. The porch rests about 8 feet above the central spine of the garden, a relationship that facilitates the flow of the cool air from the garden below into the interior porch. Two similar but smaller porches flank this central, recessed porch. The prevailing breezes ascend from the valley below, and are cooled as they pass over the pool directly in front of the pavilion (Figure III-57a).

Figure III-58a
Bagh-i Naw, Shiraz, Iran.

Recessed porch with large canvas awnings.
(Eugene Flandin, The Bagh-I-Naw at Shiraz, 1854)

Figure III-58b
Bagh-i Naw, Shiraz, Iran.

Section through porch and awnings extended
over pool.

The shaded interior porches catch the cooled air and create a comfortable summertime environment for the inhabitants.

To augment this cooling effect, the Persians employed a most ingenious, yet simple, shading device. Vertical exterior curtains hung from the facade of the pavilion, adjusted to block the hottest rays of the summer sun. The curtain was pulled back in winter to allow the lower winter sun to enter and warm the space. The Bagh-i Eram employs this shading system quite effectively, with gathered drapes easily adjusted by rope cords to control the amount of shade (Figure III-57b). These curtains impart a soft and luminous quality to the light that filters through the fabric. In addition, the cloth could also be moistened with water, cooling the interior as the moisture evaporated. Some authorities have speculated that the fabric was also sprinkled with rose water, infusing the recessed porches with the scent of paradise.

Lithographs and etchings from this era of garden building illustrate how commonly these shade curtains were used throughout Persia. In Tehran, the Gulistan Palace complex, built by Fath Ali Shah and completed in the eighteenth century, contains a garden pavilion called the Taki-i Marmar, or Throne Room. This building (also known as a Divan Khaneh) incorporates a pavilion similar in design to the structure at the Bagh-i Eram. A tall and deeply recessed porch with decorative columns sits above a stone-paved plaza, facing a pool and garden to the south. Adjustable exterior curtains were draped over the central opening and the two smaller porches on either side. The curtains were hung on the outside of these openings to deflect the sunlight and to enhance the quality of interior shade. They could also be adjusted to a variety of angles to block the changes of the sun's movement throughout the day. The filtered shade from these curtains filled the interior porches with dancing reflections caused by even the gentlest of breezes.

Figure III-59a
Hall of the Ambassadors, Granada, Spain.

Apertures in the miniature room overlook the valley.

Figure III-59b (opposite)
Hall of the Ambassadors, Granada, Spain.

Natural ventilation system.

The Bagh-i Naw garden, built in Shiraz around 1810 for the oldest son of Fath Ali Shah, also utilized fabric awnings in conjunction with pavilions and interior porches for passive cooling. A fine 1840 lithograph by Flandin illustrates the beauty of this vanished pavilion. Within the structure, one finds the typical recessed porch, fronting a large, octagonal pool with a stone edging sufficiently elevated to be used as a bench (Figure III-58a). Typical of these structures, the Bagh-i Naw faced the prevailing breezes. Three large fabric awnings, affixed to the facade of the pavilion, would be drawn out along the pool's perimeter and tied to evenly spaced stone piers. Unlike the vertical curtains of Bagh-i Eram, which can only move up or down, the stone piers allowed adjustment to accommodate changing weather conditions. When the curtain was fully extended, it acted as a large air scoop, concentrating the ephemeral breeze and capturing water evaporating from the pool. The awning extended well over the pool's edge, thereby creating a shaded area on the seating curbs (Figure III-58b). Such simple and inexpensive devices are unfortunately ignored in contemporary landscape design.

In contrast to the openness of the interior porch, cool rooms rely upon architectural mass for climate moderation. Cool rooms usually have thick walls that keep the interior cool and insulated from the torrid temperatures of summer. Small openings facing the prevailing winds direct the breezes into the interior. These small apertures are often adjacent to gardens or water features that add moisture to the air and filter dust and sand. The cool rooms discussed in this chapter are representative of the Hispano-Moorish gardens at the Alhambra and the Generalife in Granada, Spain.

Several types of cool-air rooms line the northern edge of the Alhambra on the steep hills overlooking the city of Granada. Most of these garden pavilions project out from a precarious ledge of the rocky cliffs, where air rising up the hillside reaches

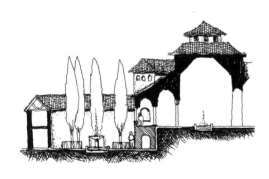

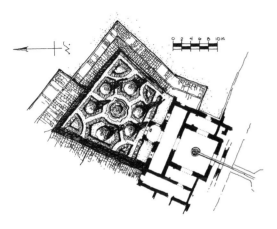

its maximum velocity. Michael Laurie aptly described this principle as "a primitive but successful air conditioning system" in his book, *Introduction to Landscape Architecture*.[16]

The largest and certainly the most massive of the cool-air rooms at the Alhambra is the Torre de Comares, or Hall of the Ambassadors. This gigantic tower protrudes out over a cliff on the northern side of the rocky acropolis. The pavilion, 56 feet square, has walls more than 10 feet thick, protecting the interior from the intense summer heat characteristic of the Andalucian region. Each wall has three sets of high, narrow openings on the east, west, and north facades to allow for cross-ventilation. The largest of these window niches, about 10 feet deep and a little more than 6-1/2 feet wide, sits in the center of the north-facing facade, creating a miniature room inside the walls. Within this arched space, carpets and pillows would be placed on the floor so that one might sit directly next to the window above the valley in the full force of the wind (Figure III-59a). The breezes are forced through the narrow window opening facing the cliff. As they pass through the small apertures of this massive structure, the wind picks up speed because of the change in air pressure. This natural ventilating and cooling system moves the air through the large interior of this hall and out a narrow doorway toward the large pool in the Court of the Myrtles (Figure III-59b).

Although not as dramatic as the pavilions facing the Albaicín hill, the Mirador of the Patio de Lindaraja projects outward on three sides into the southern perimeter of a walled garden (Figure III-60a). Adjacent to the Court of the Lions this *mirador*, or elevated porch, houses a cool room. The mirador, also called the Lindaraja Observatory, has a dimension of 8 feet deep by 16 feet wide and rests one story above a cool green garden (Figure III-60b). On the north face of the mirador, a central pair of low arched windows (called *ajimez*)

Interior Porches and Cool Rooms
Contemporary Applications

1. Integrate deeply recessed interior porches into the living and working areas of buildings. Provide openings outward to the prevailing breezes of the region to insure that the porch has access to the air currents emanating from the garden.

2. Interior porches should be 15 to 30 feet high and have broad openings, preferably to an exterior pool. The garden pool should be the same width as the interior porch. Elevate the floor above the garden level to allow the cool air from the pool to flow into the interior porch.

3. Attach vertical exterior curtains along the south facade of buildings, with pull cords to adjust the fabric to block the summer sun. Aim water misters onto the curtains so that as the water evaporates, the temperature of the air flowing into the structure will be reduced and humidified.

4. Exterior curtains can function as adjustable awnings drawn out over an adjacent pool. The awning acts as an air scoop, providing shade while capturing the chill generated by evaporating water.

5. The mirador or elevated porch should project a minimum of 3 feet and be at least 6 feet above a shady garden. Face the mirador into the prevailing breezes, above a compact garden full of aromatic plants.

look directly onto the garden. Inside the mirador one can sit on a built-in ledge at the base of these windows and enjoy the breezes rising up from the garden below, cooled by the fountain and the sound of the playing water. As the sun climbs into the sky above the Lindaraja and warms the perfumed air ascending the valley, the mirador stands ready to capture and circulate this breeze. The garden below the mirador, considered by many to be one of the most poetic gardens in the Alhambra because of its intimate scale and beautiful central fountain, rests in deep seclusion. Planted in cypress, orange trees, and low box parterres, five paths radiate from a central, polygonal pool. In the center of this pool, a round basin on a pedestal shoots a single jet of water that becomes the main focus of the court as its splashing reverberates throughout the small enclosure of the Patio de Lindaraja.

Thus we have noted many techniques for the capture, movement, and acceleration of air made possible by a variety of landscape and architectural treatments. The simple idea of cooling and moving air through a space was recognized centuries ago and realized through necessarily nonmechanical means. While uncomplicated in concept, the detail and elaboration of these passive devices are far from conservative, and completely satisfy our human need for beauty, comfort, and purpose. The potential for air to create passive microclimates will be employed in a contemporary garden context in Garden Prototype III, the Garden of Juno, which follows.

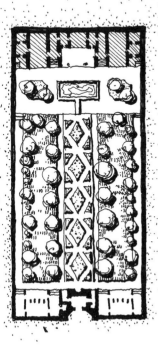

Figure III-61a *(opposite left above)*
Divan Khaneh, Shiraz, Iran.
Eighteenth century. Designer unknown.

The central porch overlooking the garden has adjustable exterior fabric curtains, and a set of stairs on either side of the porch for direct access to the garden. During the summer the recessed porch remains in shade, and in winter the lower sun warms the interior. The floors of the interior porch are elevated several feet above the ground plane for better exposure to the breezes. Immediately adjacent to the porch, a rectangular pool sits within a paved patio that extends the full width of the pavilion and stops at the beginning of the garden. From the southern edge of the patio, the garden extends along a central axis of grass with a plantation of orange trees on either side.

Figure III-61b *(opposite left below)*
Divan Khaneh, Shiraz, Iran.

The Divan Khaneh in Shiraz, Iran, is a small, urban garden that uses the same climatic principals as the large, royal porches of Persia. Strikingly similar to the layout of the Bagh-i-Eram, the structure has high garden walls enclosing a rectangular site, with the dwelling built into the rear northern wall. This wall, built thick and solid, blocks the winter winds, while the dwelling and its porch open to the south, or garden side, to catch the summer air.

Figure III-62 *(opposite right)*
Hasht Bihesht, Isfahan, Iran.
1667–94. Designer unknown.

Located next to the Chehel Sutun in Isfahan we find one of the few remaining garden pavilions along the Chahar Bagh avenue. It was realized during the rule of Shah Suleiman (1667–94), an era of great garden making. Although the gardens of the Hasht Bihesht have largely disappeared, the pavilion remains. The structure, almost three stories high, with four tall porches aligned to the cardinal points, once stood in the center of a large, formal garden. Capped with a dome, the voluminous central core sports an octagonal pool with a single jet and tall archways that connect to the porches.
(Pascal Coste, Exterior of the Hasht Bihesht, *1867)*

Figure III-63a
Hasht Bihesht, Isfahan, Iran.

The four porches, set about 8 feet above the ground, each possessed axial views into the garden. Unlike the porches previously discussed, the Hasht Bihesht does not have exterior vertical curtains, as the overhangs themselves provide abundant shade. The north side of the pavilion, with the largest of the four openings, most likely, was inhabited during the summer.
(Pascal Coste, Pavillon des Huit Portes du Paradis, *1867)*

Figure III-63b

Hasht Bihesht, Isfahan, Iran.

This structure produces a sophisticated system of natural ventilation. The large open porches allow air to enter from any direction, maximizing cross ventilation. The high central void is capped with a vented cupola that releases the hot air naturally rising from the interior. This current pulls the cooler air from the lower garden over the interior and perimeter fountains, adding moisture. Moreover, any wind that passes over the cupola will drop the air pressure inside, thus increasing the velocity of the air exhausting from the interior.

Figure III-64a

Partal Garden, Alhambra, Granada, Spain.

Fifteenth century. Designer unknown.

To the east of the main Alhambra complex, the Partal Garden includes a loggia and cool room that projects out over a cliff. This space incorporates a long, narrow loggia, open to the south, with a solid wall punctuated by six small, arched windows along the north. A rectangular pool rests directly at the southern base of the loggia.

Figure III-64b

Partal Garden, Alhambra, Granada, Spain.

The narrow loggia along the northern edge of the pool has five high arches supported by slender marble columns. Arched windows on three sides of the central room of the loggia maximize its exposure to the breezes drifting up the cliff. The loggia, with its light transparent arches, acts as a shady interlude for the breezes passing through its narrow depth. The windows, placed to face the prevailing breezes along the north wall, are also quaint apertures for viewing the hills beyond the walls of the Alcazar complex.

Garden Prototype III:

The Garden of Juno

The Garden of Juno incorporates each of the postulates found in Book III, Air, into a cluster-housing prototype designed to exist within an agricultural farmland. This experimental garden carefully harnesses and magnifies the effect of the summer breezes while foiling the cold, winter winds. Many past cultures understood wind as having an individual personality, representative of its source direction. The air from each cardinal point brought with it unique gifts or spirits. We again must recognize the distinct personalities of the wind, and consider air a fundamental principle in site planning. Creating environments that incorporate a wide variety of passive techniques to reduce energy consumption should be a driving force for community planning. The rational harnessing of the air, combined with the garden devices outlined above, represent a new garden form, a vision of a landscape where one lives in climatic harmony.

Within an avocado grove in the rapidly vanishing agricultural belt around Redlands, south of Miami, Florida, nestles the Garden of Juno — the third prototypical garden design to use passive methods postulated in this book. Given the site's wonderful tropical breezes, mild winters, but hot and humid summers, this prototype acknowledges and works with these climatic features rather than against them. The Garden of Juno is designed as a cluster of four small, residential buildings that merge into the once-abundant avocado groves that constituted this fertile landscape. The 35-acre site is entered from the north by a gravel road that travels several hundred feet to a parking lot for 10 cars. Here one finds the north side of the garden defined by tall windbreaks. Beyond these windbreaks, the garden fans outward to the south from a garden pavilion containing four individual living units. Like the format of the Persian Garden, with its strong interrelationship of dwelling to garden, this pavilion and its garden celebrate its tropical climate.

The Garden of Juno:
A Description of Passive Landscape Elements

A. Garden Pavilion and Cool Rooms
The Garden Pavilion contains four individual living units located a short walk from the parking area. Each of the four units has its own private entry along the solid northern wall. Along the back of each unit, a 20-foot-high airshaft or solar chimney heats the air at the very top, creating a natural updraft, and pulling the cooler air up from below. This airshaft also has a large exhaust fan to augment the air movement throughout the dwelling. The ceilings of the interior rooms are 12 feet high to allow hot air to rise and exit through the airshaft. These rooms also have ceiling fans to keep the air moving. Vents in the floor, connected to airshafts in the earth below, bring in cool air from the garden. When this cool air enters from the floor, it helps the natural ventilation by pushing the warmer air up toward the exhaust vent. Inside the cool, breezy, and shady spaces of the dwelling, one benefits from the cumulative effect of all the passive devices of the garden.

B. Porch
Large, operable floor-to-ceiling windows open out to the 20-foot-high screened front porch. The porch's height shades the space throughout the summer, yet receives the lower sun in the winter. A double roof over the porch adds a barrier of air, to increase the insulation from solar radiation. To repel the summer mosquitoes and other annoying tropical pests, screening encloses the porch. Adjustable canvas awnings attach to the top of the roof and can be pulled out and tied to moorings that surround the patio. The awnings can be adjusted so they can provide shade throughout the day as the sun moves overhead. They can also be used as shelters, providing a covered place to sit during the cooling summer rains. Here one can spend hot summer afternoons, sitting on the porch viewing a functional yet beautiful garden.

C. Cool Walks
A common patio unifies all four of the individual living units. Directly in front of the garden pavilion, four broad steps lead to the patio. Four small fountains with single

jets of water produce pleasant music, and a psychological sense of coolness. From the center of the patio a central cool walk enters the avocado groves to the south. The trees are planted densely to produce a shaded space where one can walk through the plantations of trees.

D. Shady Tunnels

The prevailing summer breezes in this climate come from the southeast in the morning, then gradually shift southward. In the late afternoon, when the heat builds up, thunderstorms start in the Everglades, and with them the winds change, coming from the west and bringing the cooler air generated from the storms. In order to capture this wide pattern of air movement, a series of pleached allées fans out to the southeast to funnel this air directly into the dwelling units at the garden core. These pleached allées taper gradually outward to the south in order to capture as much wind as possible. The funnel narrows as it nears the pavilion to increase the velocity of the air. Broad beds of aromatic flowers have been planted between the allées so that their aroma can float into the dwellings.

E. Pruned Hedges

A series of pruned hedges are situated along the north edge of the pavilion to block or deflect the cold winter winds that come from the north in Miami. One of the important design considerations in a hot, humid climate is to not create any air dams. Air dams are enclosed dead-end spaces, where the air will become stagnant and uncomfortable in summer. As a result, these pruned hedges are sheared at different heights and are segmented to allow the summer air to move through.

F. Cool Seats

Cool seats line the southern edge of the patio, between the pleached allées, to capture the funneled air and to provide a view of the flower gardens. These seats are perfect

Figure III-65 (opposite)
The Garden of Juno. Illustrative plan.

Figure III-66 (below)
Cross-section of garden looking north.

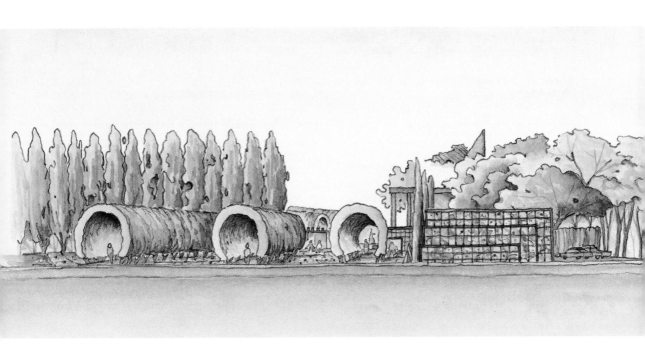

places for repose in the early morning when the sun is neither too high nor too hot. Another seat, built into a thick wall just to the west of the central cool walk, has a view out through a small opening to the plantations to the southwest. Shaded overhead, this seat takes advantage of the Venturi effect, as the breezes from the small opening rush past the seat. This enclosure performs ideally in the afternoon or late afternoon, protecting its occupant from the overhead sun.

G. Pergola

In the late afternoon solar build-up reaches its maximum, and this accumulation of heat can re-radiate into the structure. Therefore, it is very important to protect the western facade of any structure. In this case a large, overhead pergola protects the western edge of the pavilion from the summer sun. Sited to maximize shade throughout the summer, the pergola sits high enough above the building to let air circulate around it, and is planted with vines to provide further insulation from the sun.

H. Arbors

A set of ascending arbors on the east side of the pavilion protects the dwelling from morning insolation. There are three slightly curving arbors, each rising higher as it approaches the pavilion, to keep the space in shade as the sun crosses overhead. All three of these arbors are thickly planted with vines to insure as much shade as possible. The arbor closest to the pavilion has a long cool seat built into its base. With its slightly curving shape, the arbor directs the view south into the planted beds of flowers.

I. Western Pruned Hedges

Just past the western pergola we find a series of descending pruned hedges that protect the pavilion from the setting sun. The farther away from the pavilion, the shorter they are in height, to maintain the shadow patterns near the pavilion. Primarily a functional device, these areas of pruned hedges are not places to linger in the late summer afternoons.

J. Elevated Outlook

To the southwest of the Pavilion, a short walk from the patio, one discovers a hidden belvedere. Placed in the garden to provide an escape from the dwelling, the elevated belvedere can be a wonderful place to watch the setting sun. Even after the sun has set one can linger here to enjoy the coolness of the evenings and watch the stars as they slowly appear.

K. Summerhouse

To the east of the Garden of Juno, at the edge of a pine forest that borders the property, is a summerhouse. Sited to take advantage of late-afternoon shade, the summerhouse may also be used for pleasant evening dinners or parties. Trees keep the structure shaded for most of the day.

Figure III-67a *(opposite above)*
View of pleached allées and pergolas with cool seats.

Figure III-67b *(opposite below)*
Cross-section of the pavilion, showing its relationship to the garden.

Summary

In Book III, we have examined the cooling qualities of moving, active, and shaded air. Combining air, shade, and water was a defense against the harsh realities of the severe desert climate. Desert cultures developed a unique philosophy for designing with climate by fusing the dwelling and the garden into a unified whole. By reviewing the unique passive devices that were used in various cultures, we gained an understanding of their climatic context, and developed fundamental categories for their use. These devices were then interpreted and applied to a contemporary garden prototype.

Today, too many environments are sealed and removed from the landscape, and instead a totally artificial world replaces the natural air, shade, and water. With our mechanical, synthetic, and electronic climates, we move farther away from being able to harness the power of air to transform the landscape. The Garden of Juno glorifies air; nothing in this garden is still. The wind spills around the trees like water. It reveals hidden textures in the plants and flowers and the branches of the trees. The passive garden devices discussed in this chapter are all arranged to catch each hint of wind and channel it into the garden's interior. From our encounter with the invisible currents of air, we now journey into the final book, Water.

Water, as a primary element that brings life to the earth, charges the landscape with moisture, sound, and joy.

Notes

1. James Turner, *The Poetics of Landscapes*. Oxford: Basil Blackwell, 1979, p. 56.

2. Leon Battista Alberti, *On The Art of Building*. Translated by Joseph Rykwert and Robert Tavernor. Cambridge, MA: MIT Press, [1550] 1988, p. 9.

3. Giovanni Boccaccio, *The Decameron*. Translation by G. H. McWilliam, London: Penguin Books, 1972, p. 232.

4. G. A. Jellicoe and J. C. Shepherd, *Italian Gardens of the Renaissance*. Princeton: Princeton Architectural Press, [1925] 1986, p. 22.

5. Claudia Lazzaro, *The Italian Renaissance Garden*. New Haven, CT: Yale University Press, 1990, p. 211.

6. Georgina Masson, *Italian Gardens*. New York: Harry Abrams, Inc., 1961, p. 252.

7. Norman T. Newton, *Design on the Land—The Development of Landscape Architecture*. Cambridge, MA: Harvard University Press, 1971, p. 83.

8. Washington Irving, *Tales of the Alhambra*. Edited by Miguel Sanchez, Spain: Grefol, S.A., [1832] 1984, p. 44.

9. Edith Wharton, *Italian Villas and Their Gardens*. New York: DeCapo Press, Inc., [1904] 1976, p. 71.

10. Newton, *Design on the Land*, p. 126.

11. Boccaccio, *The Decameron*, p. 232.

12. Lazzaro, *The Italian Renaissance Garden*, p. 30.

13. *Koran: Interpreted*, Translated by A. S. Arberry, New York: Simon and Schuster, [1955] 1966, p. 253.

14. Masson, *Italian Gardens*, p. 11.

15. Irving, *Tales of the Alhambra*, p. 44.

16. Michael Laurie, *An Introduction to Landscape Architecture*. New York: American Elsevier Publishing Company, Inc., 1975, p. 16.

Book IV: **Water**

Water is the final, but perhaps most important, element in Plato's theories of "solids" that comprise the universe. As a conceptual model, the geometric figure representing water, the 20-sided icosahedron, is capable of holding the other "spatial" configurations of earth, air, and fire, illustrating the interdependence of elements that constitute life.

Water has the power to transform the parched earth into a rich oasis. The arid climate of the Mediterranean basin provided the perfect context for Islamic, Roman, and Italian Renaissance designers to explore the mysterious and infinite qualities of water. These designers excelled in exploiting this resource, allowing cultures to flourish where water existed in short supply. Generally, passive design solutions for the amelioration of climate became more sophisticated in response to harsher or more extreme environments. No matter what form it took, water was used not only to cool and filter hot, sand-laden winds, but also to enhance the symbolism and sensual pleasure of the garden.

Islamic, Roman, and Italian Renaissance designers developed an equally sophisticated appreciation of the metaphorical and metaphysical powers of water according to their cultural traditions. Muslims, for example, used water in their spiritual rituals to cleanse and refresh the soul as well as the body; the *Koran* itself contains numerous allusions to the divine qualities of water. This sacred text promises the faithful an eternal life in a paradise garden of lush, green grass and continually flowing rivers. Likewise, the Romans believed that numerous deities themselves imbued their presence in water, such that the gods bestowed their grace on everything touched by the liquid. The Romans erected nymphaeums and grottoes with dynamic displays of water, specially designed to celebrate the essence of these gods. In this same tradition, water was joyously displayed in Renaissance and later Italian gardens with increasing varieties of expression,

Water being available, a garden is inevitable.[1]
Donald Newton Wilber

producing ever more refined microclimates. In the Renaissance designers elevated water from the worship of an unseen deity to the celebration of the human spirit.

The manipulation of water became an art form; water was used in gardens not only for its inherently cooling abilities, but to produce such aesthetic affects as stillness, movement, sound, and light. While the philosophies and beliefs of these trail-blazing garden designers varied significantly, nonetheless, between them they developed an array of the most amazing water works ever conceived. They appreciated water as a special design medium, and refined their ideas in the design of garden elements such as aqueducts, pools, fountains, and even water jokes, that at the same time produced natural air conditioning and animated the arid climate where life is not possible without a steady supply of water.

In this last book, Water, we will analyze how water was utilized not only to support habitation, but also to sustain the spirit. The importance of water as a commodity cannot be underestimated; without water, there can be no life. In past cultures, the collection, storage, and movement of water was a priority in order to maintain a predictable supply throughout the year. Only then could passive microclimates be enjoyed and the art of the garden flourish. The first postulate will present methods that the Hispano-Moorish, Mughals, and Italians developed for the collection and storage of this precious liquid, and then explore how the collected water was used to irrigate gardens and agricultural lands. The following postulates examine the various creative forms that water can take in the garden, and the specific devices designed to modify the climate. In all the passive water devices mentioned, it is possible to capture and reuse the water with recirculation systems to further promote conservation where necessary.

Postulate I: **Water Catchment Devices and Irrigation Methods**

● To collect and store water, begin by catching as much as possible of the rainwater that falls on the site. This water, and any that flows onto the site, can be retained in underground cisterns to protect it from evaporation. Once collected and stored, this water can be available for drinking, passive cooling, and irrigation. Water can also travel great distances through aqueducts that use gravity to assist in irrigating the garden. Water catchment and irrigation patterns need not be purely functional; they can elegantly enrich the garden's lay-out through the use of such devices as the runnel (Figure IV-1).

Whatever plants grow in the garden of this world,
all of them have only one vital function, namely to
praise the grace of the water that quickens them.[2]
Rumi

● Figure IV-1
Passive water catchment device.

Historians believe that the Egyptians created the first gardens. These early garden forms probably evolved from lush fruiting oases, irrigated orchards, and the pattern of farm fields. In the quotation at the opening of this section, landscape architects Geoffrey and Susan Jellicoe emphasize the physical and spatial importance of water. The repetitive straight lines of irrigated lands certainly influenced the development of the garden as an art form and a place of cool respite. Water was the prime agent: Without an organized system of irrigation, human habitation could not be possible.

Systematic irrigation, of course, requires collecting, diverting, and storing water from all available sources. The sophistication of water collection and its retention propelled the evolution and greater complexity of garden forms. From the simple well or cistern in the Medieval cloister garden to the regional system of Roman aqueducts rediscovered in the Renaissance, advances in technical ability and hydraulic engineering occurred across time and space. Vernacular structures used for the catchment and storage of water evolved into more symbolic elements in later gardens where water became a central design motif.

The first part of this chapter presents three devices used for the passive collection of water, *qants*, *wadies*, and cisterns, that functioned as important elements in the design of garden microclimates.

The harsh environment of the Middle East demanded water collection systems to maintain predictable water supplies. For example, *qants*, or enclosed runnels, were part of an ancient system of underground, gravity-fed water supply developed by the Persians (Figure IV-2). Their enclosed channels minimized the volume of water lost due to evaporation and permitted the transport of water over long distances. This technology reflects a basic understanding of hydrologic

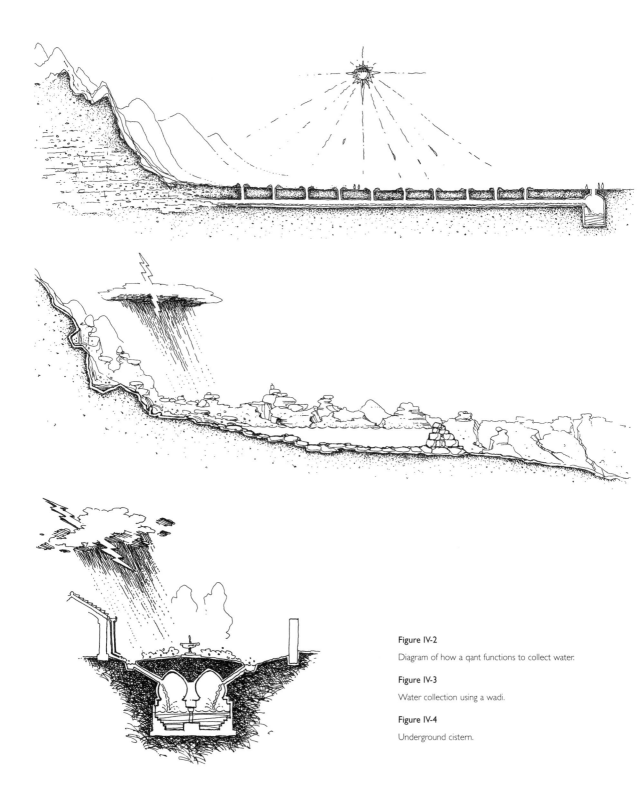

Figure IV-2

Diagram of how a qant functions to collect water.

Figure IV-3

Water collection using a wadi.

Figure IV-4

Underground cistern.

principles as well as soil science: A main shaft was dug into the subterranean aquifer, most often found in the foothills of the mountains, and extended to the point where the water was needed. Gravity would drive the flow of water through connecting tunnels toward its final destination. Every 50 feet or so, a shaft surfaced to provide air for the miners during construction and to allow the excavated soil to be removed. In porous soils, the channel would be lined with tiles. Parallel qants sometimes ran for many miles to a detention basin where it would be stored for later use.

In the desert, Persian settlers commonly collected water from naturally sloping areas called *wadi* (Figure IV-3). A wadi is essentially the channel of a dry river bed; the term also refers to small ravines or intermittently wet, sloping landforms. Dams were constructed across these dry water channels to collect water during the rainy season and divert it into large underground cisterns.

The cistern provided a fundamental method of storing as much rainwater and runoff as possible for use during dry seasons or droughts. The enclosed cistern (Figure IV-4) is an effective passive device for water collection: sunken underground and insulated from the rays of the sun, the water remains cool, and does not lose any of its volume to evaporation. Although many ancient cisterns are now derelict, two well-known examples still exist in southern Spain. These buried reservoirs are integrated into dwellings and not only store water for the dry season, but also manage the micro-climate in and around the dwelling.

The practice of using cisterns extended across the Mediterranean. An extant Renaissance cistern indicates the importance of this device to Italian architects. Vignola designed the magnificent Palazzo Farnese in Caprarola around one of these underground storage tanks (Figure IV- 5).

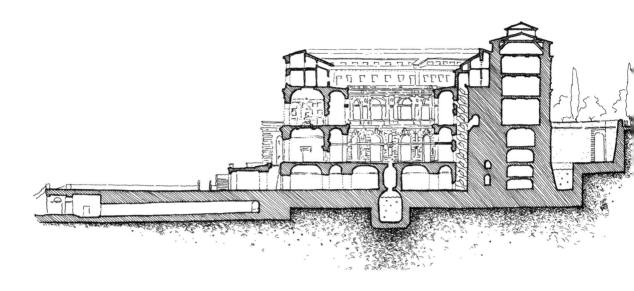

Figure IV-5
Palazzo Farnese, Caprarola, Italy.
View of cistern.

Figure IV-6a
Blanket watering techniques.

Figure IV-6b
Elevated pathway, with irrigation outlets built into the pathway.

Downspouts and surface grading directed the runoff from the roof, pavement, and courtyard into a round, metal inlet in the center of a circular courtyard at the very heart of the palazzo. This drain, adorned with a decorative grille, captured the water and delivered it to a large, underground cistern where it would then be available to irrigate the garden.

In addition to the collection and storage of water, the movement of water throughout the garden is also paramount to the creation of aesthetically pleasing, and workable, passive microclimates. The remainder of this chapter examines various irrigation methods and passive devices, such as blanket watering, *jubes*, and condensing jars, that also directly affected the specific form and composition of a garden. These principles are then synthesized in a detailed example given at the end of the chapter.

When water finally reached the garden, Islamic designers displayed innovative techniques that maximized the efficient use of water. These garden makers used a strong, symmetrical geometry to organize their unique engineering systems around the central unifying element of water. Water was generally fed into a large holding tank near the northern edge of a sheltered garden enclosure through a system of rectilinear runnels. This supply provided a reservoir for irrigation and for wetting the dust on paths and terraces, rather than for drinking or bathing. To provide the necessary water pressure for gravity-fed irrigation, cisterns were located at the naturally high point of the garden or built on a hill or berm. Often the cistern became a decorative focal point in the garden where, before irrigating the plants, the water was displayed in as many artistic situations as possible. From this central holding tank, the water traveled through runnels into a main watercourse that formed the central axis of the garden. The size of the watercourse was determined by the supply of water; the more reliable the source of water, the wider

Figure IV-7

Irrigation ditch known as a *jube*.

the canals. Water flowed from this main axis into other pools, cascades, jets, and fountains. Secondary walks and irrigation channels ran perpendicular to the central axis, while orchards of valuable orange and lemon trees surrounded the watercourses. The entire design combined beauty, utility, horticulture, and economics.

During the Roman occupation of southern Spain in the first century, elaborate canal, aqueduct, and irrigation systems were developed. Following their conquest of this region in the eighth century, the Moors reintroduced and improved upon the remains of the Roman irrigation systems. After the first emirate was established by Abd al-Rahman II in Cordoba, c. AD 750, the Andalusian plains and sprawling fertile valley of the Guadalquivir River were planted with luscious orchards, vineyards, and farms. In nearby Granada, hillsides with impressive views were chosen for gardens where water was a main feature.

Irrigation of the garden can take many different forms. For instance, in Persian gardens, walkways were generally raised above the surface of the planting beds and the edges of the pavement acted as dams to contain the precious water that moistened the beds. People could therefore still stroll through the garden while the beds were being watered. This method of irrigation, called "blanket watering," or *riego en manta* in Spanish, is still used in parts of Spain today (Figure IV- 6a).

Excavations at the Patio de la Acequia in the Generalife revealed that the original surface of the planting beds sat some 20 inches below the walkways in order to facilitate blanket watering. Sometimes, these elevated paths contained water pipes with outlets in the edges of the walks; valves could be opened to irrigate the parterres below (Figure IV-6b). A more sophisticated system involved pipes or channels built under the path with outlets that opened directly onto

the planting. In the garden of the Salón Rico in Granada, such channels were built into the sides of the stone walkways. Just below the coping of these water channels, square outlets allowed the water to irrigate the flowerbeds several inches below. This passive device served as the infrastructure for a variety of artful garden compositions, where life-giving water was considered a design element in itself.

Another simple irrigation method developed in Persia used jubes—narrow, deep furrows dug between tight rows of trees spaced about 5 feet apart—to water orchards (Figure IV-7). Water flowed along the length of the jube and seeped into the soil, watering the roots of the trees. Unlike the stone-lined channels described above, which concentrated water directly at the base of the tree, jubes allowed water to permeate the soil more broadly.

However, the most efficient method of irrigating plants and conserving water used "condensing jars," the precursor to our modern drip irrigation systems (Figure IV-8). In Yazd, one of the hottest spots on the Iranian plateau, condensing jars played a vital role in reducing significantly the amount of water lost to evaporation. Earthenware containers were placed into the soil between rows of trees, set with its neck protruding just above the surface. When filled with water, these containers "sweated" moisture through their porous earthen sides, irrigating the roots of the trees directly. These condensing jars, removed from exposure to sun and air, effectively conserved water by protecting it from evaporation.

The large Mughal garden, Fatehpur Sikri, utilized a similar water conservation and distribution system that also minimized evaporation (Figure IV-9). While most of the imperial gardens and their structures have disappeared, the ruins indicate that aqueducts were incorporated into the construction of the palace walls. Water channels, for example, were

Figure IV-8

Condensing jars as passive irrigation devices.

Figure IV-9 *(opposite)*
Fatehpur Sikri, Sikri, India.

Section of wall with water column.

carved into the stone lintels that spanned the columns. These enclosed, gravity-fed channels also eliminated unnecessary evaporation by minimizing the contact of water with hot and dry air.

As intimated above, the collection, transfer, and storage of water provided an opportunity for designers to elevate this purely functional use to the level of an art form.

The exquisite treatment of water in the Court of the Oranges in Cordoba, Spain, truly expresses the allegorical movement of water. One of the finest irrigated patios ever created, the Patio de los Naranjos, or Court of the Oranges, was built by Al-Mansur around AD 976 as part of the Mosque (La Mezquita, in Spanish) of Abd al-Rahman (Figure IV-10a). At the time, Cordoba rivaled Mecca as an important cultural, spiritual, and commercial locus. The Patio, originally designed as an anteroom for the faithful to perform their ablutions (or ritual washing) before entering the mosque to worship, is a rectangular courtyard, measuring 400 by 200 feet. The facade of the mosque rises directly from the southern edge of the patio. The vast courtyard, covering approximately one-third of the area of the total complex, is entered through a narrow gateway in the north wall, and immediately impresses the visitor with its texture and atmosphere. Intelligently, the Moors originally built the entire patio over a cistern that irrigated the trees in the courtyard.

The main constructed feature of the patio has always been the irrigation network that waters a precise grid of over 150 orange trees. This dense green mat of trees, punctuated by an occasional palm tree, decorates the ground with dappled shade. The builders grouped the plantings into three major blocks, each with its own fountain. The largest block, in the center of the courtyard, contains a pool along its northern edge. At each of the pool's four corners, stout columns with

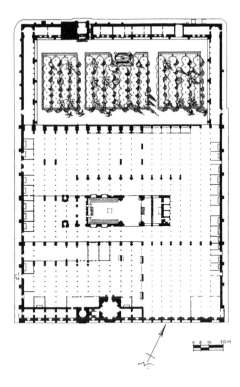

decorative caps spray water into the pool, while a single jet of water punctuates its center.

From this raised, central fountain, a recessed channel runs the entire length of the northern border of trees, then feeds into perpendicular channels along the rows of orange trees (Figure IV-10b). The brick-lined channels of this irrigation system are recessed into the pavement and link together the sunken basins surrounding the base of each tree. When flooded, water progresses through the channels into each successive basin. A wooden block placed at the opposite end of the basin retains the water. After sufficient water has been delivered, the block of wood moved near the next basin. The procedure repeats until each tree receives water.

The carefully organized grid, common in Moorish Spain, allowed efficient and convenient irrigation and also led to spatial design innovations. The rows of orange trees in the Court of the Oranges, for example, precisely align with the rows of columns inside the mosque, maintaining their visual rhythm and architectonic effect. Orange trees still frame archways on the facade that once opened to the interior forest of pillars within the mosque, hinting at the wonderful interpenetration of space that graced the original design. The integration of the interior and exterior space of this design seems, as if "the orange trees and their irrigation channels were a mathematical projection of the mystic interior into the open."[3] The paving pattern also reinforces the geometry created by the grid of trees: Rows of round pebbles, set in parallel bands, mimic the linear arrangement of the orange grove. As the sun passes overhead, dancing spots of light reflect from the stones.

In addition to its powerful aesthetic appeal, the design of the Court of the Oranges produces dramatic and powerful climatic effects. Flooding the irrigation channels, for example,

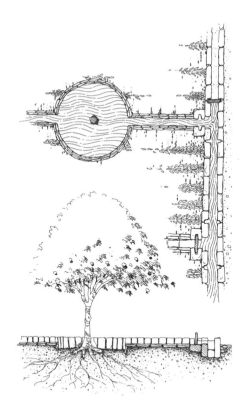

serves two purposes: First, of course, it waters and sustains the fruit trees; but equally important, it humidifies and cools the air. Growing trees transpire immense amounts of water that significantly modify the surrounding microclimate by lowering temperatures and raising humidity levels (Figure IV-11). When the leaves release water into the surrounding atmosphere through evapotranspiration, the ambient temperature cools and stabilizes. The more efficient the irrigation system, the more water will be transpired by the tree and the faster the air will cool. According to Robinette (1972), a mature orchard can transpire as much as 600 tons of water per acre per day.[4] In addition, through the process of guttation, which causes moisture to form on the leaves, the orchard acts as an air cleaner, washing the particulates off the leaves and onto the ground. The humid air around the orange trees also helps filter out wind-borne pollutants. The dense, green foliage of the oranges produces a cool shade, which in turn also helps to retard evaporation of the water in the irrigation channels and on the leaves themselves.

The Court of the Oranges offers but one example of how these cultures, through their designs, truly revered the magical life-giving qualities of water and transformed it into a major aesthetic element, flowing through the garden. They devised passive systems for collecting, storing, and moving water that ranged from simple to complex, and yet remained constant in their union of function and beauty. The next postulate, Placid Water Devices, examines the development of the water reservoir not only as a holding tank, but also as a major focal point for humidifying the air in arid climates.

Figure IV-12 *(above)*
Patio de los Naranjos, Seville, Spain.
Tenth century, of Moorish design.

The Patio de los Naranjos, in Seville, occupies a walled
enclosure quite similar to its Cordoban sibling. In contrast to the uniform walls of the courtyard in Cordoba,
the facades around the Patio de los Naranjos display
a harmonious blend of Moorish and Christian styles.
One enters from the north through a narrow opening
in the Puerto de Perdon—a transition from the urban
bustle to the tranquil orange grove which always
refreshes the visitor.
(Photo: Marc Treib)

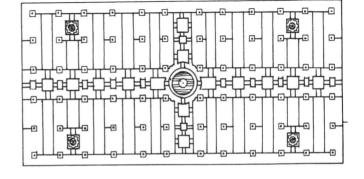

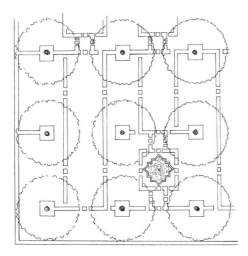

Water Catchment Devices and Irrigation Methods
Contemporary Applications

1. Catch all of the site's run-off and direct this flow into insulated, closed cisterns. Build cisterns into new structures and retrofit existing structures with run-off collection systems that deposit the water into cisterns for storage.

2. After storage in the cistern, direct the water into a central holding tank or reservoir for distribution throughout the landscape. Site the holding tank adjacent to the south facade of the main dwelling. Use the reservoir to produce water pressure for the irrigation system.

3. In all newly built landscapes, take advantage of efficient drip irrigation systems. The underground drip system conserves water and distributes moisture to the roots of vegetation with little loss of water.

4. Where possible, recycle filtered gray water into the irrigation system.

5. Combine the irrigation system with an efficient network of shade trees. More efficient irrigation increases transpiration by trees to quickly cool the air.

Figure IV-13a *(opposite below)*
Patio de los Naranjos, Seville, Spain.

Although the Patio de los Naranjos is much smaller and has fewer orange trees than its counterpart in Cordoba, its climatic effect is similar. Water gently cascades over a raised basin into a surrounding pool. From there it spills slowly over a rounded coping, into a channel sunken around the base of the pool. The water then enters the irrigation system, which in the Seville patio is a masterpiece of geometric precision and sophisticated decoration.

Figure IV-13b *(above)*
Patio de los Naranjos, Seville, Spain.

The patio surface is paved in a herringbone pattern of brick, as are the narrow water channels. The basins surrounding the trees are sunken beds of earth edged with brick. The trees are irrigated in the same manner as in Cordoba: Water from the central fountain fills the brick channels linking the circuit of trees; a block of wood placed at one end of the tree well restricts the water flow and floods the bed with water. When the tree has received sufficient irrigatation, the watercourse is shifted. Here again, the patio, cooled by the evaporation of water from the irrigation channels, is blanketed by the pleasant air under the shade of the aromatic orange trees.

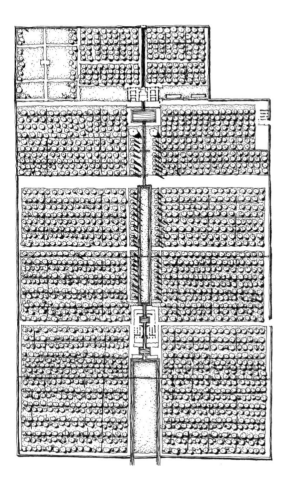

Figure IV-14b *(below)*

Bagh-i Eram, Shiraz, Iran.

The water dropped in three small cascades before the channel divided into two smaller canals, bordered by slender cypress trees that cast shadows across the water. These canals merged, passed through a small garden pavilion, and separated again. On either side of this central water axis were immense orchards. Periodically, at right angles to the central channel, smaller irrigation channels passed through these plantations. The orchards were further subdivided by even smaller irrigation channels into a total of 198 garden plots; everywhere, water seemed to flow. The water supply was used ingeniously for decoration, irrigation, and cooling. This garden clearly illustrates how water can be used efficiently and beautifully to create and sustain wonderful microclimates.

Figure IV-14a *(above)*

Bagh-i Eram, Shiraz, Iran.

Nineteenth century. Designer unknown.

The Bagh-i Eram in Shiraz used an extensive series of irrigation channels to water its extensive orchard plantations. A continuous channel over 2000 feet in length unified the upper and lower terraces of this enclosed complex, and provided water to the smaller irrigation channels that subdivided the site.

The garden was entered from the north, through a pavilion. Along the south face of this pavilion a rectangular reflecting pool stored water for irrigating the garden. Water flowed outward in a wide channel from this pool to the plantations below.

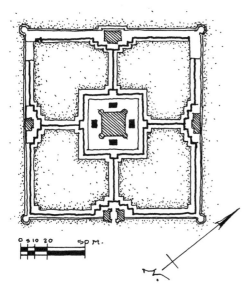

Figure IV-15a *(above)*
Tomb of Itimad-ud-Daula, Agra, India.
1628. Designer unknown.

The Tomb of Itimad-ud-Daula, on the banks of the Jumna River in Agra, India, was built for Emperor Jahangir's prime minister. A marble sarcophagus, placed on a slightly raised plinth in the center of the garden, was encircled by a narrow water channel, from which four other runnels radiated into the garden to divide it into four equal squares.

Figure IV-15b *(above right)*
Tomb of Itimad-ud-Daula, Agra, India.

To irrigate the garden, water was lifted from the Jumna River and fed into these water channels until they flooded, causing the water to sheet over the causeway and spill into the garden.

Figure IV-16 *(right)*
Ram Bagh, Agra, India.
Date unknown. Designer unknown.

The Ram Bagh, in Agra, had platforms raised about 10 feet as part of a gravity-fed irrigation system. These walks had decorative, stone-lined water channels down their center; water, diverted from them, irrigated trees planted at equal intervals along the walk.

Postulate II: **Placid Water Devices**

● Large pools of placid water within a garden can transform a hot or arid landscape into a life-sustaining microclimate by adding moisture to the air. Often the main focal point of the garden, these cool pools and reservoirs capture the run-off from streams and springs. Through its physical and psychological effects, placid water can provide comfort to those people and structures that dwell at the water's edge or linger on islands set within the tranquil liquid (Figure IV-17).

Iram indeed is gone with all his Rose
And Jemsyd's Sev'n-ring Cup where no one knows;
But still a Ruby kindles in the Vine,
And many a Garden by the Water blows.[5]
Omar Khayyam

The idea of water as an ornamental garden feature developed with its employment for agricultural purposes. Gardens and agriculture shared a parallel history: The terms were often interchangeable in recognition of the life-sustaining gifts provided by both landscape forms. Water quenches the thirst of both the parched soul and the dry plant.

Large volumes of water are necessary to maintain a predictable supply of water for irrigation throughout the year. Early hydrologic engineers directed water from mountain streams or springs into large basins at the highest point in the garden so that gravity could power the fountains and supply the irrigation. Primarily a Persian invention, these tanks became so large that they were referred to as *daryachen*, or "little seas." Persians admired the daryachen for the dark, reflective sheen of their placid waters as well as their more pragmatic applications. Kept brimming with water, they created gigantic mirrors set horizontally. Boats were taken out on the "little seas," completing the illusion of leaving the hot shores behind. In order to take advantage of the spiritual and physical properties of water, garden pavilions were constructed in the center of the pool on a small island or along the water's edge.

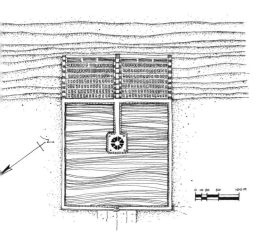

An impressive example of a "little sea" still exists in the Persian garden of Shah Goli, which translates as "royal pond," in Tabriz (Figure IV-18a). The name of the garden is taken from the Persian and Turkish languages. The royal pond measures over 700 feet on each side and has an octagonal pavilion at its center. A wide, stone-edged causeway connects the pavilion to a series of eight lush terraces, each planted with poplars and willows that sway and shimmer with a breeze. A stream originating at the uppermost terrace fed the pool; water channeled through each terrace came to rest in the pond below (Figure IV-18b). Due to its size, this artificial lake produces an immense quantity of moisture that surrounds the pavilion, providing it with cooled air regardless of the wind's direction.

The Bagh-i Takht, or Garden of the Throne, built north of Shiraz in 1789 for the Qajar ruler Aqa Muhammad, also included a rectangular pool, measuring about 460 feet by 213 feet (Figure IV-19). The stream-fed pool is placed below a series of hillside terraces and acts as the central feature of the garden. This daryachen dramatically alters the garden's microclimate by utilizing a simple, but effective, principle of temperature and pressure differential. The large area of cool, evaporating water created by such an immense pool draws the relatively warmer air from the hillside. The resulting breeze passes directly over the pool, cooling the air and creating a distinct microclimate.

Thus, the pool or reservoir can be considered an essential device in the modification of climate. The sheer size of a large storage tank of water makes it a prominent feature in a garden, while its large capacity humidifies vast quantities of air, creating a thoughtful and cool passive microclimate. Placid water also has important decorative and functional uses in a garden. The next postulate will present devices for the movement of water and examine the effects of active water in the garden.

● Figure IV-17 *(opposite)*
Placid water as a passive microclimatic device.

Figure IV-18a
The "Little Sea" of the Shah Goli, Tabriz, Iran.

Figure IV-18b
Shah Goli, Tabriz, Iran.

Plan of garden.

209

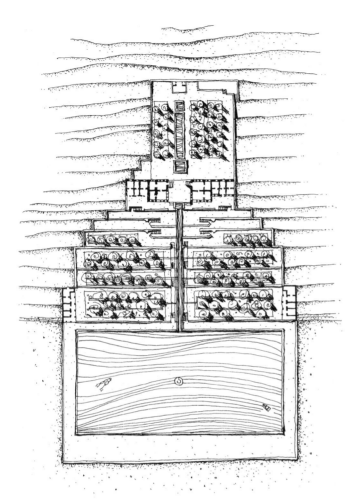

Placid Water Devices
Contemporary Applications

1. Retain large volumes of water to create a predictable supply for irrigation.

2. The reflective sheen of a wide plane of water creates the illusion of tranquility and imparts a calming effect upon the visitor.

3. Construct pavilions with ample openings for cross-ventilation in the center or along the edges of placid water. Locate shady sitting areas adjacent to the pool border.

4. Design the garden so that the air will move over large areas of water, cooling it, and creating draughts into adjacent structures and gardens.

5. In hot, dry climates, use large, flat water surfaces to create quantities of humidified air to decrease ambient temperatures. Shade the pool area as much as possible, with broad overhangs or shade trees with horizontal, spreading canopies to help retain the evaporating moisture from the pool.

Figure IV-19
Bagh-i Takht, Shiraz, Iran.

Plan of garden.

Figure IV-20
Garden of the Cuba, near Palermo, Sicily.
Twelfth century. Designer unknown.

The palaces of the Saracen emirs and Norman kings
also boasted immense pleasure gardens that commonly
included large canals or artificial lakes. A painting by
Lentini depicts the Garden of the Cuba near Palermo,
with a domed, three-story dwelling placed in a rectangular pool. A drawbridge connected the structure to
the shore. Shown close by, in the very center of the
water, was a smaller open-air kiosk with a dome, and
a small group of people relaxing.
(R. Lentini, Garden of the Cuba, *Gabinetto Nazionale
delle Stampe*)

Figure IV-21
Garden of Shah Abbas, Sari, Caspian Coast.
Nineteenth century. Designer unknown.

Nothing remains of the garden built by Shah Abbas
at Sari, on the Caspian coast, save a drawing executed
by Hommaire during his visit there in 1847. The image
shows a square pool combined with a long rectangular
pool extending the length of the garden. Stone paths
about 6 feet wide with finely carved stone curbs encircle the pool, with a decorative gravel band running
parallel. The combined water system of the two pools
cooled the garden as well as the pavilion.
(Hommaire de Hell, Garden Palace in the Chehel
Sutun Area, *1854–60)*

Figure IV-22a
Vernag Garden, Kashmir, India.
Date unknown. Designer unknown.

At the Vernag Garden in Kashmir an icy spring feeds
an unusual octagonal tank located at the base of a
mountain. Its designers built shaded niches into the
thick walls of this enclosure to utilize evaporative
cooling from the central pool. No matter where the
sun passed overhead, one could find a cool enclave in
which to retire from the heat.

Figure IV-22b
Vernag Garden, Kashmir, India.

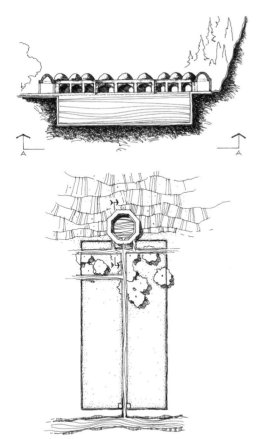

Water flowed from the octagonal pool under a central arch into a long canal that traveled the length of
the garden before dropping as a waterfall into the
Jhelum River. Trees along the canal shaded its flanking
paths and the water itself, heightening both the physical
and psychological sense of coolness. A visitor, renewed
by the movement of the water, could stroll the length
of this linear pool, stopping at the base of the mountain
to contemplate this unusual retreat.

● **Figure IV-23** *(opposite)*
The waterfall as a passive microclimatic device.

Postulate III: **Active Water Devices**

● The microclimatic effects of placid water are further enhanced by using gravity to create more complicated effects of motion, sound, and light. Rapidly moving vertical sheets of water excite the air in the garden, reducing summer warmth. Waterfalls, featured in grottoes, banisters, stairs and walks, lower the ambient temperatures and insulate the space from the sun's heat. These devices, while creating pleasant microclimates, can also be stunning focal points in the landscape (Figure IV-23).

Everywhere in these paradisiacal places fountains and waterfalls made the summer air cool and pleasant.[6]
Eugenia Salza Prina Ricotti

From the observation and contemplation of natural waterfalls and steep, hillside streams, early designers and engineers developed techniques to recreate in the garden the natural properties of rapidly falling water. The Mughals, Roman, and Italian designers regulated their microclimates with a vast array of active water innovations. Active water humidifies and reduces air temperature as it plunges downward in vertical sheets, rushes over serrated surfaces, or cascades down chutes and hillside watercourses.

The use of active water was an integral design element in early gardens. Triggs noted how naturally sloping sites were exploited for "the display of terraces and for the decorative treatment of water, for the Romans always delighted in the presence of cooling fountains and cascades."[7] The Roman emperor Hadrian widely incorporated cooling fountains and active water in his villa near Tivoli. The most spectacular use of active water was in the triclinium, or dining area, enclosed in the southern end of the *canopus*, one of the most unique waterways in Hadrian's complex (Figure IV-24). The canopus was a long, rectangular pool, designed to resemble a majestic and peaceful river, sited in a little valley whose steep banks were once covered with green lawns and shrubs. This pleasant miniature valley offered an idyllic setting for summer dining and entertaining (Figure IV-25a). Guests sat along the grassy banks of the canal and contemplated the reflections of the Greek and Egyptian statues that surrounded the pool, while Hadrian himself entertained in the rooms of the triclinium.

Along the southern edge of the canopus rose the umbrella-like ceiling of the semicircular triclinium. Built into the hillside behind the exedra form of the triclinium, was a second deep, rectangular dining room once covered by a barrel vault (Figure IV-25b). This was a place where Hadrian dined amid a "veil of water, falling in cascades, spreading like a glittering carpet over marble steps and rushing in gurgling rivulets through small canals that surrounded the couches of the diners."[8] A dramatic waterfall, fed by an aqueduct running along a hill just south of the canopus, filled the room with aerated water. The waterfall emptied into a basin beneath the room. Hadrian positioned his dining platform over the central portion of the room so water could flow directly underneath, cooling the interior as it passed on its way to the central canal.

Another dining area cooled by active water was located in the eastern portion of Hadrian's Villa, in the luxurious Piazza d'Oro, or "Golden Plaza." The Piazza d'Oro, a series of buildings now in ruins, once enclosed a courtyard designed for summer use and intimate entertaining (Figure IV-26). Bacon describes the architecture of the main pavilion in this complex as "illustrating the [Roman] mastery of the plastic design of space . . . a complex, sinuous form interlocking the rectangular corridors and the curved chamber."[9] While water remained the major climatic and architectonic element of the Piazza d'Oro, the nymphaeum dominated the main hall of the pavilion. This water feature, placed along the base of the gently curving rear wall, contained a series of rectangu-

Figure IV-24 *(opposite above)*
Hadrian's Villa, Tivoli, Italy.

The miniature valley of the canopus.
(Photo: Author)

Figure IV-25a *(opposite below left)*
Hadrian's Villa, Tivoli, Italy.

Plan of canopus.

Figure IV-25b *(opposite below right)*
Hadrian's Villa, Tivoli, Italy.

Section of canopus.

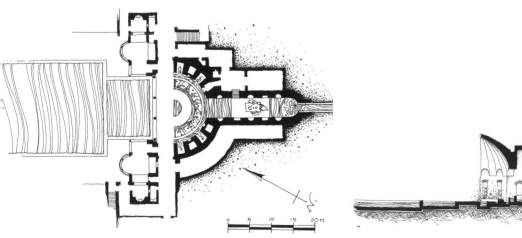

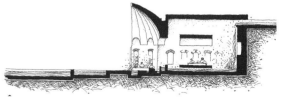

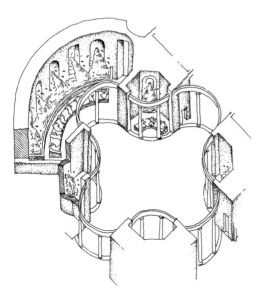

lar niches positioned over semicircular splashing waterfalls. In front of each pool, an elevated dining platform invited guests to a sumptuous meal in an interior environment cooled by sensibly placed fountains and the sound of crashing water.

Fifteen-hundred years later, Persians incorporated active water throughout the design of the spectacular Nishat Bagh, or "Garden of Delight." Asaf Khan designed the complex in 1625 as his summer palace on the shores of Lake Dal. One of the largest gardens in the Kashmir lake region, Nishat Bagh still brims with exuberant and animated water courses (Figure IV-27a). The snow-capped Himalayas are reflected in the lake and provide an exquisite backdrop for this walled garden. The lush green of Nishat Bagh set against the barren slopes of the mountainside prompts a unique dialog between built form and landscape. The views from this garden make it one of the most unusual Mughal gardens, which typically are more inwardly focused. Originally, one approached the complex by boat and entered on the lowest terrace, where a two-story pavilion spanned a central canal. From the lake, twelve terraces of varying sizes (thought to represent the twelve signs of the Zodiac) rose up and eventually disappeared into the hillside. The rectangular garden was organized around a central canal punctuated by a line of water jets and edged with stone. At each change of grade along this central water axis chutes accelerated the flow of water and created a rhythmic composition. Flanking panels of grass and formal beds of luxuriant flora visually reinforced the composition. Chenar trees and orchards framed the lawns, providing architectonic mass and shady retreats from the open central areas.

Located on the lowest terrace, a shady arcaded pavilion was set directly over the rapidly flowing central canal, while jets sprayed water into the canal to cool the air (Figure IV-27b). From the arcade, one witnessed a breathtaking view of the

Figure IV-26 *(above)*
Hadrian's Villa, Tivoli, Italy.
Axonometric of Piazza d'Oro.

Figure IV-27a *(opposite above)*
Nishat Bagh, Kashmir, India.
Plan of garden.

Figure IV-27b *(opposite center)*
Nishat Bagh, Kashmir, India.
Water-filled pavilion.

Figure IV-28 *(opposite below)*
Nishat Bagh, Kashmir, India.
Detail of *chabutra*.

garden and, in the opposite direction, beheld a panorama of the lake and towering mountains. From this vantage point, the visitor was caressed by the cool breeze and mesmerized by the continuous sounds of spraying jets and rushing cascades. On a sunny day these cascades and fountains reflected the sunlight like a million silver mirrors, and created a spine of silver that contrasted dramatically with the dark-green expanse of the surrounding trees. Spray from the jets and cascades alongside the rapidly moving water axis provided a continuous mist. Raised stone platforms, or *chabutras*, lay at the center of the canal where the torrent of water underneath dramatically chilled the air (Figure IV-28). Similarly, steps along the sides of the cascades also provided access to the splashing water so that one might romp in the cool mists.

Active water uses the force of gravity to draw water, often at great speed, back to the surface of the earth. The next postulate, Aerated Water Devices, examines how certain devices counter the effects of gravity with high pressure to produce cooling mists and sprays. These elements of motion, which engage both active and aerated water, increase the vocabulary of the designer and enrich the language of passive design.

Active Water Devices
Contemporary Applications

1. Humidify the air with active water cascading in vertical sheets over serrated surfaces.

2. In interior spaces use waterfalls to cool the microclimate. Place a waterfall on a wall so that the water drops the full height of the room and flows under the floor, cooling its surface.

3. Rapidly flowing canals can pass through the center of open, arcaded pavilions. The interior canal should be full of water jets. As the canal exits the room it can cascade into a waterfall, filling the room with cool air and the sounds of crashing water.

4. In garden watercourses, evenly space water jets to create a mist about 4 feet high. Shade these misty canals with a tree canopy or canvas awning. Place walkways along the canal edges.

5. To create a water-cooled passive environment, place 5-foot-square sitting areas in the center of water basins filled with water jets. These platforms can be placed at the edge of waterfalls that drop at least 4 feet for maximum effect.

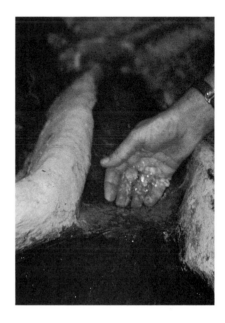

Figure IV-29a *(opposite above)*
Camino de los Cascades, Generalife, Granada, Spain. Date unknown. Designer unknown.

Under the shade of laurel and hazel trees in the northern corner of the Generalife gardens, a set of stairs climbs a steep incline called the Camino de los Cascades, or Street of the Cascades. The steps transect the top three terraces of the garden, terminating at a small mosque. A white-washed banister with a waterfilled trough built into its "handrail" runs along the top of the parapet, using terra-cotta tiles to create a narrow channel for the rushing water. The three flights of stairs also have small, circular fountains with bubblers in the center of each landing.

Figure IV-29b *(opposite below)*
Camino de los Cascades, Generalife, Granada, Spain.

The mere act of ascending these steps under the shady canopy on a hot day, and feeling the cool water running between one's fingers, is a heightened sensory experience. The concave treads and risers allow water released from hidden locks to cascade down on the visitors' burning feet.
(Photo: Elizabeth Boults)

Figure IV-30a
Villa d'Este, Tivoli, Italy. 1550–70. Designed by Pirro Ligorio.

The swooping staircase of the Dragon Fountain on the central axis of the Villa d'Este features a water banister. Water streams down stepped channels in the handrail and flows into the mouth of a frog at the middle landing. Water then emerges from the mouth of a dolphin at the top of the next staircase. The cascades continue down stepped channels, disappearing into the mouths of sea monsters at the base of the stairs.

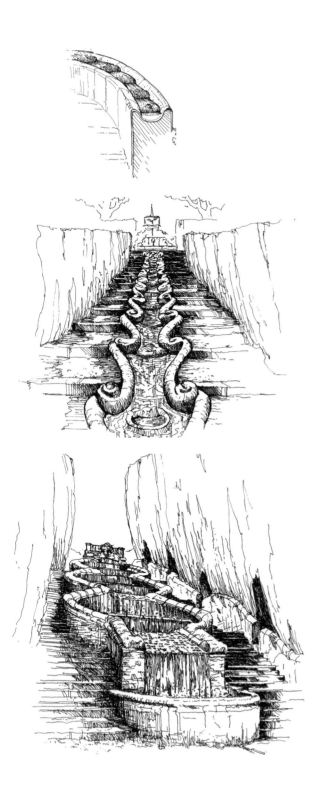

Figure IV-30b
Villa d'Este, Tivoli, Italy.

As the water flows down this continuous chain of weirs, graced with an elegant curved coping, one can dip one's hands into the chilly water. At the end of the cascade, the water disappears into a drain, then emerges from the mouth of a comical face on the final pilaster. Inside the base of the Dragon fountain, jets along the side of the stairs shoot arcs of water 20 feet overhead and over the Dragon Fountain court, creating an enclosure of mist.

Figure IV-31
Villa Lante, Bagnaia, Italy. Sixteenth century.
Reputedly designed by Vignola.

The water chain is a variation on the Italian Renaissance water staircase, and sensuously recreates the effect of bubbling mountain streams. The water chain at the Villa Lante structures the villa's central axis and dominants the upper terrace. Under a shady bosco, this magnificent cascade flows down the center of a gently sloping staircase lined by neatly clipped hedges. The chain broadens and narrows repeatedly, reflecting the ebb and flow of water. At each of these sections an up-turned shell acts as a weir. The shells' undulating shapes cause the water to flow in curvaceous patterns, swirling over the weirs, lapping as it passes to the next terrace. As the water reaches the last weir, it spills out between the claws of another giant crayfish, and falls into the Bowl of the Giants on the next terrace.

Figure IV-32
Villa Torlonia, Frascati, Italy.
Date unknown. Designer unknown.

The Villa Torlonia has a larger version of the Lante- and Farnese-style waterchain. The water originates at the crown of a hill in a balustraded basin with a gigantic fountain in its middle. It flows into a grotesque face, where it begins its descent by blasting out of the mouth and falling into four beautifully sculpted, oval basins. Between each basin, the water tumbles into a carved stone incline, causing the water to ripple as it becomes a waterfall, dropping into the basin below.

Figure IV-33

Palazzo Farnese, Caprarola, Italy.

Date unknown. Designed by Vignola.

The southwest garden at the Palazzo Farnese contains
a subterranean room designed to reproduce the sight
and sound of a rainstorm, thus giving it the name
"Fountain of Rain." The grotto, set on the central axis
of the garden, tunnels into a terrace along the rear
of the garden. Inside, stone satyrs, nymphs, and other
creatures that stand above a dark pool of water support rusticated vaults dripping from the rocky ceiling
and walls.

Figure IV-34

Shalamar Bagh, Lahore, Pakistan.

Date unknown. Designer unknown.

An imitation of falling rain becomes the transition
space between two terraces in the garden at
Shalamar Bagh in Lahore, Pakistan. The water from
the main reservoir of the garden flows into the *sawan
bhadun,* a sunken, three-sided room, and cascades
over three white-marble walls honeycombed with
chinikanas (small marble niches). As water flows over
the recesses in this vertical cliff, the sound of a raging
thunderstorm fills the air. The crashing sound amplifies
as it bounces off the marble walls of the sunken
room. The floor of the room forms a pool and five
fountains agitate the surface of the water, simulating
rain falling on the ground. Water flows beneath a
narrow open walkway on the fourth side of the
sawan bhadun before emptying into the central canal
on the lower terrace. The room, accessible from this
lower terrace, provides the sensation of being in a
torrential downpour—a welcome relief in a landscape
of infrequent rain!

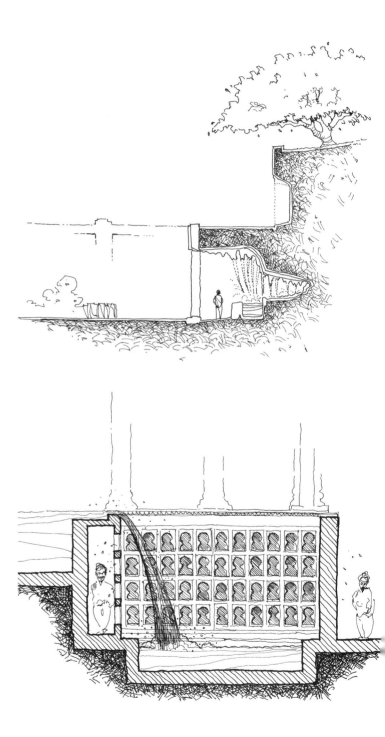

Postulate IV: **Aerated Water Devices**

Like active water, aerated water creates unique effects of light and sound that psychologically cool the body. In addition, moist, cool environments are produced by physically restricting the flow of water under pressure through a variety of methods. Forcing water into space through tiny openings suspends thin veils of fine mist in the air, thus lowering the ambient temperature (Figure IV-35).

This playing fountain, like the hand of the Shah,
fills the earth and the sky with a shower of pearls.
I asked, "Is this the life giving water?"
And the answer came,
"Yes."[10]
Saba

The microclimatic effects of aeration depend on a consistent supply of water under high pressure. The development of aerated water for climatic comfort most likely paralleled the refinement of early hydraulic systems that harnessed the natural energy of water pressure for human uses. Islamic, Mughal, and Italian gardens all used some type of aerated water device to affect microclimatic design. Though their respective designs varied substantially, each of these cultures developed techniques to aerate water for natural air cooling. Forcing water under high pressure through miniature openings, small nozzles, or thin slots suspends fine drops of water in the surrounding air, humidifying it and lowering the surrounding temperature.

Water, an extremely propitious cooling device, as well as an important decorative element, became the central theme of many gardens. The gardens of the Villa d'Este at Tivoli possess perhaps the greatest and most nuanced example of this practice. Miller describes the choreography of water in this garden as follows:

> Nowhere is water more truly the queen of all the elements than at the Villa d'Este in Tivoli… The dynamic aspect of the water and its sonic range is paralleled and underscored by our movement to

● Figure IV-35 *(opposite)*
Misting water jets as a microclimatic design device.

Figure IV-36
Villa d'Este, Tivoli, Italy.

The Centro Fontane, view toward the Ovata.

and away from this theater of infinite works of every manner, shape and contrivance.[11]

The first major water feature encountered in this garden is the terrace of the Centro Fontane, or the Hundred Fountains (Figure IV-36). This wall of fountains contains over 300 water jets set into a continuous, two-tiered stone trough running 450 feet across the entire slope of the garden. Decorative finials on the upper trough expose a variety of jets that shoot water in vertical columns and project aerated spays in fan-like shapes. In front of the finials, water arches forth from spigots and sloshes into the trough. Another series of nozzles directs water neatly into arches falling into the lower trough. The water then gently spills over the stone wall and collects in a channel built into the walkway. Water splashes onto the mosaic walkway, glistens in the sun, and reflects the sky.

The Fountain of the Oval, or Ovata, one of the largest water features at the villa, terminates the lateral axis of the Hundred Fountains (Figure IV-37a). This fountain was designed by Pirro Ligorio and is said to be directly inspired by the triclinium in the canopus at Hadrian's Villa nearby (Figure IV-37b). A large, semicircular waterfall excavated out of the hillside is the focal point of this outdoor room. The waterfall cascades over an arcaded nymphaeum where transparent sheets of water fold into the oval pool before dispersing to the rest of the garden (Figure IV-38). Between the niches of the arcade, statues of nymphs pour water from their amphorae into the oval pool that frames a view of the Centro Fontane. On top of pilasters that surround a balustraded walkway above the nymphaeum, raised circular water basins send a single jet of water arcing down into the pool below.

At the lower level of the garden, toward the east end of the reflecting pool, looms the incredible cooling device known

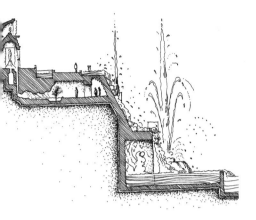

as the Water Organ (Figure IV-39). Occupying six distinct terraces, the sound and force of this massive structure, replete with torrential vertical sprays, water slides, a waterfall, pools, and basins, overwhelms the visitor. On sunny days rainbows float in the mists of the vertical jets that spray nearly 30 feet into the air. On the second terrace, one can walk through the sides of the waterfall into an archway directly beneath the torrent and look out to the lower pools. A myriad of flying droplets cools the pavement, steps, and railings, and bathes with a fine mist those who venture near.

Behind the Water Organ, on the second level, water fans out into huge, misty veils from the back wall of three long, narrow grottoes (Figure IV-40). In the lower garden, at the terminus of the central sight line to the villa, towering cypress trees and a ring of clipped ilex form a circular garden room. Within the remains of an older fountain, lush ferns surround a ring of single water jets. In this serene room, one can sit and gaze up through the magnificent central allée and view the fountains and villa set against the Mediterranean sky.

The Persians also devised techniques to cool temperatures with aerated water. The Shalamar Bagh in Kashmir used water in many inventive ways. Shah Jahan built this Shalamar Bagh (or "Garden of Love") in the seventeenth century as a series of descending terraces along a main water axis. At the upper level of the garden, the main watercourse led into a large water basin which surrounded a structure known as the Black Marble Pavilion (Figure IV-41). This 165-square-foot structure was an excellent example of a Mughal *baradari*, or open-air pavilion, and was the focal point of the entire composition. On all four sides of the pool, a field of 122 raised jets threw water into the air, creating a "forest of silver lances around the kiosk ... the feast and the apotheosis of water."[12]

Figure IV-39
Villa d'Este, Tivoli, Italy.

Section of Water Organ and three grottoes.

Figure IV-40
Villa d'Este, Tivoli, Italy.

Water fan in grotto behind Water Organ.
(Photo: Marc Treib)

Aerated Water Devices

Contemporary Applications

1. To humidify the air and lower surrounding temperatures, force water under high pressure into the air through miniature openings, small nozzles, or thin slots.

2. To create a water wall, install a continuous row of water jets to aerate water in fanlike shapes along the top of a 5-foot-high, and at least 10-foot-long, wall. Below these water finials, insert a line of nozzles that arc water into a trough 12 inches below. At the base of the wall, collect the overspray in a channel along a walk. Construct the walkway out of a material that will reflect the overspray. Plant a row of canopy trees along the wall's back, keeping the trough in continuous shade.

3. Equip arcaded walkways or rooms with wide, arched openings covered with a water curtain flowing from the roof.

4. Provide window openings with jets that spray water into fans, filling the void with a thin liquid veil. These water fans cool the air that passes into interior spaces.

5. Insert open-air pavilions into the center of pools, eight times the size of the pavilion's footprint. Within the pool place raised jets on 4-foot centers, to throw out a 6-foot diameter mist.

On the middle terrace level of the Shalamar Bagh, just above a cascade of water, a chabutra extends over the main watercourse. Elevated stone steps lead to these platforms where a visitor relaxed on cushions and pillows surrounded by rushing water. At the lowest garden level, another open pavilion, the Diwan-i-Am, was sited so that the water from the central canal flowed right through the room and cascaded over a waterfall (Figure IV-42). There at the edge of the waterfall, in the shade of the pavilion, another chabutra offered respite from the searing heat. The pool in front of the cascade utilized many fountains similar to those surrounding the Black Marble Pavilion. Aerated by thousands of misting jets in every corner of this garden, water created a tranquil oasis for the body and mind.

From the grand displays of the Renaissance to the more contemplative compositions of the Muslims, aerated water modified the microclimate in an infinite number of ingenious and imaginative ways. The next postulate presents a more subtle device for passive cooling, the Wet Walk. Perhaps less visually stimulating than the action and motion of aerated water, this device nonetheless cools and calms the garden's occupants in a quiet and soothing manner.

Figure IV-41

Shalamar Bagh, Kashmir, India.

Section of Black Marble Pavilion.

Figure IV-42

Shalamar Bagh, Kashmir, India.

Section of the Diwan-i-am.

Figure IV-43 *(opposite above left)*
Palazzo La Zisa, Palermo, Sicily, Italy.
Date unknown. Of Mughal design.

An excellent example of a water chute called a *selsebil* exists in the vestibule of Palazzo La Zisa, built by the Muslim emirs during their occupation of Sicily. Examples of these natural air-cooling devices from as early as the thirteenth century have been found built into the walls of sunken rooms or basements of dwellings. The raised designs of a selsebil's decorative panels aerated flowing water. At the bottom of the selsebil, water collected in a small pool. Seating generally faced this feature. Evaporation increased the humidity, also lowering the temperature of the room.

Figure IV-44 *(opposite above right)*
Aerating Columns, Museum of Islamic Art,
Cairo, Egypt.
Date unknown. Designer unknown.

Water was also integrated into the structural elements of buildings to create a primitive form of air conditioning. A pavilion's columns were punctured with thousands of tiny holes through which water would spray, gently caressing and cooling the room with an almost invisible mist. In an excellent example of this type of column, preserved at the Museum of Islamic Art in Cairo, 10 jets propelled the water pumped inside the polychromed marble column into a sunken basin at its base. Along the edges of this basin additional jets shot 3 feet up into the air.

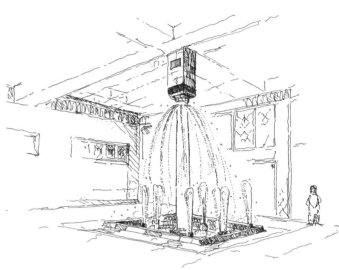

Figure IV-45 *(right)*
Chehel Sutun, Isfahan, Iran.
Sixteenth century. Of Islamic design.

A similar misting effect was employed at the Chehel Sutun in Isfahan. Four fluted cedar columns rose from massive stone lions which occupied the corners of a rectangular pool. From the mouths of these animals a gentle arc of water produced a fine mist as it splashed into the marble pool. Another fountain featured three stepped basins of cascading water originating from a bubbler at an upper level. Mirrors built into the ceiling of the room reflect the shimmering water to increase its effect.

Figure IV-46
Villa Pliniana, Lake Como, Italy.
1570, built for Count Anguissola.

In 1570, Count Anguissola of Piacenza built the Villa
Pliniana along the deep, shady banks of Lake Como
in the Lombardy region of Italy. The villa, reputed to
be the coolest in the region, lay on a small bay in the
eastern section of the lake and faced north. Placed on
a narrow foundation, the structure projected into the
lake as a high terrace. The rear of the villa faced an
almost vertical cliff, effectively shading the structure
during the summer, its primary time of occupancy.
On the northern side, a torrential waterfall cascaded
down the cliff and passed right through the center of
the villa.

● **Figure IV-47** *(opposite)*
Wet walk with jets and runnel.

230

Postulate V: **Wet Walks**

● In the midst of a hot summer day, delightful sprays of water can cool walks, paths, and patios. Water jets can intermittently operate throughout the day, releasing just enough water to make a surface appear as if it were a shimmering stream. This intermittent wetting settles the dust on a path, and imparts a refreshing coolness to the air. Small irrigation channels may also be adapted into wet walks (Figure IV-47).

Glitt'ring the streams reflect the Vision of beatitude, [13]
William Blake

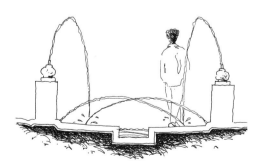

The creation of wet walks was most likely inspired by observations of the moistened ground between irrigated rows of plants. The earthen irrigation channel evolved over time into a shallow stone- or marble-lined runnel, which distributed water efficiently to all parts of the garden. Where these channels bisected a pathway, water splashing out of the runnel transformed the path into an abstraction of a shallow streambed. This idea translated easily to the design of garden paths. The placement of jets on either side of a paved walkway further enhanced the idea of a wet walk. The jets, spaced so their arches would mist the path and gently splash a person's ankles with water, recreated the sensation of walking in a brisk stream in the middle of summer.

A perfectly scaled wet walk exists in the Moorish Jardin de las Infantas at the Alcazar in Seville (Figure IV-48). Here, small jets are placed at the intersection of four pathways around a tiled, hexagonal pool; a raised, iron fountainhead shoots jets of water in all directions and into the pool's basin. Flowers in clay pots along the top of the basin shimmer with beads of water. Forty-eight invisible nozzles, sitting flush with the pavement surface, discharge water 3 feet up into the air. The water falling onto the tiled surface creates a glistening puddle; when the wind blows, the water flickers to the ground in an even wider circumference. Excess water collects at the base of the fountain in a narrow trough. In the shady corners of this intersection, tiled benches, cooled by the waters flowing across the walk, face the fountain.

The Moorish influence persisted in the design of gardens on the island of Majorca, despite the wresting of its control by the Spanish in the thirteenth century. A particularly exquisite example of the synthesis of Moorish and Baroque design principles can be found in the garden of La Alfabia. Designed in the Moorish tradition, the garden includes eight terraces reminiscent of the eight stages of paradise in Islamic teaching, as well as a fantastic wet walk. Here, 2-foot-high parapet walls support octagonal stone columns and a gently curving, vine-covered wooden arbor that borders the path (Figure IV-49). Wisteria and other vines wrap themselves around the supports, contributing to the shade. Between the octagonal columns, above the parapet, stone "capitals" spray fine mists of water that crisscross each other and arc downward. The shady arbor retains the moisture from the damp walkway while water splashes the feet of the visitor.

Perhaps the most elaborate and sophisticated system of wet walks and runnels in Spain remains at the Alhambra complex in Granada, begun by Mohammed V in 1377. For example, the runnels and fountains of the Patio de los Leones, or Court of the Lions, create a splendid microclimate through a fabulous interrelationship of garden and building. This intimate rectangular courtyard is entered from a dark corridor that connects to the nearby Court of the Myrtles. An arcaded portico of finely scalloped arches, resting elegantly on pairs of slender alabaster columns, encloses the Court of the Lions. On the east and west ends, the portico expands into two small, square spaces that extend into the main space of the

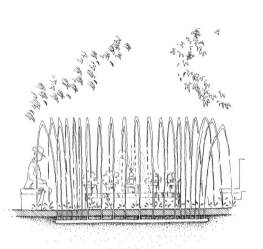

Figure IV-48
Alcazar Gardens, Seville, Spain.

Section through the Jardin de las Infantas.

courtyard. Looking out into the center of the courtyard, a circle of 12 stone lions faces outward, supporting a fountain with a single jet of water that "rises lazily into the air, seems to give up, then topples back with a soft lapping sound... Indeed, the whole affair glistens and drops and looks exceedingly wet..."[14]

From this central focus, four marble runnels, glimmering like quicksilver, radiate outward and divide the garden into quadrants. Along both sides of the troughs, marble walks provide just enough space for one person. The runnels narrow slightly as they enter the adjacent pavilions and interior rooms where the water terminates in circular pools set into the floors (Figure IV-50). At the end of these wet walks, bubblers agitate the surface of the pool, splashing water onto the floor and cooling the marble. The water channels that traverse the court link the interior with the exterior spaces to "form a cross under the central fountain and complete an image of delicious coolness."[15]

These interior wet walks and fountains help keep the room cool in the summer months, making the space quite comfortable in the hottest weather. In addition to the excellent climate modification, the transparency and balance of space created by the delicate architecture and proportions of the built elements, as well as the envelop of sound created by the soft rhythm of flowing water, combine to make the Court of the Lions a serene and tranquil refuge.

From the subtleties and refinement of wet walks and placid water, to the more energetic and ostentatious displays of active and aerated water, we have explored how this basic element functions as an art form and as an effective passive climatic mechanism. The final postulate, Water Jokes, examines the art and engineering of passive microclimates through the use of playful water devices.

Figure IV-49
La Alfabia, Majorca, Spain.

Detail of a wet walk.

Wet Walks

Contemporary Applications

1. To transform a path into an abstraction of a shallow streambed, bisect paved pathways with runnels filled with enough moving water to splash from the runnel.

2. Place water jets on either side of paved walkways to mist the path and gently splash the passerby with water.

3. At the intersection of pathways, place nozzles flush with the pavement surface to shoot water 3 feet into the air. Direct the jets to fall onto the paved surface to create a glistening puddle. In the shady corners of the intersection, place benches facing the jets.

4. Between the columns of vine-covered arbors, construct 2-foot-high parapet walls. On top of the parapet, place water jets every 2 to 4 feet spraying fine mists of water that crisscross each other and arch toward the intersection of the pathways.

5. When possible, use glazed tiles or other reflective materials on walks to increase the illusion of water.

Figure IV-50

Alhambra, Granada, Spain.

Interior pavilion of the Patio de los Leones.

(Photo: Marc Treib)

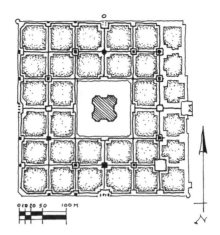

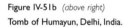

Figure IV-51a *(above left)*
Tomb of Humayun, Delhi, India.
Sixteenth century. Of Mughal design.

Placed on an arcaded platform in the center of a traditional four-square garden, the tomb is surrounded by a grid of water channels, using extensive runnels to create wet walks.

Figure IV-51b *(above right)*
Tomb of Humayun, Delhi, India.

Single runnels in the center of broad walkways inscribe the perimeter of the grounds and receive the additional channels that subdivide the grounds into square lawns. Water flows throughout this system — interrupted by miniature waterfalls that create a ripple effect similar to mountain streams — and cause the water to splash onto the adjacent walkways. The constant movement of water moistens the area surrounding the ruler's tomb and animates this extremely flat site.

Figure IV-52 *(right)*
Red Fort, Delhi, India.
Seventeenth century. Built for Shah Jahan.

Water from the adjacent Jumna River fed into a large white marble chute intricately carved to agitate the flow. A variety of wet walks connected the palace's interior with the gardens. The water collected in a basin and traveled along a 10-foot-wide canal beneath the emperor's throne and throughout the remainder of the estate.

Figure IV-53
Alcazar Gardens, Seville, Spain.
Date unknown. Designer unknown.

The Alcazar Gardens contain one of the most delicate
and beautifully scaled wet walks of Moorish design,
which radiates from a single jet in the center of a
square sunken pool. A shallow central runnel extends
the entire length of the pathway which is raised above
the adjacent planting beds to irrigate the garden without disturbing the surface of the walk. The sides and
bottoms of the runnel are paved in a zigzag pattern
that creates an illusion of quickly flowing water. The
surface of the wet walk is paved with handsomely
glazed polychrome tiles to enhance the shimmering
effect of the water.
(Photo: Author)

Figure IV-54 *(opposite above)*
Carmen of the Purification, Granada, Spain.
Date unknown. Designer unknown.

On the southeastern slope of the Albaicín hill, the
Carmen of the Purification contains a beautiful and
poetic garden in the corner of an estate. Within this
small garden enclosed by shrubs and clipped hedges,
a runnel connects a row of three low fountains.
Sunburst patterns of black and white pebbles radiate
out from the raised, circular basins. Simple jets fill the
pool with water that overflows into a trough encircling
the base. A stone bench near the central fountain rests
against the clipped shrub border, and invites one to sit
and reflect.

Figure IV-55 *(opposite below)*
Villa Medici, Pratolino, Tuscany, Italy.
1569. Built for Grand Duke Francesco I.

The central axis of the Villa Medici at Pratolino once
contained one of the most spectacular wet walks in
garden history. An eighteenth century drawing of the
Pratolino gardens depicts an arc of water that once
covered this axis below the villa. Water shot from
fountains in a wide arc and landed at the opposite
side of the walkway. In the drawing, this arc appears
sufficiently high for a person to ride through on
horseback.
*(B.S. Sgrilli, Pratolino (Firenze): stradone delle fontane,
1742)*

237   WET WALKS

Postulate VI: **Water Jokes**

● Water jokes add another dimension of levity and spontaneity to the landscape. The effectiveness of their operation hinges on the designer's ability to choreograph movement through space, and to use the element of surprise. Well-designed water jokes appear where one least expects them, disguised by a sense of tranquility. On a quiet walkway, open patio, or comfortable bench, an invisible hand mischievously activates the *giochi d'acqua* that suddenly saturate the area and scatter its victims throughout the garden (Figure IV-56).

One hundred little jets (in the theater) and on the stairways, where water sprayed the entire length from left to right, Legovitz, a member of his party ran to the top to turn on another valve but was deceived and soaked himself with a jet of water the thickness of an arm. [16]
Judith Chatfield

Only a thorough understanding of hydraulics combined with a dose of mischief could have produced the distinctly Italian device of *giochi d'acqua*, or water jokes, in the garden. The beguiling nature of water jokes reflects the Italians' willingness to integrate water into their social events as sensual celebrations of life. Garden designers often concealed nozzles in the anatomical parts of sculpture, grotto ceilings, or stone benches, where a sudden burst of water, ranging from fine mists to cascading arcs, was used for calculated effect (Figure IV-57). Artfully choreographed, the design of the water jokes could move visitors through the garden. When the first jets erupted, perhaps from a walkway or a bench, the astonished guests would naturally try to avoid the spray of water and move to a dry section of the garden. The stunned visitors would then seek refuge in another garden site, such as a conveniently placed grotto, only to receive an additional soaking from cascades of water tumbling from the ceiling. While often a shocking surprise, these wonderful devices cooled visitors with their playful mists, wet down dusty paths, and created stunning visual effects in the garden. And, as pointed out in the quote to the left, at times even the trickster was fooled by his own devices.

The gardens of the Medici villa at Castello, near Florence, featured many sophisticated water jokes. Jets hidden in walkways and steps sprayed a mist of water so fine, it was almost invisible. Triggs describes the experience of walking on the central flight of steps that lead to a grotto:

> …whence may issue tiny jets of water. These secret fountains, which are to be met in nearly every Italian garden also serve the very useful purpose of keeping the hot parched stone work occasionally moist.… That was all the more grateful in the scorching heat of the summer sun.[17]

An accomplice would turn on these tiny jets just as someone started to ascend the steps. The guests would hastily make their way into the protection of the grotto that, as good fortune would have it, lay directly ahead (Figure IV-58). Once safely inside this grotto, more jets in the floor would come on, chasing the poor souls to the back of the cavern, where another barrage of water would finish the soaking. Exquisite sculptures of animals covering the walls of the grotto also emitted jets of water from their mouths and other body openings (Figure IV-59). This underground room with its complex waterworks and maddening games was also a welcome relief from the summertime heat.

The elegant double staircase leading into the sunken garden at the Villa Torrigiani in Camigliano contains a series of spectacular water jokes that chase the visitor into the garden using a barrage of water (Figure IV-60). Once inside this elegant, sunken garden, an octagonal grotto comes into focus (Figure IV-61). Of course, this attractive grotto employed an arsenal of water jets that drenched the visitor from all sides. Inside, a waterfall cut off any escape from the interior; on the roof, a statue of Flora — itself containing many jets—released water in a chandelier-like spray that cascaded down from the tile-covered cupola. If the visitor should leave by the flanking stairs, the water jets followed his or her retreat.

Figure IV-57b *(below)*

More forms of water jokes.

Figure IV-58 *(right)*

Villa Medici, Castello, Italy.

The grotto and its water jokes.

Figure IV-59 *(opposite left)*

Villa Medici, Castello, Italy.

Animal sculptures covering the walls of the grotto emit jets of water from their mouths.

(Photo: Marc Treib)

Figure IV-60 *(opposite right)*

Villa Torrigiani, Camigliano, Italy.

Double staircase containing water jokes.

Figure IV-61

Villa Torrigiani, Camigliano, Italy.

The playful grotto: four actions.

Left to right:

a. Hidden jets surprise the naive visitor.

b. Blasts of water back the unfortunate one into a dark grotto.

c. Lips of large sculptures around the perimeter of the room continue the assault.

d. As a final insult, water cascades downward from the dome. There is no escape; a sense of humor is mandatory.

Figure IV-62 *(opposite)*

Villa Aldobrandini, Frascati, Lazio, Italy. 1598. Designed by Giacomo Della Porta and by Carlo Maderno.

Villa Aldobrandini, at one time, had some of the most renowned water jokes in all of Italy. Hidden surprises were part of a complex system of hydraulics that constituted the axis of the garden. The water for these features issued in a woodland high above the villa; it filled a pool and disappeared beneath a terrace, reappearing as a series of cascades along the garden's central spine.

(Photo: Marc Treib)

Water Jokes

Contemporary Applications

1. In the garden, disguise nozzles in anatomical parts of sculpture, or in ceilings or benches where sudden bursts of water ranging from fine mists to cascading arcs can be turned on to surprise the visitor.

2. Choreograph the timing of water jokes to orchestrate the movement of people through the garden as they try to avoid getting wet.

3. Locate water jokes not only to surprise and cool a garden's guests, but also for wetting down hot, dusty pathways. Space the water jets along a path so they will lay a light, even coat of water on the walk. Time the jets to go on just long enough to wet the pavement every hour.

4. In staircases, hide water jets in the base of the tread to spray a fine mist that is activated when stepped on. Space these nozzles 8 to 10 inches apart and aim them at a 60-degree angle.

5. On the roofs of buildings, arcades, or arbors, attach radial nozzles that produce chandelier-like sprays, cascading down the roof and cooling the structure. These cascades should erupt when garden visitors pass by or stop to rest.

This last element in Book IV, Water Jokes, contributes the important element of fun and play to our ever-expanding vocabulary of passive design. While the design of micro-climates is a serious endeavor that seeks to accommodate human needs and reduce energy consumption, it must also strive to enliven the imagination and nourish all aspects of the human spirit.

Figure IV-63

Villa Aldobrandini, Frascati, Lazio, Italy.

At the beginning of the last cascade, just above a semi-circular nymphaeum, special grooves direct water to spiral down and around two slender columns. A print by G.B. Falda from 1683 illustrates how water once shot from the tops of these columns, then wound its way around the spirals, splashing onto the heads of visitors. The Falda print also shows a stone banister containing a cascade of water racing over small weirs. The base of this railing also contained hidden jets of water that chased the visitors up and down the steps.

Figure IV-64 *(opposite left)*

Villa Mondragone, Frascati, Lazio, Italy.

Date unknown. Designer unknown.

A famous first-hand account by Michel de Montaigne describes a central water feature at this villa that is a truly Italian water game: the idle hose pipes around the pool suddenly began to stand up and "piss fresh water non-stop." The aquatic weapons were grabbed by the guests and aimed at each other until all were drenched.

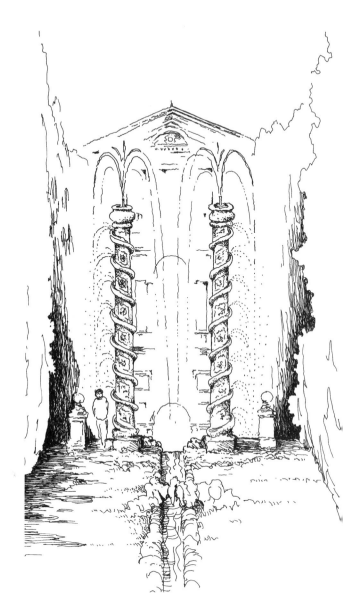

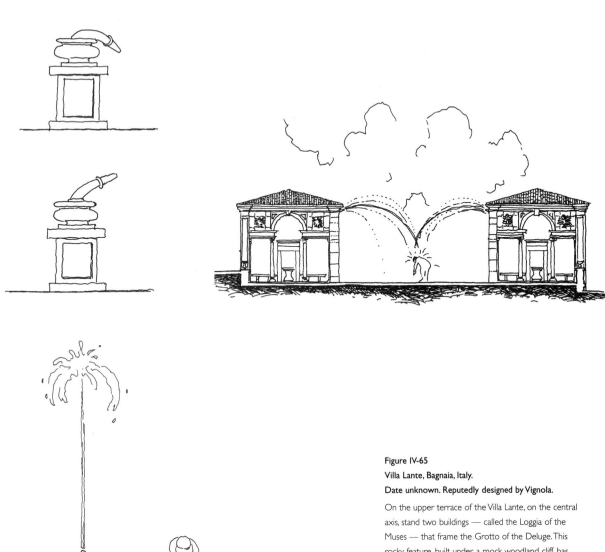

Figure IV-65
Villa Lante, Bagnaia, Italy.
Date unknown. Reputedly designed by Vignola.

On the upper terrace of the Villa Lante, on the central axis, stand two buildings — called the Loggia of the Muses — that frame the Grotto of the Deluge. This rocky feature, built under a mock woodland cliff, has three arched niches covered with mosses and ferns. A stone head drips water from its mouth to a pool below. Numerous hidden jets of water shoot out from beneath the roofs of the two buildings, creating a torrent of water which arcs across the entire width of the space, soaking the lawn. The field of jets creates a roof of water overhead and produces a space quite unlike any other. When viewing the garden from the open-air casinos that support the jets, the abundance of water appears as a powerful rainstorm.

Figure IV-66a
Villa Lante, Bagnaia, Italy.

Another hidden waterworks in this garden nestles between the two lower villa buildings overlooking the lower parterre.
(Photo: Author)

Figure IV-66b
Villa Lante, Bagnaia, Italy.

An unseen attendant opens the valves causing 30 jets of water to burst forth, wetting any visitor who pauses to enjoy the view of the lower garden.
(Photo: Author)

Garden Prototype IV:

The Garden of Neptune

The Garden of Neptune rests at the base of the Sierra mountains, northeast of Bakersfield, in the central valley of California. The hot, dry climate of this region, and its proximity to a mountain stream and an underground spring, make it a perfect site for exploring the potential of water for passive cooling. The flat valley, made fertile with massive irrigation projects, stretches into the distance, gleaming with the image of productive agriculture. However, leapfrog housing developments and the ubiquitous strip mall have eaten away at the fertile landscape at an increasing rate, forever eroding this once-agrarian paradise. The Garden of Neptune perches in the foothills of steeply wooded peaks facing in a southwesterly direction just above farmland. The site, with its proximity to a constant water supply and agricultural lands, bears a strong resemblance to the landscapes that Mughal, Islamic, and Italian gardeners generally selected for their gardens and dwellings.

The Garden of Neptune exploits water as a passive landscape device. This ultimate garden prototype engages water throughout its site, collecting, storing, and activating it with gravity and pressure to moderate the climate of its dwellings and gardens. The collected water, stored in cisterns, irrigates the gardens and the fields; any excess water is returned to the land to replenish the aquifer. Too many modern landscapes hide the movement of water; sanitized and contained in pipes, water has generally been removed from our view. We no longer understand where it comes from; we simply turn on the faucet and out it flows. This contemporary garden attempts to develop efficient uses of water by joining practical and aesthetic elements in an innovative partnership that makes the path of water legible. Celebrating water at every juncture, we are able to follow its movement and partake of its bounty.

However, occasions to partake of water's refreshing and life-giving properties may be severely limited in our future. Widespread water shortages have already occurred. California experiences persistent droughts and the control and disbursement of water there has become a politically explosive issue. Perhaps only enlightened watershed management and a change in public attitudes toward consumption can preserve a dependable supply of clean water. Continued ecological research of innovative hydrological processes and sustainable agricultural approaches is a first step toward redefining our relationship with water. Changing cultural attitudes poses a more profound challenge. Water is not merely a resource to be exploited for human convenience, but rather a nurturing force that links and sustains all life on earth.

The Garden of Neptune:
A Description of Passive Landscape Elements

A. Water Collection
Located in proximity to a mountain stream and an underground spring, the Garden of Neptune captures water in sunken pipes at the top of the site. The emergence of this water above ground bursts into a miniature nymphaeum dedicated to the beloved. The captured water flows through channels into a large, underground cistern at the top terrace level. A portion of this water is diverted into an elevated aqueduct connected to a water tower which forms the upper edge of the dwelling and produces the pressure necessary to disperse the water throughout the garden.

B. Grotto
Directly below the water tower, a portal in the northeast facade of the dwelling leads into a deep grotto. In its cool depths, a tall veil of water crashes into a pool. The cooled air from this water drifts from the grotto into the main living area, filling its large, central space.

C. Air-Misting Columns
Water from the aqueduct curves downward through pipes that force the water into circular columns supporting the roof of the central room. Thousands of tiny holes are pierced into these columns so that the descending water will spray into tiny arcs throughout the room. Filling the air with these almost invisible mists gently cools the air in the dwelling.

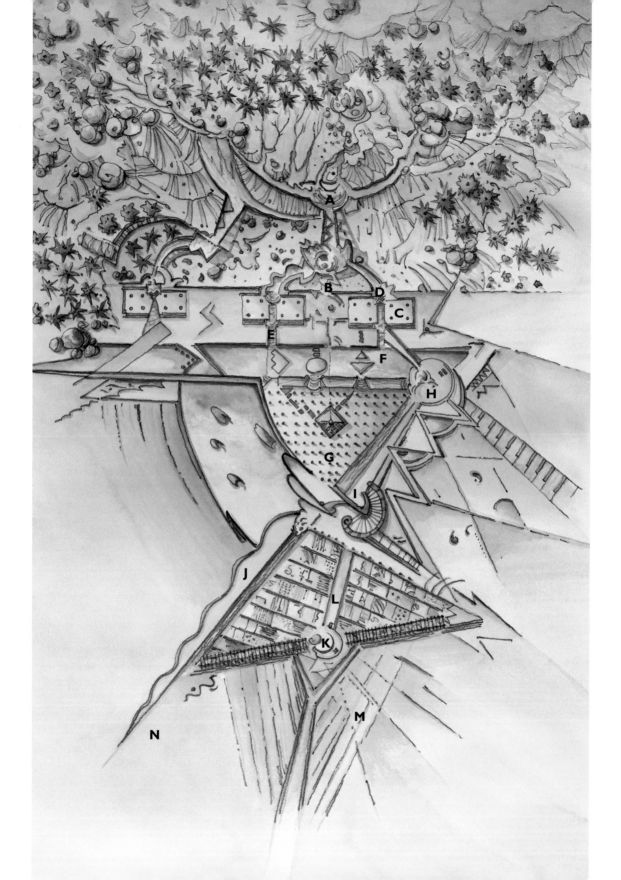

D. Cascade

Along the northeast interior wall of the dwelling, water makes its first active appearance in the form of a selsebil. Water cascades down an 8-foot-high chute, splashing into a pool at its base. The lively churning of the pool amplifies the psychological and physiological effects of aerated water.

E. Runnels

Water leaves the selsebil and flows into a narrow runnel edged with smooth terrazzo flooring. As it flows along, water splashes onto the floor making it shimmer like a brook in summer.

F. The Giant Chadar

The runnels exit through the center of the dwelling, where water cascades down three terrazzo steps and into a rectangular pool. The water flows directly under an open-sided pavilion at the center of this pool, before crashing down a 15-foot-high chadar. The serrated surfaces of the chadar aerate the water, and cooled air drifts upward into the pavilion. One can sit here looking down into the lower garden and be cooled by the churning, frothing water below.

G. Pool of Forty-Nine Jets

The water cascading down the chadar splashes into a large, square pool. In the center, a raised platform sits just above the surface of the water. The platform rests on four slender columns built just high enough for the water to flow beneath. The surface of the platform has slots for wood posts to support a canvas roof. A total of 49 jets surround all four sides of the platform. Fan-shaped jets throw arcs of water four feet up, cooling the air.

H. Lower Cistern

Below the aerating jets and pool sits the garden's lower cistern. Every effort has been made in this garden to capture each drop of water that falls from the clouds or

Figure IV-67 *(opposite)*
The Garden of Neptune. Illustrative plan.

Figure IV-68
Section of the garden's water features.

250

traverses the site. The surface grading of the site directs run-off into catchment pipes that connect to cisterns. This store of water can be used in times of drought for essential irrigation and "natural" air conditioning.

I. Water Banisters
Stairs spiral down from the Pool of Forty-Nine Jets to the garden terrace. Built into the handrail, a cascade of water rushes along channels just deep enough to allow the cool water to flow through the fingers of one's hand.

J. Water Curtain
A narrow cryptoporticus forms the retaining wall separating the Pool of Forty-Nine Jets from the garden terrace 15 feet below. A curtain of water drapes from the pool above, forming a wall of water 40 feet long.

One can walk behind this aqueous plane in the coolness of the cryptoporticus while its spray splashes over the body. Looking through this water curtain, one perceives an almost psychedelic image of reflected color from the garden beyond.

K. Wet Walk
An arbor-covered wet walk bisects the garden terrace. From short parapet walls that border the path, jets arc outward wetting the stone path shaded by the arbor. The arcs of water gently lap at one's feet.

L. *Giochi d'Acqua*
Spread throughout the garden terrace, water jokes lay in wait to delight and astound. One never knows just which, or from what direction, one of these delights will erupt. Hidden in the benches placed throughout the garden,

they quietly soak one's backside while resting during a summer's walk. When strolling down a path jets might suddenly explode, chasing one into a shelter, where unexpectedly a cascade of water will drop from the ceiling.

M. Irrigation
The fields of the farm emerge 8 feet below the garden terrace. Here, water from the cisterns irrigates the orchards and vineyards. Woven into these fields, a drip irrigation system irrigates the fields with maximum efficiency. Based on the same principles as its historic predecessors, the condensing jar and jube, this modern system slowly leaks water into the soil, minimizing evaporation.

N. Aquifer Recharge
All of the water that runs off the site, that has not been captured or used, is directed to a series of aquifer recharge tanks. These subterranean tanks are placed along the southern border of the site at the garden's lowest elevation. Even the water that has not been used in the gardens above has been diverted and stored in the recharge tanks. The water slowly soaks back into the earth to recharge the aquifer.

Figure IV-69a *(opposite above)*
Details of climatic devices.

Figure IV-69b *(opposite below)*
Section showing passive water collection techniques.

Summary

Water, the final and concluding element in this study, has revealed its power as a superior medium for climate modification. In past cultures, the applications of water as a passive design element assumed an astonishing variety of forms, from calm pools of placid water to kinetic displays with humorous intentions. Each one of these passive devices was analyzed for its specific characteristics that reduce summer temperatures and help produce cool microclimates. Garden Prototype IV adapts these historical techniques into a modern garden context. The inhabitants of the Garden of Neptune are able to live within the midst of the magical properties of water.

In Book IV, we have reviewed how water effectively cooled a variety of warm climates through its efficient collection, storage, and movement. With its infinite possibilities for climatic design, water can cool both physically and psychologically. The attraction of water throughout history has been not only spiritually profound, but integral to the conduct of our daily lives.

Water holds the power of possibility; where a droplet falls it may unlock a sleeping seed, or, at the point where a stream meets a river, a village may spring up and flourish. However, the welcome raindrop may indeed become the deluge. The catastrophic flood and the gentle rain differ only in degree. From a different perspective, water can destroy as easily as it can foster. Its essential purpose is to move, purify, replenish, and cool. We must learn to work with these natural tendencies instead of against them in order to continue to enjoy the many graces water bestows upon us. The sacred properties of water, fluid and powerful, must reemerge into the climatic garden of the future.

Notes

1. Donald Newton Wilber, *Persian Gardens & Garden Pavilions*. London: Longmans, Green, and Co., 1979, p. 5.

2. Jalalu-D-Din Rumi, *Mathnawi-yi ma'nawi*. Edited by R.A. Nicholson, London:Leiden, 1925-40, Volume VI, verse 4542.

3. Geoffrey Jellicoe and Susan Jellicoe, *Landscape of Man*. New York: Van Nostrand Reinhold Company [1975] 1982.

4. Gary Robinette, *Plants/People/and Environmental Control—A Study of Plants and their Environmental Functions*. Washington: National Park Service and American Society of Landscape Architects Foundation, 1972, p. 17.

5. Omar Khayam; quoted in Wilber, *Persian Gardens & Garden Pavilions*, p. 17.

6. Eugenia Salza Prina Ricotti, "The Importance of Water in the Roman Triclina," *Ancient Roman Gardens*. Edited by Wilhemina F. Jashemski, Washington D.C.: Dumbarton Oaks, 1987, p. 174.

7. Inigio H. Triggs, *The Art of Garden Design in Italy*. London: Longmans, Green, and Co., 1906, p. 7.

8. Georgina Masson, *Italian Gardens*. New York: Harry Abrams, Inc., 1961, p. 30.

9. Edmund Bacon, *Design of Cities*. Penguin Books, [1967] 1974, p. 88.

10. Saba, Fath Ali Shah; quoted in Wilber, *Persian Gardens & Pavilions*, p. 20.

11. Naomi Miller, *Heavenly Caves: Reflections on the Garden Grotto*. New York: George Braziller, Inc., 1982, p. 45.

12. Robert d'Humieres, Vicomte, *Through Isle and Empire*. New York: Doubleday, 1905, p. 215.

13. William Blake, *Milton*, Boulder, CO: Shambhala Publications, 1978, p. 104.

14. Norman T. Newton, *Design on the Land—The Development of Landscape Architecture*. Cambridge. MA: Harvard University Press, 1971, p. 46.

15. Marquesa de Casa Valdes, *Spanish Gardens*. Woodbridge, Suffolk, UK Antique Collectors' Club Ltd., [1973] 1987, p. 39.

16. Judith Chatfield, *A Tour of Italian Gardens*, New York: Rizzoli International, 1988, pp. 209–10.

17. Triggs, *The Art of Garden Design in Italy*, pp.79–80.

Conclusion

In the garden one could come to know all the elements of nature, the animals, vegetables, and minerals, and the 'four elements', air, earth, fire, and water, and thus rise through the spheres and finally reach God.[1]
Bartolomeo Taegio

I started this manuscript as a Fellow at the American Academy in Rome many years ago. It is strange, but also appropriate, that I finished it where it began. I have learned much from Rome and been inspired by all of Italy. My journey toward a design philosophy has been long, but with many interesting and fortuitous diversions along the way.

In some ways, the conditions that motivated this research have improved; there is an increased awareness about certain environmental issues and a budding consciousness of "green" living, but little action has been taken by the general public to ensure a sustainable future. For example, during the last several years, summertime heat waves have caused power outages across the country as energy companies struggle to keep up with the growing demand for electricity. The "rolling blackout" has become part of daily life in California. Everyday, newspapers around the globe report of some shortage or crisis affecting our natural resources and the world's supply of clean earth, air, and water. Still, particularly in the developed world, people are reluctant to make the changes in their lifestyles that would ease the dire situation. Gas-guzzling sport utility vehicles have replaced the more economical compact cars and, unfortunately, the technological revolution is not solar-powered.

My hope is that in the near future, new climatic gardens will begin to appear, fusing the four elements of this book into a new world order. The gardens of this new order will be not only functional microclimates, but artful and spiritually enlightening places as well. The garden has the potential to reverse the destructive patterns of our past. The answers to our environmental challenges lie within the garden, if only we choose to recognize them.

Such recognition came as a gift to me, as I finished the illustrations for this book at the Bellagio Study and Conference

Figure V-1
Villa Serbelloni, Lake Como, Italy.

Climatic orientation of the villa's south-facing terraces.
(Photo: Author)

Notes

1. Bartolomeo Taegio, *La villa*. Milan, 1559, pp. 9–10.

Center on Lake Como, Italy, on a Rockefeller Foundation fellowship. Describing the essence of my work to the other scholars there, I would simply note the climatic orientation of our residence at the Villa Serbelloni (Figure V-1). Built into the southern face of the hillside, all our rooms had exposure to the low winter sun, while the wooded crest of the hill above us blocked the cold northern winds. Below the villa, gardens and terraces of olive trees reach down the hill to the south to maximize solar exposure and capture the cool breezes that flow from the lake in summer. I was stunned to learn later that Pliny the Younger had not only visited this area but lived on this very site. His recommendations for the full integration of landscape and architecture were first developed here. Now, coming full circle, his timeless principles of climatic design are still in effect today.

Bibliography

Acton, Harold, *The Villas of Tuscany*. Italy: Thames and Hudson, 1973.

Alberti, Leon Battista, On the Art of Building in Ten Books. Translated by Joseph Rykwert and Robert Tavernor, Cambridge, MA: MIT Press, [1550] 1988.

Alberti, Leon Battista, *The Family in Renaissance Florence*. Translated by R. N. Watkins, Columbia, SC: University of South Carolina Press, [1433–1439] 1969.

Ardalan, Nader, and Bakhtiar, Laleh, *The Sense of Unity*. Chicago: University of Chicago Press, 1973.

Bacon, Edmund, *Design of Cities*. Middlesex, England: Penguin Books Ltd., [1967] 1974.

Baldesar Castiglione, *The Book of the Courtier*. Translated by George Bull, New York: Penguin, 1967.

Berrali, Julia, *The Garden: An Illustrated History*. New York: Viking Press, 1966.

Blake, William, *Milton*. Boulder, CO: Shambhala Publications, and New York: Random House, Inc., 1978.

Boccaccio, Giovanni, *The Decameron*. Translated by G. H. William, London: Penguin Books, 1972.

Byne, Mildred Stapley, and Byne, Arthur, *Spanish Gardens and Their Patios*. Philadelphia: J.B. Lippincott Company, 1924.

Chatfield, Judith, *A Tour of Italian Gardens*, Part I. New York: Rizzoli International Publications, Inc., 1988.

Coffin, D. R., *The Villa in the Life of Renaissance Rome*. Princeton, 1979.

Colnagh, Sir Dominic, *A Dictionary of Florentine Painters*. Firenze: Archivi Colnaghi, 1986.

Comito, Terry, *The Idea of the Garden in the Renaissance*. New Brunswick, NJ: Rutgers University Press, 1957.

Coste, Pascal, *Souvenirs de Voyages*, (2 Volumes). Marseille: Typographie et Lithographie Cayer et Cie, 1878.

Crescenzi, Piero de', *Liber ruralium commodorum*. Venice, 1309.

d'Humiers, Robert, *Vicomte, through Isle and Empire*. New York, 1905.

Doyle, Jim, "Hot: Heat Rising from Cities Appears to Be Changing Regional Weather Patterns," *San Francisco Chronicle*. March 6, 2000, Science, Health and Environment, pg. 1.

Elgood, George S, *Italian Gardens*. London: Longmans, and Co., 1907.

Falda, G. B., *Le Fountane di' Roma*, II: *Le Fontane della Ville di Frascatti*. Rome, 1675.

Falda, G. B., *Giardini di Roma*. Rome, 1683.

Fauré, Gabriel, *The Gardens of Rome*. Translated by F. Kemp, New York: Brentano's Inc,

1924.

Franck, Carl, *The Villas of Frascati 1550–1750*. London: Alec Tiranti Ltd., [1956] 1966.

Goethe, J. W., *Italian Journey*, London, England: Penguin Books, 1962.

Gothein, Maria Luise, 1928. *A History of Garden Art*. Vol. I. Translated by Laura Archer Hind, New York, 1928.

Gromort, George, *Jardins d'Espagne*. Paris: Vincent & Cie, 1926.

Harvey, John, *Mediaeval Gardens*. London: B.T. Batsford Ltd., 1981.

Hawthorn, Hildegarde, *The Lure of the Garden*. New York: The Century Co., 1911.

Heschong, Lisa, *Thermal Delight in Architecture*. Cambridge: MIT Press, 1979.

Irving, Washington, *Tales of the Alhambra*. Edited by Miguel Sanchez, Spain: Grefol, S.A., [1832] 1984.

Jashemski, Wihelmina F., *The Gardens of Pompeii, Herculaneum and the Villas Destroyed by Vesuvius*. New Rochelle, NY: Caratzas Brothers, 1979.

Jellicoe, G. A., and Shepherd, J. C., *Italian Gardens of the Renaissance*. Princeton: Princeton Architectural Press, [1925] 1986.

Jellicoe, G. A., and Shepherd, J. C., *Water: The Use of Water in Landscape Architecture*. London: A. & C. Black, 1971.

Jellicoe, Geoffrey, and Jellicoe, Susan, *Landscape of Man*. New York: Van Nostrand Reinhold Company, Inc., [1975] 1982.

Jones, Owen and Goury, *Plans, Elevation, Sections and details of the Alhambra* (2 volumes). London, 1842–1845.

Junius, Manfred, *Practical Handbook of Plant Alchemy*. Translated by Leon Muller, New York: Inner Traditions International Ltd., 1985.

King, Ronald, *The Quest for Paradise-A History of the World's Gardens*. New York: Mayflower Books, Inc., 1979.

Koran: Interpreted. Translated by A. S. Arberry, New York: Simon and Schuster, [1955] 1996.

Lane, John, *Mediaeval Gardens*, (2 volumes). London: The Bodlethead Limited, 1924.

Latham, Charles, *The Gardens of Italy*, Volume I. London: Country Life Ltd., 1905.

Laurie, Michael, *An Introduction to Landscape Architecture*. New York: American Elsevier Publishing Company, Inc., 1975.

Lawrence, D. H., *Sketches of Etruscan Places and other Italian Essays*. London: Penguin Books, 1999.

Lawrence, D. H., *Twilight in Italy*. New York, Viking Press, [1916] 1958.

Lawson, W., *The Country Housewife's Garden*. London, 1626.

Lazzaro, Claudio, *The Italian Renaissance Garden*. New Haven, CT: Yale University Press, 1990.

Lehrman, Jonas, *Earthly Paradise: Garden and Courtyard in Islam*. Berkeley: University of California Press, 1980.

Marx, Leo, *The Machine in the Garden*. New York: Oxford University Press, [1964] 1971.

Masson, Georgina, *Italian Gardens*. New York: Harry N. Abrams, Inc, 1961.

McHarg, Ian L., *Design with Nature*. Garden City, NY: The American Museum of Natural History, Doubleday/Natural History Press, [1969] 1971.

Michell, George (ed.), *Architecture of the Islamic World, Its Historical and Social Meaning*. London: Thames & Hudson, 1978.

Miller, Naomi, *Heavenly Caves: Reflections on the Garden Grotto*. New York: George Braziller, 1982.

Moore, Charles, Mitchell, William J., and Turnbull, Jr., William, The Poetics of Gardens. Cambridge, MA: MIT Press, 1988.

Moynihan, Elizabeth, *Paradise as a Garden—in Persia and Mugal India*. New York: George Braziller, Inc. 1979.

Newton, Norman T., *Design on the Land—The Development of Landscape Architecture*. Cambridge, MA: The Belknap Press of Harvard University Press, 1971,

Phillipps, Evelyn March, *The Gardens of Italy*. Edited by Author Bolton, London: Counrty Life, Ltd., 1919.

Plato, *Phaedrus*. Edited by Harold North Fowler, Cambridge, MA: Harvard University Press, 1960.

Plato, *Timaeus and Critias*. Translated by Desmond Lee, Middlesex, England: Penguin Books Ltd., 1962.

Radice, Betty, *Who's Who in the Ancient World*. Middlesex, England: Penguin Books Ltd., 1986.

Ramelli, A., *Le diverse et artifiose machine*. Paris, 1588.

Robinette, Gary, *Plants / People/and Environmental Control—A Study of Plants and Their Environmental Functions*.Washington, D.C.: National Park Service and American Society of Landscape Architects Foundation, 1972.

Rumi, Jalalu-D-Din, *Mathnawi-yi ma'nawi*. Edited by R.A. Nicholson, London: Leiden, 1925-1940,Volume VI, Verse 4542.

Salza Prima Ricotti, Eugenia, "The Importance of Water in the Roman Triclina," in *Ancient Roman Gardens*. Edited by Wilhelmina F. Jashemski, Washington D.C.: Dumbarton Oaks, 1987.

Scamozzi, Giovanni d'Vincenzo, *L'idea della architettura universale*. Venice, 1714.

Shakespeare, William, *King John*. New York: Penguin Books, 1962.

Sitwell, Sir Osbert, *On the Making of Gardens*. New York: Charles Scribner's Sons, 1909.

Steenbergen, Clemens, and Reh, Wouter, *Architecture and Landscape: The Design Experiment of the Great European Gardens and Landscapes*. Munich: Prestel-Verlag, 1996.

Taegio, Bartolomeo, *La villa*. Milan, 1559.

Tanser, H., *The Villas of Pliny the Younger*. New York, 1923.

Thompson, Clay A., "Power Hungry in Silicon Valley," *San Francisco Bay Guardian*. June 2, 2000, p. 13.

Treib, Marc, *Sanctuaries of Spanish New Mexico*. Berkeley: University of California Press, 1993.

Triggs, Inigio H., *The Art of Garden Design in Italy*. London: Longmans, Green, and Co., 1906.

Turner, James, *The Poetics of Landscape*. Oxford: Basil Blackwell, 1969.

Valdes, Marquesa de Casa, *Spanish Gardens*. Translated by Edward Tanner, Woodbridge, Suffolk, UK: Antique Collectors' Club, Ltd., [1973] 1987.

Van der Ree, Paul, Smienk, Gerrit, and Steenbergen, Clemens, *Italian Villas and Gardens*. The Netherlands: THOTH Publishers, 1992.

Vitruvius, *The Ten Books on Architecture*. Translated by M. H. Morgan, New York: Dover Publications, [1914] 1960.

Wharton, Edith, *Italian Villas and Their Gardens*. New York: DeCapo Press, Inc., [1904] 1976.

Wilber, Donald Newton, *Persian Gardens & Garden Pavilions*. London: Longmans, Green, and Co., 1979.

Index

Note: *Figure numbers shown in italic*